UNLOVED AGAIN

UNLOVED AGAIN

Breaking Your Serial Addiction

ELAN GOLOMB

UNLOVED AGAIN
BREAKING YOUR SERIAL ADDICTION

iUniverse books may be ordered through booksellers or by contacting:

iUniverse
1663 Liberty Drive
Bloomington, IN 47403
www.iuniverse.com
1-800-Authors (1-800-288-4677)

Author picture by Gary Golkin.

ISBN: 978-1-4917-6596-8 (sc)
ISBN: 978-1-4917-6597-5 (hc)
ISBN: 978-1-4917-6598-2 (e)

Library of Congress Control Number: 2015906226

Print information available on the last page.

iUniverse rev. date: 11/30/2015

To my dear Malcolm,
Who died two years ago and is with me still,
Thank you

Contents

Preface .... **xi**

The Repetition Compulsion xiii

Chapter 1 Some of Us Lose the First Thing That We Love **1**

Forced to Surrender What You Love 1

Then It Was My Dog 5

Heart Sealed Off from Loving 10

Raised to Cater 20

Married Despite Wanting to Escape 25

Hyperactive to Avoid Feeling Pain 29

Raised to Hide 33

Winner Equals Loser 37

Ever-Deserted Victim 46

Afraid to Be Seen and Known 50

Sometimes He Does What He Wants and Still Loves You 55

Exploitation as Love 60

Loving from Behind Walls of Hate 63

Chapter 2 Developing Your Sense of Love **69**

The Freezing Parent and the Frozen Child 69

The Warming Parent and the Warmed Child 71

Janus Faced: Presenting a False Image 73

Slavery Continues 74

Chapter 3 Your Defenses Can Hurt You **81**

Your Defenses 81

The Iceberg of Bad Attachment 84
Swallowing the Bad 85
Learning to Cover Hate with Love 88
Blind to Your Repetitive Choices 91
The Need to Destroy Love 93
We Hold on to Being Unloved 96
Fear Keeps You Holding On 100
Fear of Being Rejected 102

Chapter 4 Forced to Serve 105
Parents Who Must Be Served 105
Arms Outstretched to Hold You Back 107
Addicted to Pain and Suffering 109
Their Feelings Are More Important Than Your Own 112
Guilt about Separating and Leaving 116
The Need to Heal Your Parent 119
Change Is Frightening 120
It Feels Easier to Give Up 124

Chapter 5 Leave the Trap 126
You Cannot Force Someone to Change 126
Submitting to Them Makes Them Weaker 128
Hatred Is a Form of Attachment 129
Your Anger Has a History 131
The Grief of Losing Unreal Love 133
The Courage to Say No 134
Feeling Like a Failure Links Us with Our
Abusive Parent 137

Chapter 6 Awaken 140
Sometimes It Takes a Dream to Wake You Up 140
The Self 142
Their Pain Is Not Your Pain 144
How to Deal with Fear 146
How Are Your Gifts Received? 147
What If You Don't Know Love? 149

Each Time You Go into Confusion 152
Recovering Your Pain 153
Whether to Stay or Leave 156
Growing the Self 157

Chapter 7 Choose Love 159
Do Not Accept Bullying 161
At War with Your Partner as if with Your Parent 163
The Power to Disconnect 165
Unhealthy Connections 167
Time to Warm Up 171
Don't Think of Yourself as a Commodity 172
Don't Let Age Stand in Your Way 174
Are You Not Good Enough? 177
Mourn the Loss of the Loving Parent You
Never Really Had 178
Early Places of Adaptation 181
You Feel Compelled to Comply 183
Choose Love 184
We Love and Heal Together 187
How I Learned to Love 189

Index 195

Author Biography 207

Preface

I am a clinical psychologist who has worked with people who are trying to understand why their love lives are so miserable. I do not dismiss my many years of education, but reading another person's theories and even his or her self-descriptions has little power compared to knowing your own. So I found the answers by studying my own history.

I loved those who could not love me. I now see it as a matter of choice, not chance, that I rejected those who loved me and chose those who could not. I lived in expectation of a disaster that eventually happened. When they were incapable of love, I demanded what they could not give. When they were able to love, I knocked them out of my life by focusing on what was wrong. I always ended up alone.

When I first began my study, I did not see my pattern. I regarded each of my unhappy love affairs as unique, each as if it was happening for the first time. Then awareness that I was repeating a pattern began to seep inside my brain. I could no longer call it an accident or bad luck.

This awareness raised deeper questions into the why of it, which led me to study my childhood, since parents offer our first and deepest experiences of love. However, most parents at times subject their children to their tempers, and the children react with grief. But always those parents are sorry and turn their regret into better behavior. Other parents, caught in their own maelstroms of childhood abuse and lovelessness, offer little love, or none at all, to their children and do not make amends. Or they offer the wrong kind of love, which further undermines their children.

A parent who loves thc wrong way or offers too little love often is in a state of rage. Because a parent's aggression causes the child to be afraid, development of the child's ability to love is arrested. It is a kind of deer-in-the-headlights experience in which the child seeking love, combined with its need for safety, is frozen in place. The child's notion of love becomes twisted in a way that predetermines endless misery. Abuse is conflated or confused with the kind of love that shapes its dreams. If we experience this as children, we become blind to what we can see, feel, and do. We don't want to see. It is too frightening. We are too weak and helpless. We lack the ability to see, and this condition remains.

Based on the childhood condition of arrested love, our adult love lives invariably are unhappy. We replay aspects of our childhoods without knowing it. We mistreat others or are mistreated. There are moments of loving, but mostly we feel unloved and/or unloving, empty, abandoned, and alone.

We are living in the past but do not know it. Who and how we love represent an interaction within our minds of the original abusive "parents" and our terrified, trapped, and stricken "children." The "children's" needs—combined with fear of the "parents," along with the real parents' strictures—are put into our minds and followed as if they represent our inner truths. Because these early emotions are so powerful, we think that our intuitive selves are speaking.

Our active adult selves must exist in the now. They need to separate from the past as active forces. Which parts of their minds are commanding them what to feel have to become clear; their minds need to make this analysis so that the adults can choose behavior that is compatible with their need to share love rather than be destroyed by love or to destroy it.

You need to see if you are submitting to the internal "parent's" angry, needy demand for ever-increasing power over your frightened internal "child." You need to recognize that you have a right to make your own choices and that your fear of doing this represents an unholy alliance between your internal "child" and "parent." Separate from your "parent" and "child" no matter how much your "parent" threatens your "child" and your "child" cowers.

The mind is very powerful. It remembers and causes you to recreate now what happened then as if it now is real. It is like going to a good movie that makes you shiver and weep … until the lights go on. Only your adult lights stay off. Get a calendar on your life. Then is then, and it becomes now only if you make it so. Claim your life and your ability to love.

Unloved Again tells people's love stories, including the ability to love only your pet, falling for those who abuse and use you, and falling in love with someone who is ruthless and against whom you have to be emotionally armed; it tells the stories of people who settle for crumbs of love because they think themselves unworthy, and it tells of endless submission to save yourself from the abusive "parent," which only leads to more abuse.

Unloved Again describes the issues that underlie these self-punitive choices and what you must do to change. *Unloved Again* explains why it is so hard to change due to the fear of your "internal child." But loving miserably is and remains your choice. Changing self is also your choice. The fear you have about change comes from your ancient "child," whose emotions stand in the way of freedom.

Change is made by your adult self, which is oriented toward the present. *Unloved Again* ends with the story of one who made the change. If she could do it, so can you.

The Repetition Compulsion

Many people, men and women, suffer from the same kind of emotional disorder without knowing it. This experience is so common that songs are written about it; sufferers hum the melody and trudge to its beat.

This emotional plague has to do with loving. It has to do with choosing people who cannot properly love you back. It has to do with mistreating those who love you. The in-love person argues and begs for more; he or she switches lovers and switches again but always chooses the same kind of person as a replacement. These people complain about the ones they are now rejecting but are agog with ecstasy over the next, until their eyes are open and they see what they have chosen. Then the complaining begins again.

How can so many people suffer from the same disorder but no one understands it? Confusion comes from not knowing the origin of this behavior. It is an action of the unconscious mind. People cannot imagine that they are led by their unconscious. Many do not believe they have one. The actions of their minds remain an enormous mystery. They like to think that they are the ones who choose, but they cannot explain the repetitive misery of their choices. Aren't we supposed to learn from experience?

The very expression "falling in love" indicates that it is not a conscious doing. "Falling" means that you lose control. What pushed you off the cliff of conscious reason? The mind may be conceived of as having many kingdoms. Two of these kingdoms whose impact we deny are those of the internal "child" and the internal "parent." We are falling out of our conscious minds and into the unconscious or barely conscious minds of our "child" and "parent." If we always choose people who render us miserable, who do not love us at all or who love us poorly, or if we do the same to those who love us, we are falling into the world of the internal "freezing parent" and the internal "frozen child." The "freezing parent" attempts to control the "frozen child," who largely submits. We, the conscious adults, experience the outcome of this battle and let it guide us toward whom and how we love.

The "child" and "parent" are as powerful as they are unknown. This condition is the origin of our falling. We can fall into something great and wonderful, but then there is no negative "parent" calling the shots and no frightened "child" submitting. We learned early to love, and we love that way again when similar captivating stimuli appear. If open love was felt with our parents, as adults we do not regret our repetition.

We call a repetitive unhappy love choice a "repetition compulsion." The word *compulsion* is affixed to the idea of being unhappy. You go where your inner forces summon. They pair you off with users and abusers, with poor lovers, or with self-centered people who are unable to make a commitment. You fall in love with people who are "stars" who sometimes drop in on you. You never know when they are coming and when they will go, or with whom. Or you compulsively take the negative position and do the same to others.

Your painful longing, your confused and unsettled mind that is preoccupied with another, is what we call "being in love." Many people associate falling in love with pain. You long for something you cannot have. That person is out of reach. You believe that the one you are in love with will treat you better than the one who went before, but since you have drawn one from the same barrel of faults, this hardly ever happens and the relationships rarely last. You do not question what drives your preoccupation. You enjoy the agony of being driven. Nice people, considerate people, do not set your love wheels turning.

People do not sufficiently question their repetition. They attribute whom they choose to fate, to bad luck, or to something they cannot change. It is not your conscious adult mind/self that does the craving, although it surrenders to these pangs. The conscious mind is confused about what is happening. It rationalizes and justifies what it feels and how this causes you to act. It sometimes is suspicious of its reasoning, but it cannot stop following its edicts.

Many "fallen-in-love" people, even though they see some parallel with how they felt in their childhoods with their parents or caretakers, cannot put this knowledge into action. And even if they are able to see the current choices as embodying the parents' faults, and knowing that these will make them unhappy, they still choose to remain in harness. They say, "I can't help what I feel."

They are trapped by their internal "freezing parents'" definitions of what they need. The internal "parent" is modeled upon the original rejecting parent(s). This modeling causes the adult to play the child who searches for love from the same kind of person as the parent who did not and could not give it. Or the internal "parent" traps the grown-up into playing an unloving "parent" role with partners whose own internal "parents" cause them to play the roles of helpless "children."

Mimicking the role of the original unloving parent, as now exemplified by the internal "freezing parent," is an example of identification with the aggressor. It says, "I am not weak. I am strong." Sometimes the grown-up swings back and forth between "freezing parent" and "frozen child" with the same lover or with another. Neither role prevails, possibly because the actual parents went from one role to the other as well when they were children. There can be no happy ending as long the adult wavers between "parent" and "child" or when either's dominance continues.

Chapter 1

Some of Us Lose the First Thing That We Love

Forced to Surrender What You Love

The first person loved by the child is his or her mother/father/caretaker. The next step in developing attachment is loving an object that represents the parent. This embodiment is a necessary developmental step on the path to committed love.

A child's experience with the beloved object should not be overlooked, as it so often is by parents who think that love begins when we are grown. Love begins in the womb when the child hears familiar voices and cottons to them. Love begins after birth with every kind word and pleasant touch. Children experience loving caretakers as extensions of themselves. For parents who do not provide sufficient care, the world is felt to be cold and rejecting, the self in retreat and in danger.

The next step in developing a love connection is when you love an object—be it your doll, toy, blanket, and so forth—and cannot be separated from it. This beloved thing is a *transitional object.* Its function is symbolic. The ability to have a transitional object is an intellectual leap in developing a love connection. The transitional object represents the parent, who even when absent is there for the child. Children can put their arms around the transitional object and can sleep with it that way. They can set the object on their pillow or somewhere close at hand. Children choose an object to adore from those that are available. Once the choice has been made, that's it. There is no trading it in for another.

Parents who are empathetic accept their children's connection to the beloved object. The child carries it around, leaves it in a certain place, and knows that it will be there. If the child doesn't want the object taken away to be washed, the parent leaves it dirty. "Dirty" is an adult concept that is often reacted to with exaggerated feeling. The parent who believes a "good child" (and all he or she possesses) is a clean child is out of touch. After a period of time, the "transitional object" goes inside the child's mind. The child has bonded. Attachment is ongoing.

Parents who interrupt the developmental sequence often are repeating their attachment trauma. Children whose "transitional objects" are taken away, once grown into adulthood, will doubt the enduring presence of their loved ones so that their attachment will be shaky or nonexistent. They even may choose to love people who will abandon them, which is in keeping with this ancient childhood experience of losing their transitional objects. For them, love is always lost, so why not choose people who will flee them and have none of the pain of waiting for love not given or rarely given and not sustained?

People put mountains of forgetfulness in front of their early pain. But suppressed memories and miserable, frightening experiences vibrate everywhere in what we see, feel, and do. Myriad events in the adults' lives remind them of things to be avoided, events painful, repugnant, and ancient. The things and people they love, strangely cause them to move away. Why? It makes no sense. To solve this riddle, they need to get hold of painful memories via mental associations. They need to act like a dog that has found something fascinating half-buried under a rock. They need to find an edge to it, dig and sink their teeth in, and pull until the entire thing appears.

Especially important is the question of what happened to the transitional objects we loved as children. Our ability to hold on to whom and what we love as adults without hysterical grasping or a tendency to give it up is learned in early childhood. Back then, we needed to count on the security of specially adored things to which we clung and attributed great significance. We kept these objects where we could get at them, clearly seen and available when needed.

That doll, or this ball or blanket, our beloved objects represented our parents, usually a mother or someone on whom we felt dependent. We always had our parent substitutes to hold on to so that we could blithely go our way. Their availability and our control gave us a sense of security. What are the consequences of loss?

Here is my story of Effie.

I was about four and in a nursery school that I little enjoyed. I didn't like to go along with rules that had nothing to do with my desires and needs at the moment, such as "lie down on the floor now and take a nap" when I wasn't sleepy.

I had been raised in a rather extreme fashion. My parents either largely ignored me or jumped down my throat for things I couldn't help, didn't know about, or couldn't understand, like speaking with food in my mouth. I quickly learned that when war is coming your way, it is best to be invisible. So I would grow quiet in response to their barrage of words. Much of my life concerned escape.

My father made grandiose speeches about "important things," except when he descended from his throne to study and criticize. There was no time when my mind and body were not being scrutinized. For example, take my posture: Why are you slumping? Stand up straight. I slumped between my shoulders as if they were two boulders to hide from his verbal darts. It was my constant thought that these really weren't my parents, that they took the wrong child from the hospital after the baby's sojourn in an incubator for premature newborns.

When Dad greeted me, he grasped my head on either side like a stereotaxic device for inserting electrodes. He bestowed a kiss on my cheek that allowed him to see himself as loving, although his words were full of hate. But why did he immobilize my head? Was he afraid of his own sexuality, of falling into wild kissing and who knows what else that he projected onto me? Many sexually critical parents who tell a child she is ugly and tie her down are attempting to tame their own sexuality.

I always wanted to escape from both parents' attacks, but how could I do it? They would make me pay for such rebellion. Instead of saying no to them, I gave in with silent submission. Our worlds bumped against each other but did not meld.

My mother was a distant woman who broke into rages over actions she labeled unacceptable that seemed quite trivial to me. She acted on her impulses and carried out her notions without first inquiring how I or anybody else felt about it. She was a human centrifuge who spun me into a blank and threatening universe.

There was little in my life that was calm and wonderful, except for Effie. Effie was my beloved doll. I always had Effie, my mainstay in life. I talked to her and loved her. Effie would say mama when you bent her over and straightened her up, until I gave her a bath and stilled her voice. Although she no longer spoke aloud to me, I still heard her talking in my head and loved her just the same. She was Effie! I have to admit that Effie's pink cheeks also had been washed away. I was big on bathing her. I poured my love into her via all my ministrations. I knew that she enjoyed them.

I related to Effie as a representation of all good things in the world, which I now understand to mean my mother's reincarnated love. But changes in her appearance meant nothing to me. I loved Effie from the inside. I should add that Effie's name was a contraction of my own, Elan Phoebe. I was in Effie, and she was in me. Effie represented the loving parent I saw little of but whose loving moments lingered in my brain. Effie was Mommy and I combined.

I went to a boring nursery school with its silly games and enforced naps. I was not that kind of game player. The games I played I made up in my head, but the school was too controlling to allow that kind of sharing. After my daily stint was over, I came home to Effie, who was always there waiting for me, sitting on my pillow. Effie was my point of security in an otherwise chaotic, destructive, unreliable home life.

But one day I came home to Effie and did not find her. I was distraught. Where was she? I never put her away. I looked under the bed, behind my desk, and on the closet shelf. My mother came home to find me frantic. She didn't comfort me. She saw no reason for my grieving and so ignored it. She informed me that Effie was so old and worn that she had been given to the Russian Wore a Leaf (Russian War Relief). Mom had gotten me a new doll, an expensive Tony doll that she produced with its golden hair and fancy clothes.

But no, the Tony doll meant nothing to me and never would. I was in mourning. I couldn't totally let my mother know this and be subjected to her rage. How could she do such a thing to me? She was totally out of touch. She was going to "improve" my doll experience. Had she never been a child with her own beloved doll? Had it been taken away? Without careful observation and self-understanding, we tend to do to our children what was done to us as a form of emotional denial.

When she made up her mind, nothing could penetrate and contradict it. I said nothing and wept inside. My beloved doll was gone. Tony was merely a "thing." My loving self had been uprooted. The connection to my mother as represented by the doll had been given away. It was like having a limb chopped off. No, it was worse. It was like having your self chopped off.

I learned from this experience not to reach out for love, which inevitably leads to its loss. A state of loneliness took over me then and has not left me yet. Lovers will desert you. If they are not the cause of this separation, someone else will remove them. There is no secure bonding with the one you love. Do not allow yourself to hope. Be empty and accept it.

Then It Was My Dog

The powerless and threatened experience of a child with aggressive parent(s) lives on inside the adult's mind. The internal "child" makes terrible decisions based on the sense of vulnerability at the hands of the internal "parent" or in accordance with the "parent's" worldview. The internal "parent's" attitude is modeled after the actual rejecting, controlling, and worried parent who saw tyranny as the proper way to handle a child. The internal "parent" continues to want the same kind of childish dependency, which should not be engaged in no matter how fearful and tentative the adult feels. Childish dependency includes giving to another what that person wants from you, even though you do not want to give it and would be terribly hurt by doing so.

Childish dependency has its roots in fear. You need to recognize that you have an exaggerated fear of taking an independent stand against someone whose wishes contradict your own. The tyrannical parent, whether within or without, is asking you to betray yourself. You find yourself becoming vague in your thinking, ready to do what the parent asks for with a smiling face. You are falling into a semiconscious state of being-doing to avoid your "parent's" wrath.

You are not to surrender what you love because people who desire it bellow their pain at you for withholding. Their pain is not more important than your own. You are not to give them what you love because that is the only way to keep a friend or lover. What kind of lover or friend is that? Wake up. The minute you see the fog of surrender rolling in, you have to say no, and if you can't yet say no, say, "I'll think it over." Then gather your self-respect, and seek outside support if it is needed in order to say no.

The woman in this story (me!) was overwhelmed by the other's need, while feeling that giving in was an act of suicide. She (I) gave away her (my) dog.

I told a friend about my mother's taking my dog. The friend was shocked to hear it and became totally up in arms. She said, "Your mother stole your dog. Can't you call it *stealing?*"

"No. I can't. *Stole* is not the right word for it. What happened is far worse. I gave my mother the dog. She begged and pleaded and argued, and I succumbed … against my will. My mother didn't steal the dog, which I adored and couldn't imagine living without."

You should not be surprised that I named the dog Effie. Losing Effie, the doll that my mother had given away, my transitional object, was such a tremendous loss. Naming the dog Effie was an experience of renewal. I had my Effie back again.

Effie was part of my life. She was always in my heart and mind, and of course she waited for me at the door expecting a good, long walk. She rested her head on my lap while looking into my eyes. She ran with me in the park. She was my companion and my friend. I would put my arms around her to laugh or cry, and she remained there. We were together.

The experience with Effie was my second experience of feeling the closeness of a transitional object and then having it taken away—by the same person who removed the first one. Once as a child, and now as an adult, I experienced the same heartache and loss.

It was not a coincidence that losing the most important thing in my life was due to the need of an insensitive parent. The first loss, trading my doll, Effie, for a new one, Mom claimed was done for me. The second loss, taking away my dog, Mom claimed was done for my dog. Who could fight it? Or rather how can a child of any age fight it when the parent demands something and acts threatening or wounded if you don't give in? It is a giant step to say "enough of that" to a functioning parent, no matter what the child's age. Childhood trauma lives on in the adult mind particularly when it is repeated. The emotional scab on the old wound was scraped off, and it began to bleed again.

The problem was that my mother had become attached to Effie, for whom she babysat when I was away for several months on a trip. I was celebrating getting my doctorate and knew such an uncommitted time would never happen again.

Now that I was back, I learned that she wanted my dog. That was always her way ... whatever she loved, she had to totally possess. Without exaggerated ownership, she loses interest and ignores or feels rejected and attacks the chosen object with the fervor of her antilove. Now she loved and needed to be with Effie.

She built her case for ownership on how she offered the dog better treatment. She pushed me out of the picture "for Effie's sake." She said that Effie loved her more than she did me because of how she treated her. The creature I loved so much and loved me back, loved her more? The creature I embraced and against whose fur I'd laughed and cried? The creature I knew felt what I felt and even had a fiendish sense of humor—like when she would walk behind the Chinese blue-and-white vase standing a few inches from the living room wall, to shake it a bit and make me scream? (My dog Effie did this many times. She had a wicked sense of humor.)

Saying Effie loved her more stabbed me in the heart. There had been no stable love relationship in my family life except for the one with my doll Effie. Dad was disinterested and was mostly away. My mother also was usually somewhere else, and when she was home she didn't talk to me. Was I loved by either parent? It's hard to say. Now she reported that my dog had abandoned me. Effie was the single being whose love I counted on when the major figures in my life repeatedly failed to give me love and togetherness. Effie was no longer there for me?

Effie loved my mother more? I didn't believe it. Or did I? I was always assigned by both parents to the "unloved seat," whose validity I accepted. I was impressed and defeated by people who said they were better than I at doing almost anything. I accepted negative judgments as correct. But love seemed not to be open to such judgment. You felt love when you were loved, and that is how you loved. Love has no parameters. It just is. Effie was glad to see me, wasn't she?

My mother was deliberately and intensely inserting a wedge between me and Effie, between my feelings for her and, as she stated it, Effie's feelings for me. I was growing numb. My mother went on and on about how great she was for Effie. She got home from teaching a little after three. I got home from work in the early evening. She said that living with me, Effie spent too much time alone. I used to find her snoozing on the rug, and then she would leap up hugely excited to greet me, after which we went for a long walk. What was wrong with that? And we spent time together on weekends.

They were together only a few months while I was away. Effie and I had been together for years, including during her puppyhood. German shepherds never lose allegiance to their primary owners. She had always known my mother and related to her as one of the "family." But I was number one.

I don't know if I said all of this aloud. I was too frightened and easily trounced. I thought that fighting back guaranteed defeat. She presented a wall of sound. I hoped that my mother would grow exhausted and stop talking, that she would move on to some other topic, but that happened only in my fantasy. My mother didn't stop talking about Effie. Her speech became loud and threatening. She said that she took Effie everywhere she went, which symbolized their connection. She made a speech on a platform to the teacher's union with Effie at her side, as if she were blind. My mother was unique in breaking rules that stood in her way. But I felt only grief upon hearing this. She was establishing her primacy for Effie in everybody's mind.

I felt trapped by her expectations. It always was that way. My thoughts and feelings fell into a maelstrom. Was my mother "better" than I was for Effie? Did she love my mother more? A piece of my heart was chopped away by this notion. Would I be depriving Effie of what she needed by taking her home with me? Would taking her hurt my mother, as if that was the only hurt that counted? What about *my* pain? I felt anxiety, confusion, and guilt.

Also, there was the fear that my mother would overwhelm me if I refused her. She was a major bully who fought to have her way. I lived too much of my life hiding from this person. She acted like a commanding general. I'd be court-martialed and then hanged if I persisted. I already was in prison.

Then there were other influential people who demanded I thrust myself aside. My mother's sister, who lived with her, said, "Leave Effie." Bella had always been a friend to me, but she was a timid person who avoided conflict. She wanted to live with my mother in peace, so she shared Mom's demand for the dog. She resembled her own mother, a smiling silent woman. "But Bella, what about me?" I didn't figure in her thinking.

Worst and most serious was the opinion of my psychotherapist. This was a man who so long had stood for my taking my own path. I trusted his opinion, which was usually so objective and free. But it wasn't this time, although I couldn't allow myself to see it. I always had to trust those I depended on, even if their actions turned them into enemies.

As I heard his destructive words dressed in the garb of compassion for another, I lost my only friend … or rather my second friend after Effie. Did he not see how I felt? Did I not speak of it? Possibly I spoke too little. Couldn't he see that I was in agony? He gave his instructions coolly: "Let her have the dog." I accepted his judgment and went into deep freeze. I paid the dues for membership in his club of nonexistence.

Now as I look at why he did this, I have to assume that he had some underlying issue in his own life, probably pertaining to his mother. Instead of facing his sense of guilt and emotional debt, he pseudo-resolved it by advising me to submit. I was the sacrificial lamb he murdered to quell his internal "parent's" anger and to whitewash his sin.

In my habitual thinking, I am always wrong if I don't support another person's needs. Would it hurt my therapist if I disagreed with him? If only I had done so. Would I lose him as my friend? This has been my chronic worry. Was he my friend at all if he couldn't stand my disagreeing with him, particularly if it revealed his unsolved problem? Was it more important to agree with him than to honor myself?

These questions were not discussed and clearly did not cross his mind. He forgot he was there to help me heal and grow, which meant to stand up for my rights. Instead, I was led to act against and ignore my wounded heart to relieve another's pain.

Do I have the right to disagree with those whose love I seek? Do all my relationships depend on fitting in to their needs? I hate the therapist, whom

I also love, for doing this to me, or rather for suggesting rather strongly that I do it to myself. I hate myself for giving in. Being led and giving in remain problems. Those who would have me accede to wishes that please them but do me harm have to be correctly seen as not my friends.

I left Effie with my mother and lived feeling empty for a long, long time. I did not enjoy seeing Effie on my visits. I was anesthetized. The part of me that was connected to Effie, my feeling of union with her, was numb. The Effie I saw when visiting my mother was not the Effie of my experience and my dreams. She had been demoted into an object with four legs, ears, and a tail … a stranger.

This book is about the intrusion of the past into the present. The book attempts to help you see the difference between what you are feeling now and what you were experiencing then. Thus, the shifting tense is to imply the intrusion of the past into the present thinking, feeling, acting.

When does my obligation to sacrifice and submit come to an end? What must *I* do to end it? One part of my giving in to my mother has to do with maintaining my image of her as a loving individual. If I don't feel sorry for the person who is set on taking away what I hold most dear, her image changes into that of a monster. How can I relate to a monster that devours? How can I resist her control and fury after being trained to believe that I am helpless? I need to see through the mask of helplessness and remove it from my face.

How can I disappoint her if she threatens to not support me … should I ever need it? Feelings of dependency turn me into fragile prey. I am torn by ambivalence, to do or not to do? My mother is weak and needy. I have the power to help her. My mother is a monster who wants to devour me. I have to give in. About my self's existence, it means less than nothing to her. To give her my dog means that I agree with her, that I am nobody.

Heart Sealed Off from Loving

It is strange that a great loss to you can be seen as self-protective. Giving up something that all the world deems valuable can be an act of hiding. If I do not show you my feelings, if I deny them to myself, you will not get a bead on who I am and kill me. This kind of depersonalization occurs for people whose parents are destructively invasive. To the child it seems that nothing escapes their notice. The parent projects "I see all and know all" to control the child. "Don't even think of doing that …"

The most powerful form of existing is to show whom or what you love. Nothing puts you more out front than loving. Love means that you take a position regarding the one you love, especially if that person is not the choice of your dogmatic and controlling parent. Some parents even regard it as an error if your love is directed at yourself. The parents want all that love for themselves. Giving love to anyone else is regarded by them as a theft that has to be stopped, your love snuffed out.

Everything you do is run through the parents' hopper to see if it is good for them. Neutral behavior is considered bad because it does not serve them. Being neutral may be adopted by a child in lieu of giving in. Unfortunately, if this behavior is used pervasively for a long time, the child also forgets who he or she is.

You are attacked for not being/doing what such parents want. After endlessly appearing in their hanging court to hopelessly state your case, it becomes an automatic decision by your defenses, not to be seen and known. You become a moving statue, a lifeless clone of yourself. What can parents do about that?!

You act like a shell person, which frustrates parents who want to erase your sense of separation. Your shell-ness gives the parents nothing to grab and change. Your blankness and ignorance protects you from their devouring intrusion. You believe that your sense of self has gone inside so that you can no longer reach it. You are out of touch with your feelings. The protective shell has turned into a prison, and you are the loser.

However, as an adult, the idea that your internal "child" has to emerge and declare itself before you can exist as a feeling/acting person is an excuse and a subterfuge. This is the same kind of reasoning that led you to create this defense in the first place. Your real self is your current self, how you act in the world and how you feel about it. It is reaching out to people, sharing good times and bad. It is the battering as well as the caresses of life in the world that establish your existence.

To some extent you claim you are unfeeling. It takes a lot of practice to remain so numb. Now and then something arouses your feelings, but you find ways to dismiss them as not expressed by the "true" you. Whom are you kidding? Most of all you are kidding yourself. Your self may feel unreal to the extent you have kept it on mothballs. But shake it out and use it despite all your statements of not being present, and you will learn something about your existence. Not to say that you won't be awkward. Anybody would be awkward who has so long avoided human interaction.

Your "child" fears the rejecting "parent," whose rage is projected onto those you meet. But thinking they all will reject you is not supported by what happens. You cannot depend on the workings of your "child" and "parent" to know what people think and feel. You have to show yourself to learn it.

Take the life of Ida:

Ida is a woman who claims that her "freezing parent" has taken over. She says that her adult self is a shell devoid of feeling and personality. She claims that her sense of self lacks identity.

Part of this statement is a lie. It is a self-protective lie even though it seems to be lodged against the self—but that is what you do when you think you are surrounded by an enemy that can destroy you. Ida lies to fool the internal "freezing parent" about having an outside existence. She works hard to believe the lie so as not to betray her vulnerable existing self.

Most of us attempt to believe defenses that shield us from unpleasant reality. It is like children who put their hands over their eyes to deny the existence of other people. Peekaboo. Now I see you, so you are real. I cover my eyes and don't see you, so you do not exist. The children have not learned "object constancy," that something continues to exist when it is out of sight, and the children adore the power of shutting their eyes to make the world go away. Some adults continue to use childhood defenses that are magical and unreal.

Take Ida who claims to be unable to love. For starters, she clearly loves her huge and friendly long-haired cat called Henry, the most recent of a series of Maine Coon Cats, each one having achieved a full life span under her loving care.

Although she radiates love, she discredits what she does as signs of loving attachment, using a variety of defensive mental perambulations. She claims that she is emotionally restricted, which is sometimes but not totally true. It certainly is not true all of the time. Any gap of behavior in a self-description that negates one's view of the self as limited—as if the limitation is set in stone—essentially eradicates it. Being emotionally unavailable sometimes is not always. Other reactions are possible.

Ida is a tiny, extremely shy woman, child of Jewish parents who fled at the onset of World War II to Buenos Aires, a city with many refugees. Although she was born in Buenos Aires, Ida was raised by her parents in a timorous, keep-yourself-hidden atmosphere. Her upbringing deeply affected Ida's view of existing and relating with others, permeating it with the unsafe nature of being seen.

Ida is very tentative and shy about what to do and say to nonfamily people because of her sense of not fitting in. With her husband, her attitude represents another facet of self-hiding. She rejects her husband first. She is frequently dissatisfied with his behavior. She and he perpetually argue over petty things, like his share of household chores being done incorrectly or not being done at all. She frequently doesn't do her share of chores or does them to a perfect level, which is one aspect of how a couple will share a common defense. Overdo or underdo, the attack remains the same, with the partners doing a do-si-do between critic and criticized. You perpetrate, and I criticize … or vice versa. The main goals of this dance are mutual rejection and distance.

Such arguing also is a shield against talking about the truth. They do not argue about "big things" that have to do with what is wrong between them. In response to her verbal barrages, he calls her crazy and disrespects her words and deeds, but they do not discuss their real problems. It is like there is an unstated pact between them, which can lead only to the mounting hostility of short but open warfare. Unmet needs fester in her husband's mind.

Ida was raised in a one-person household, although she had two parents. Dad was mostly away at the office. He worked fourteen-hour days to make a living, but that never sufficed since his wife was a compulsive spender, a bottomless pit of need. Since Dad's own parents had been self-centered, he was raised to carry the other person's bricks of desire, not to relate to that person as a fellow human being to whom he could say "enough."

Ida's father rarely protected his daughter from her mother's onslaughts and seemed unable to make a connection. There was none of the attitude of "we stick together in the interest of being fair." This was the father's defense against feeling his own grief and deprivation. You deny damage at the hands of your parents by similarly mistreating your child. Dad had been ignored by his father the way he ignored Ida.

Dad's father had been bossed by his wife, and Dad followed suit with his wife. He knew how to surrender, to follow orders, and retreat. Ida had this behavior as a model, so she did not learn how to show herself as a person. The inability to show your self leads to losing self-awareness. You simply do not pay attention to self, another form of infantile peekaboo in which you think that what you do not see does not exist.

Ida's mother was a supremely controlling person who smiled when things went her way. Her smiling and simultaneous grasping for what she needed others to give her confused Ida and ate away at her trust. Mom always was out to get something and otherwise did not seem to enjoy Ida's company. People, including Mom's in-laws, kept giving her the objects she spoke about, some which were quite expensive; finally they got fed up with her demands and dropped her. Most of her relationships with could be friends were ended by them for that reason.

The absence of her working husband and friends is part of the reason her need was turned to Ida, from whom she didn't want things. Ida was too young to have possessions Mom desired. Instead, she sought intangibles like adulation, the right kinds of attitude and speech, and endless kowtowing. Ida was raised in the bottomless pit of her mother's needs. She hated her mother for asking and herself for giving. It was an irresolvable conflict.

As a child, the only break she had in her mother-cornered life was when she visited her father's parents, who lived quite some distance away. Both grandparents seemed different from her mother. They tried to give her what she wanted, which was seeing her as an independent person. Of course, as self-centered people, they mostly gave Ida what they liked, which luckily coincided with Ida's desires.

They were cat lovers who gave her a Maine Coon kitten. These cats are very large, hairy, calm, and extremely friendly. They genuinely seem to like people. Ida fell in love with this cuddly animal, which followed her everywhere and slept in her lap. She brought the kitten home with her, and her parents let her keep it. She could totally love this creature, which loved her back, giving unmistakable affection without a price tag. Bliss.

When he got home from work, Dad followed Mom's orders to beat and correct the girl for her reported misdeeds. Dad lacked the courage to fight for his own autonomy, as well as for his daughter's, and he didn't understand the impropriety if not abuse of rendering punishment. He maintained a distant albeit punitive position. One of the ways you deprive your emotionally needy child is by maintaining distance.

By the time Ida was four, her mother's reign of terror made having an independent existence impossible. She had to fall in line. Like a marine sergeant, Mom wanted Ida, the new recruit, to be obedient and chatty, to answer all her questions, and to be on call. When her mother didn't need her, she was to be a silent statue. At other times, the reverse was true. She put Ida through cruel indoctrinations to keep her in line. As a seeming religious fanatic who will seize on her philosophy as a weapon, she threatened Ida with going to hell for being "bad." She terrorized in order to manipulate.

Ida became a religious fanatic in turn. When a parent gives you no way out, identification with the aggressor is a solution. You won't hate me because I am you, so there is no one here to attack. She accepted that she would go to hell for being bad. Agreeing with Mom's accusations and accepting punishment for misdeeds put her in the antiself position her mother seemed to require. It also confused the child about whether she was bad, since Mom required it, and furthermore she was confused about whom she was.

After Ida returned from the visit to her grandparents, Mom's regime was stronger because Ida had better command of English. Mom's demands could be more to the point, and her child's rebellions were ineffectual. Ida remembers the day her internal "freezing parent" decided to cut off her mother's access. She became silent and withdrawn. Mom demanded and pleaded with Ida to talk, but it was of no use. Ida felt that she had no control over her lack of speech and was incapable of speaking. Control had gone inside.

Ida's notion of punishing her mother also entered her thinking, since a sword can cut two ways. She fantasized a strange juxtaposition of the two of them trapped together in hell. She punished Mom for mistreating her and rewarded her by putting them together.

Her self-centered mother regarded Ida as a parent who would provide maternal care. Ida felt the conflict of this enforced symbiosis. The persecutory fantasy that started in childhood remains with her in adulthood. She provides excessive care to her husband, whom she hates for receiving and presumably needing it. She probably would have surrendered this enforced symbiosis with her mother a long time ago if she hadn't felt so guilty about feeling hate. Sometimes to free yourself from the past, you have to let hate be. You hate that person for what he or she has done to you, and that is that. Your hatred will grow less only when you stop acting in the constricted role he or she imposed on you. Freedom is a healer.

Eventually, Ida went to college, where she deliberately did not follow the family pattern and become an accountant. She chose a field without real choice, not one that her self called for. She mechanically does the work of an undersecretary. It is a typical halfhearted negation of her parents' expectations by not choosing to do what she loves. It is part submission and part rebellion, with the result that she emotionally exists in a nowhere land and claims not to know what she likes. The internal "freezing parent" does not allow her to try new things in order to find what she wants to do, so that inner emptiness continues. She dares not venture forth.

After college, she met Schmuel, son of another family of Jewish refugees. They dated for a while and had sex after drinking a lot of beer, when Schmuel declared his love. Ida said she loved him too. Then as now, she claims to love and then disowns her love as due only to their drinking or to some other uncontrollable outside factor. It is back and forth with her, like the peekaboo of a child. Now you feel love and admit it; now you don't feel so you deny its existence. She clings to Schmuel, who allows the relationship to continue while despising his wife for her critical and frequently detached state.

Schmuel clings to her because, as the son of war refugees who taught him that he might be killed for being Jewish, he fears that no one else would have him. Ida clings to him because she cannot admit to feeling love … and who else would want to be with her? She loves Schmuel but denies it still, except when she guiltily says, "I love him." Then she again denies it.

Raised by a very disapproving we-don't-touch family, Ida developed an approach/avoidance, I need/I don't need attitude about sex. Schmuel took her inhibitions as a permanent state, which allowed him to maintain emotional distance. After an initial flurry, Schmuel did not say much about her recalcitrance. Ida did not talk about or seek his help to overcome her inhibitions, and he did not insist upon it. Perhaps Ida was afraid that once she accepted her sexuality, he would still reject her. That would have been her mother's law.

Problems that can be corrected often are allowed to remain by adults who were rejected in childhood. They'd rather keep problems than correct them and relive their childhood experiences of personal rejection. Beneath most inexplicable adult anxiety and procrastination lies serious childhood trauma.

Schmuel and Ida stayed silent, which is one of the ways they maintained their distance. Sex with the one she loves may have been too intimate for Ida. Her internal "frozen child" needs to keep a protective relationship with the "freezing parent" which dislikes loyalty to anyone but itself. Schmuel dealt with his rage at a relatively sexless marriage by coming home late from work, eating out, losing jobs, and living on restricted pay.

He would engage in nitpicking about the careless way she did things, like tracking mud into the kitchen, but he didn't deal directly with his rage. This couple was all about indirect communication. His meant, I hate you for sexually rejecting me. Hers meant, Your hatred is a good excuse for my sexual withdrawal and selfless coexistence.

By surrendering to her internal "parents" demand that she be celibate, she cannot reach out to her husband. According to her mother's religious interdiction, she will go to hell if she experiences sexual pleasure. What her mother really was against was Ida's separating from Mom's ownership and rule. Pleasure would put her daughter in touch with her self, an experience that would endanger the potency of the internal "freezing parent." Her terrified "frozen child" had to reject the experience of sexual desire.

Her husband's self-esteem cascaded to her level of rejection, although secretly each of them felt love. Schmuel sometimes plays the role of a rejecting mother and often that of rejected child, with Ida playing the cruel parent. Then Schmuel expresses his wife's helpless self. In most conflicted and often unloving relationships partners sometimes play one role and sometimes the other, that of the destructive parent or helpless child.

In their act of replaying painful mother/child relationships, Schmuel does not develop his adult self-identity. People often marry those whose defenses interlock with theirs. They can be angry at each other for not helping them escape the childhood terror that lives on inside their minds. At the same time, they have the security of living the restricted emotional life to which they are accustomed.

The punitive voice of her "freezing parent" and the terror of her "frozen child" continue to determine Ida's choices. She is a master at creating a sense of hopelessness. Being unable to fully love or to get into the kind of career she would like represents punishment by the internal "parent" for rejecting the living parent's orders, as well as Ida's doing penance for this act.

Ida states her lack of self over and over again like some kind of mantra. She says that before she can have a sense of self, she has to heal the "mother" she injured by withdrawing and to transform the "frozen child" into a warm and loving being. Stating that this condition has to happen first guarantees her never having an interactive emotional life.

The "freezing parent" and "frozen child" are unchangeable mental remnants from the past. To think you can change them is an act of rewriting history. Your mother was unloving, and you reacted to it. What happened to you is not an act of your imagination. Ida's determination to change the internal "parent" and "child" melds past and present.

Ida claims there is a wall between her depersonalized world-self and the internal world of her "freezing parent" and "frozen child." Her body, her speech and actions enact the movements of a person conducting life's business but her sense of self is lacking.

Is such a thing possible? It is not as impermeable and absolute as Ida claims. Her adult self is wearing a mask of emptiness. It is like her sense of self is hiding behind a straw-filled scarecrow. Her mind is playing tricks upon itself. You know yourself by interacting with the world, which includes in your fantasy of being in a prison cell or spaceship. As long as Ida's self hides behind a scarecrow of nonfeeling, it can claim to not exist.

The mind of a relatively autonomous adult receives messages from its internal "child" and "parent" but has a sense of distance from them. The "parent" and "child" are experienced as distant tendrils of early experience and feeling that are fed into the self that exists in the now. We all grow out of as well as carry some of the past within us. The self's current relationships, feelings, and interactions have priority over emanations from the past, those mental relics stored in the mind's dusty room.

When she looks into the world of her "freezing parent's" rages and the "frozen child," Ida cowers. Regarding them as her real self, which is an enormous error, she causes ancient feelings and directives to become her current problem. Especially, she is pulled into a sense of detachment as her abusive "parent" turns away from the world. This abusive "parent" determines the course of her life.

Ida claims to be devoid of love feelings, but this isn't true. She cares about her Coon Cat, Henry. She doesn't see that these love feelings represent her true self. She claims that love for the cat doesn't exist, because the cat has to climb into her lap to get her to feel. According to her mental schema, this requirement puts love's occurrence out of her control. She thinks that control over one's feelings establishes their reality, that feeling love has to come before physical touching. She has to go to the cat, not have the cat come to her.

Ida doesn't know that love is not an experience we control. Love happens to us all. We respond to different things, including fantasy and memory. Whatever triggers our love feelings, love exists. She doesn't recognize that when she loves Henry, she is emotionally present. She is in her self. People who cling to a defensive self-image often are blind to their contradictory behavior.

She repeats the litany of not knowing how to change her internal "child" and "parent" as if these must come first. Her reaching out and experiencing events in the world would not please her "parent." Her "child's" terror of displeasing the "parent" blocks awareness of that desire. Many deny the reality of their need to act. They hope to magically become emotionally strong and then to act. But the truth is that you have to act to develop strength.

If Ida learns to disregard her "parent" and "child" and to pay attention to what moves her, she will develop a greater sense of self. If she can love only Maine Coon Cats, so be it. However, affection remaining constrained to a single creature is unlikely. The ability to love usually spreads. She might feel aroused by her husband and know that he deeply loves her. To feel and know that you feel means to know the self.

She might feel affection for other people if she dares to imagine that they like her back. She has to stop enacting the rejected/rejecting role. She needs to be on alert for present feelings and not hide behind the mental scarecrow of "I don't feel anything at all." She may find herself full of emotion if she stops cohabiting with her husband like a ghost. They may want to drink some wine to relax enough to have sex in whatever way they can do it. Introducing sex will change the restricted emotional tone of their marriage. If she keeps procrastinating, she will remain stuck in an emotion-denying state of mind.

The self is revealed and developed by human interactions. It is the current self that loves.

Some of the needs that bind Ida to her "freezing parent" represent a frightened child crying for its mother's love. Her adult self needs to surrender this wish as impossible to achieve. The past is past, and so it will remain. She needs to orient herself toward seeking love in the real world. She has to forgive herself for failing to meet the unreal expectation of fulfilling her mother's every wish. She has to mourn her mother's love as unattainable and forever missing. Mourning will put an end to waiting for it.

Raised to Cater

The need to fit in is with us all. Many animals are social beings that honor the habits of their group. Elephants, wolves, and other animals have all kinds of rules. For wolves, their uncle babysits the kids when the parents have had enough with their playing around. In humans, there is additional pressure to surrender your individuality if you have come from a different country and need the group you have joined to accept you so that you survive.

Under these conditions, you entirely absorb their rules and habits. You take on their protective coloring. You learn and speak their language. You celebrate their events. You volunteer for service. You are happy and relieved if the group accepts your efforts and requests even more. You sell or volunteer the skills you learned in the Old Country. And you have children.

These children know only the environment in which they are raised, although they feel their parents' anxiety about fitting in. This feeling overrules any tendency on their part to rebel and go their own way. They, like any animal, feel their parents' anxiety, which causes them to conform to the parents' rules.

But what if the group they have joined is excessively programmed and they have to carry out its objectives to belong? Everything required is emphasized for the children by their parents, who fear group ejection. This fear and the inability to adjust have an element of truth, but they are greatly exaggerated. It is pathological to deeply believe in an outside threat with insufficient reason.

Any aberration in the society, as well as in the outside world, can be focused on to support the generalized notion that one must "watch out"; so the group psychology gets tighter and tighter to the point that no suggestion for change can be made. The only option is to fit in or get out and leave the society, which is supposed to protect you from an immoral and destructive world.

Take the case of Wlodek, a third-generation immigrant to this kind of society.

Wlodek is a tall and handsome man of about forty. He is the grandson of Polish immigrants who came to the United States to escape severe poverty. Grandpa was a man who fixed things. Grandma was a seamstress. They saved enough to pay for steerage in a boat to the United States. Once they arrived and got through customs, they hopped a bus going south. After living through endless freezing Polish winters, they wanted to live where it was warm.

When they got off the bus in a city they chose by chance, they met no one who spoke their language and, of course, no one from their village. They felt isolated, even stranded, and they were unclear about where to live and how to support themselves. As churchgoers back in Poland, they saw the steeple of a local church and went in to Sunday service.

After services, they joined the parishioners for coffee and cake in the church basement, where they were approached by the minister's wife, who saw they needed help. They were welcomed into the church community, which hired the husband to do physical labor, including maintaining the church; his wife was hired to clean the church and to mend church things made of cloth, including the minister's vestments.

The church gave them a sense of belonging, of having a home. As a result, the couple became totally involved with the church community, giving them a sense of membership that was passed on to their children and to the generation after. Wlodek was from the third generation.

He is pleasant man, perhaps too pleasant, like an actor playing the role of servant. He has a flat, emotionless voice. As a child, he observed his parents doing "important" work for the church's social outreach program, which included collecting money to support residences for the elderly. He took their selfless outreach as his model. The organization focused on converting new members around the world. Every church member was considered a missionary.

Wlodek's father was a church officer and had a lot of work to do, which took him away from his wife and son. His wife had an important church job as teacher, which took her away as well. Work for the society absorbed both parents. They were happy that their boy was able to endlessly entertain himself. He didn't remonstrate about their absence. He loved to take things apart and to study and then reassemble them. They would give him an object to play with and wouldn't hear from him for the rest of the day. He was a perfect kid. Right?

This society wore a cloak of morality behind which their behavior frequently went awry. Many drank and had extramarital sex. Wlodek's father did it, and his wife, like most of the women, put up with it as long as she could. Some of the wives strayed as well. No one talked about it. People were ejected from this society for divorcing. Remaining married was a religious principle. Playing around was something else. It was a look-the-other-way society. Everything was image.

Wlodek's immediate and extended family didn't speak about anything unpleasant. They told half-truths or lied about things they couldn't avoid discussing. People who dropped out of the society were no longer mentioned. They simply vanished. Drug addiction was overlooked. A suicide of someone's child who had given warning signs of despair was formally described as an "accident"; it was said that the child "went to God." Once you get onto the bandwagon of falsehood, it is very difficult to get off. The password is *cover-up*—don't admit; avoid what rankles and exposes you.

Wlodek's father did not know his son. His mother was a close second in this "I don't know you" behavior. He was a "good kid" who was preoccupied with taking things apart. Give him something to disassemble, and he'd be busy all day. Not a word was said. There were no demands. His ability to entertain himself freed them from having to provide contact.

Did he have any friends? No. He looked funny on Sunday in his dark suit and tie, his buttoned-up white shirt, shoes so fastidiously shined they seemed to glow, and a little dark hat with a brim. It was the hat that he thought did him in. None of the local kids dressed like that, even if they went to church. In his mind he was automatically rejected, so he didn't try.

Due to his life of isolation, he had no idea about how to approach his peers. Rather than join the crowd, he developed a false front to hide behind. He was the most giving, the most considerate, the most "whatever you need and I can do it for you" kind of person. People couldn't complain about him … unless they were looking for a real person.

He got so used to exhibiting a false front that he lost connection with what was true. Of course his true self was full of needs and rage and tears. It felt the pain of disconnection. The true self was forever calling out, "Daddy, Mommy. Look at me and know me," but over this bleeding sense of self were layers on layers of falsehood. There were the lies he had to believe about his father and his mother, about their marriage, about all the people who had dropped out of the organization, and about the kid's suicide, which had hurt him deeply but had been brushed away as God's will. His self-awareness was misted over by years of playing with objects because no one wanted to relate to him, by years of feeling lonely under a cloud of feigned indifference.

So then he married. But whom would he marry, and how does he love? He knows all about putting himself aside and serving. So he married a woman who was spoiled by her family, the super "last child" who used tantrums to get her way … and when that didn't work, escaped over the wall to a neighbor's property whose family catered to her.

She moved away from her family as an attempt to find out who she was, since parents who offer you everything keep you from figuring it out. People learn about themselves through struggle. They develop selfhood by venturing forth and trying to make things happen, and by investigating what interests them; they live through endless mishaps and adventures in order to figure out what is important just for them. Selfhood is a consequence of this struggle. If parents step in and do it for you, you remain an unformed baby at some level, holding on to their hands or apron strings.

Once she was away from her family, the struggle began between her internal "child's" fear of being incompetent and her emerging self's desire to try. She fell in love with her husband's serving personality and remained so until the plaster around their childish union began to crack. At that point, nothing he did could satisfy her. It was rage stimulated by her helpless dependency and his catering to it. She asked him to take her out. He said, "Where would you like to go?" If she didn't know, he'd ask, "How about *x* or *y*? Which one would *you* like?" The choice remained hers.

She'd weep in frustration but couldn't state what was wrong. After they went to her first choice, she had a fit about waiting for a table. There were too many people and too much noise. So they went to another restaurant directly across the street. She had the blues there too—went to the ladies' room and came out crying. Wlodek kept asking what was wrong. He got angry at her for not telling him when she said she didn't know. The slave mentality so early acquired awaited his master's decision. This is the consequence of a child's fitting in too much.

As he saw it, the answer had to come from her. He could label her unreasonable and wash his hands of it. He always was Mr. Fix It. What more can you ask for? When she asked him to do what she could easily do for herself, he answered yes. He felt used but submitted. He also felt a bit of anger but only a small portion of the rage that actually spun within.

He was like a hamster running on a revolving wheel that got him nowhere. He would get home from work and sit down on the couch, and she would join him there, plunk her feet into his lap for a massage, and then turn her back for more. If he didn't massage quite right, she whined a little and said "Harder ... up ... no, down." After his wife was satisfied, his cat and then his dog lined up for stroking. They all were waiting to get theirs. He was proud of his facility in pleasing them but didn't recognize he had trained them to act this way. The part of him that rebelled against being on call was stuffed into unawareness.

Wlodek didn't recognize it, but aside from his anxiety about not pleasing his wife, aside from being exasperated by her, he felt bored. Everyone who lives beneath a false façade is bored. Only life that is lived by the heartfelt self is interesting. Playing the role of servant becomes shallow and meaningless. It merely is a gesture. He had been raised to do this all of his life. It was just like childhood, with parents who mostly got away from each other and from their child. The result of this behavior is the solitude (and emptiness) to which he was accustomed.

Wlodek stated that he wants to find his true self but cannot because it is not possible given the way he enacts the search. He is speaking from his "fit in" training. It is his head that tells him to conform and serve. His head is alienated from his heart. He needs to bore down through endless layers of subterfuge till he reaches his feelings. His heart is where self lives. He asks, "How will I know if it is the true me?" He will know it is his true self because he will feel grounded and real. Whenever you lose that sense of being real, grow quiet and seek inside until you find it. Finding the self is a necessary exercise for all of us. You need to settle there.

A man who is true to himself will sometimes tell his wife what *he* wants to do. Self will say that she is free to join him if she wants to. If she does not, he will do what he wishes without her. He does not automatically drop his plans to find what suits her. Self sometimes will tell her that he wants to do it alone or to simply be alone, which is not an attack on her, even if she angrily remonstrates with him. Perhaps she will explode in rage, which actually would be a test to see if he means it. She tests his independent action as a path that she too can follow. The right to be separate is part of having a self. Only an autonomous self can create true union. True union is not an act of surrender.

A man who is true to himself can have a real fight with his spouse. A fight can wear down some of the rough edges that exist between them instead of covering them up and pretending they fit together when they don't. The true self may find that his wife does love him—or that she doesn't and can't. If the latter is the case, he can leave her or vice versa. It wouldn't be a disaster. Then he will be free to find someone who knows and loves his self. A bond between two false selves is not a bond of love.

Married Despite Wanting to Escape

She does not fight back. She adapts, adapts, adapts to what is set against her. She puts up with endless mistreatment, deprivation, and false attacks. She tries to look on the bright side, a habit that is like wearing kaleidoscopic glasses that break things into pretty patterns—when one is looking at a tornado approaching. As she describes it, she is walking a narrow line, so as to avoid the inevitable rejection. But she must always be rejected. Rejection is what is called for by the internal "parent."

Denying mistreatment and personal pain causes her to float in clouds of illusion. She was taught to deny her reality by a mother who said, "I do what I do because I love you." This includes having screaming tantrums and slapping her in the face. Seeing the bright side causes her to deny the pain of her children, who need her to protect them from the attacks of the vicious brute she married. She has to see the child's immediately inflicted pain, but the bully uses his remembered mistreatment as a child which is displaced onto his own child with him playing parent and giving an exaggerated response to the child's behavior, all which force the mother to give in. She falls for the children's smiling with their vicious father as if they like his company. She falls for this action, so obviously phony, because she has abandoned the part of herself that knows better. We all smile at virulent tyrants to ward off further attacks.

She was raised by an utterly self-centered mother who bitterly attacked her for disagreeing with her and even for having friends. Mom frequently stated, "I am your best and only friend." There was no place for the child to have an independent point of view. The daughter hid behind her beauty and talent, which impressed others. Her adult is hiding still.

Raised by such an invasive and rejecting parent, she had no way to develop independent vision. Love is the essence of a developed self. Love cannot happen when one's self is crushed beneath a lid of fear. Submitting to abuse is not an act of love.

The woman's adult self is diverted from having clear perceptions by the statements of her internal "parent." Her self wants to escape this negative influence, but the "parent" overwhelms her and fills her mind with doubt. It tells her, "Everything you do is wrong," and she believes it, even when what she does is ostensibly successful. Confusion is one of the attitudes induced by a negative "parent" who wants to run you. This woman needs to get clear of parental attitudes in order to possess her life.

Here is her story.

Janine is slim, strong, and beautiful. As a dark-haired goddess, she had amazing adventures before she married an abusive man. She survived on her own in a primitive, distant country by starting a business that sustained the local culture.

Why would such a creative and courageous person marry an egotist and a bully? The answer lies in her childhood. It was a punishing, unreliable experience with two ill-equipped parents. Her father was mostly off somewhere, a gambler and a criminal type. Her mother was an utterly self-centered person who went into rages and would turn against the child for any act she deemed disloyal. Life with Mom was like living at the base of an active volcano, flames spewing acrid smoke and steaming lava ever ready to pour down. The child was waiting to be engulfed. Years later, she found another volcano and married him.

Mom reiterated that she was her daughter's only real friend, that Janine should trust no one else. Mom inculcated in her the habit of putting up with outbursts of rage and accusatory tears, and of losing her current home, school, and friends when Mom chose to take herself to a warmer state almost every winter. Mom was a snowbird. The daughter had the flimsiest security. Sometimes Dad followed them, but he never stayed very long. Janine abandoned hope that her parents would consider her in their plans. She had many fleeting friendships, of which her mother disapproved. Mom wanted to be her only person. Janine developed her talents. She had a "prepare for the worst by developing your skills" philosophy. This attitude served her well but also served her badly, since she learned to expect nothing in return.

As a grown-up, she claimed to be seeking a reasonable mate, but her internal "freezing parent" ran the show and turned her away from adequate, sweet, handsome, kind, and respectful men. Such dependable types didn't offer a continuation of the experiences of her early abusive home. She met many excellent men during her years of working abroad. But she didn't take them seriously. Something in them was lacking.

Once she was back, she met a man who was "full of himself," furiously overreactive to anything she did that did not support his current opinion about anything and the image of his idealized self. He was not unlike her mother. They went on a trip to Italy. The trip was full of jealousy, accusations, and mistreatment. He walked out when she spoke ill of a restaurant he had chosen. He accused her of looking at other men when they sat at an outdoor cafe with a view of an ornate church façade and the statues that filled the square. He threw her out of his car and left her standing there for disagreeing with him about the right road to take. She pleaded with him to get over it. She apologized as she always had had to do with her mother. Eventually he came around, once it was established that she was the one who was in error.

She knew she had to get away from this man, but she didn't. She felt fear, hatred, and even loathing for him. She saw that he was all about image, that he would exaggerate and lie to sustain it. She saw that he did not remember what he said and could easily change his story. He had to come out right and as a winner. He lived in each self-idealizing minute. She saw that he would treat her as his enemy for disagreeing with him over the smallest thing. There might have been a secondary motive in his continual attacks. He needed an adversary to trounce and prove his might.

Yet she rolled into his clutches like a pebble down a barren slope. Why did she do it? She talks about doing what was familiar to her, which was giving in to tyrants. The repetition of self-destructive behavior due to strength of habit has some truth to it, but it is not the root of the problem. There is another world inside the mind that calls for abuse and submission to the self-proclaimed "superior" person. In that world, the abuser abuses, the abused person submits, and both call it "love."

It is the underlying demands of the internal "freezing parent" and the fears of the internal "frozen child" that drive the locomotion of choice. It is the commands of the "parent" that call the shots. The fear of nonsurvival that plagues every child who has unloving and threatening parents makes the adult move in ways that, to a stranger, do not seem sensible. It is different in the "child's" mind that exists inside the adult. A slave does not rise up against the master. A child who has been abused and frightened is in a similar state.

Janine's bullying, self-centered fiancé so much resembled her original parent that her internal "freezing parent" accepted the man as a kindred spirit. The "freezing parent" has the original parent as its model. Accepting this man as her suitor protected her "frozen child" from her "freezing parent's" rage. A person raised by a bully marries a bully and remains consistently unhappy.

Contracting in this unhappy marriage has meaning that the conscious adult does not surmise. She cannot understand why marrying a persecutor brings relief, but there is relief in the misery of cohabitating with one who punishes. It is like life in a prison camp. You have to get along with those armed-to-kill-you men with their dogs and guns. Life depends on the smile of a prison guard. If you are born in a prison camp, despite seeing other parts of the world, your sense of love still exists behind these walls.

The underlying compulsion of loving the abusive guard to save your life is disguised by the conscious mind, which uses the defense of denial. Denial is like gluing a piece of white paper over a black painting to make it look white. The blackness beneath still exists. By marrying an abusive person while pretending that all can be worked out and that love will triumph, Janine is placating the ravening beast of her internal "parent." The message implicit in this terrifying marriage was, "I still love you, Mom. Please don't destroy me."

Hyperactive to Avoid Feeling Pain

Defenses are behaviors our mind constructs to take us away from pain. Defenses minimize the experience and distract us. The pain continues outside awareness. Some of our early defenses continue throughout life to serve us in ways that prove them useful. Others cause more problems than they solve.

Feeling pain is a service. That is why the body retains the pain experience as part of its operations to ensure survival. Pain tells us that there is something we need to fix or take care of. When pain comes to a child from being with rejecting parents, denial of these feelings keeps the child from succumbing to grief and despair. Once they are grown, people retain the same defensive blindness, which doesn't sound the alarm in similar rejecting situations and therefore keeps them from getting out.

Pain calls attention to the fact that we are pounding our head against the same unyielding wall. Pain keeps us from saying, nothing I can do about it. The ringing phone must be answered. Pain forces us to ask why we are trying to get an unloving person's love. It is necessary for us to get enough of a perspective of our history which brings our attention to the fact that we are with a person who is in a deeper but familiar ditch than we are and is pulling us down.

Take the life of Tommy as an example. He avoids feeling pain through sleeplessness and drugs. He staggers on, confused.

He has a tiny farm in the Northern California hills far away from his family, from people who do not accept him. Tommy works like a dog, asks for almost nothing, and receives almost nothing. He doesn't plan ahead, doesn't act on his own behalf and especially doesn't ask for more. Tommy doesn't think that he deserves more. He is always friendly and suffering. His posture in life started a long time ago.

He sees life as a persistent kick in the ass. He fights his pain through induced insensitivity. He drinks, smokes grass and cigarettes. In this "land of plenty," despite hard work and talent, he can't make enough money to fix his teeth. A vital man in his early forties, he is losing his teeth. It doesn't help that he eats a lot of sugar. He uses sugar and coffee to start his engine in the morning, and then to keep it running. He thinks no man should sleep more than four hours a night. Any more time spent in bed "is wasted." As a result he walks around as if asleep with eyes open, a body that is working.

He is committing suicide by inches. That's what happens when self-hatred gets so great. Directly or indirectly, you will try to do yourself in. Indirectly, he attacks his self through his love relationships. His most recent attempt is with the woman who employs him. She is self-preoccupied and cannot love him back. He doesn't have the mental ability and economic clout she needs to be attracted. He doesn't have the throw-his-weight-around personality she looks for in a man as part of her own unconscious need to "kill someone" she thinks has power to prove her might. This man surrenders right off. No contest.

She can't get into his nonverbal artist's world, which might enrich her life. She enjoys buying and displaying his work, but her emotional life is untouched. She needs to be with a man who acts superior to her, jousting with her for the throne so she feels challenged in a way that she calls love. Her love has a lot of fight in it. It is a win/lose proposition. Once she has become the winner, her love just fades away. If she is the one who is rejected, she feels enormous anger. She can't believe anyone would reject and does not give up the battle. Featuring hurt feelings is one of her approaches to winning a match. "How can you do that to me?"

Tommy works ever harder for her, weeding and planting and pruning, in hope that this will turn her on. But it doesn't, although she always comes up with a new project and a new request. She feels okay about this situation, since she pays him well. She is not a person with whom to relate heart-to-heart. Then she would feel his pain. She pays him for his services. Her conscience is clear.

Sometimes, he makes love with her. She uses him to "get her off" but feels little interest and certainly no love. If he has had a glass of wine, he will fall asleep before achieving orgasm. Sleep is more important to him than coming. In addition, he only can have an orgasm in the female below position, his legs spread apart. He needs to be passively taken, a position that turns this woman off. He has to assume a submissive role before he can receive anything that is given. He cannot take it for himself; he cannot be aggressive.

His self-esteem is too poor to think of taking something. He suffers from ADD which makes it hard to have a larger view. He knows how to plant, to grow, even to sculpt, but he cannot dwell in abstract thought. Part of this narrow vision causes him to accept being used as his lot in life. He doesn't ask, Am I doing this to myself? Why am I not earning enough? How am I to work toward achieving that goal? He doesn't ask why he is chasing a woman who does not love him.

Before this self-centered woman, he cohabited with an alcoholic with whom he had a child. She was always screaming at him and was mostly out of it. Their child clung to him as a point of sanity. After a while, the need to escape distracted him from his role as parent. He left the woman by *catting* around. He didn't show up for days, until the woman and their son returned to her mother, another screaming alcoholic. Now his son lives in a nest of alcoholics sans his father. Enraged at his abandoning father, his son now avoids him—another source of torture, since he greatly loves the boy. He feels overwhelmed by loss.

He slaves to stay alive. He planted a wide variety of plants and fruit trees on a one-acre garden, which used every inch. He makes all kinds of vegetable relishes with the heat of jalapeno peppers and gives his creations explosive names. He sells them at a weekend summer market and earns about one hundred dollars a day, standing by his raft of jars, one jar open to give samples while he chats with those who stop by.

This is a man of many talents. He can create concrete miracles with hand and eye. Incidentally, he can always find a four-leaf clover in your lawn but it certainly doesn't bring him luck. Aside from gardening he does stone work. He says that his life is hell now that he is estranged from his son. He can't make a living despite doing excessive work. His extraordinary talents as a mason largely go unsung. He has no idea how to advertise his skills and set a miserable price.

He fails at love. Twice he told Alice, a self-centered woman who is his regular employer, that he loved her after they had sex. She responded by arrogantly inquiring if she correctly heard him say the words "I love you." He then apologized. He said that he sometimes needed to say it, as if it was a ridiculous supposition. She repeated his words "I love you" with a supercilious tone to shame and silence him. Her mockery delivers a terrible blow. She put more fuel into the hell of his unreciprocated love.

Does she know it? Perhaps. The woman has a dim awareness of taking an aggressive and rejecting role as a defense against feeling her own pain. Her childhood was one of reaching for love and not receiving it from her duty-bound but unemotional mother. Her emotional requests were similarly disregarded. She described her father as a friendlier man but incapable of making close contact. He saw himself almost exclusively as a provider of money.

Her mother was studiously indifferent. She taught Alice what she needed to teach and then departed. Alice had no option to change her mother's mind. She took on Mom's indifference as a disguise beneath which lurked sadistic urges. Wearing the banner of intellectual prowess became her way of life and interfered with further emotional development. She could put anybody down and mostly did. Her mother's attitude—"Learn this right away … without making a mistake, or I will hate you"—became the shape of her internal "freezing parent." It turns the same demand for perfection and subsequent hatred onto would-be lovers and friends, on anyone who hopes to get close to her. She disregards and frequently despises them for their neediness the way her mother disregarded and despised her when she reached for Mom's love.

It is the arrows of her "freezing parent" that she shoots into rejected and vulnerable lovers. The "freezing parent" harms a vulnerable person. The "frozen child" keeps out of the way, while identifying with the victim. Alice's reaction to a request for help from a friend or lover has a demanding "freezing parent's" style to it.

Her approach is opposite this when she is the asker. Then she weeps and asks them to hold and comfort her, and to ignore their schedule, their work, and obligations. They must "sacrifice" for her, give up survival functioning and conflicting needs to placate her *now*. And this is not the end of it. There are everlasting requests for more.

She does not take responsibility for curing herself of her neediness and insensitive demands. She turns away from its necessity. If you are the lover, she symbolically draws the arrow of pain from her heart and plunges it into yours. She is the "frozen child," and you are the "freezing parent."

Forced to see that she has hurt you, she quickly speaks of your hurt and takes credit for her verbal recognition as if speech is everything. But she does not long dwell in the land of guilt. When lovers seek emotional recompense from her for wounds inflicted in a way that intellectual directives, money, or gifts do not suffice, her internal "freezing parent" runs the show. She apologizes and demands immediate forgiveness so she can get back onto the demanding throne. She is a master of lip service, stating apologies and regrets. Her apology must be accepted wholesale; you must surrender your pain. The speed of her apology has a defensive quality to it. It is a get-with-it approach.

Tommy still works for her. Frequently he sounds angry without clearly stating his case. She is very seductive and knows how to jolly him out of it, which includes providing him with grass and booze. He comes to see her less frequently, which is a form of indirect speech. He says that he fell asleep at home, which probably is true but is not the whole story. She says he doesn't visit because he's tired, and she avoids the rest of the message. Alice says he is tired because of overwork. Doesn't add there is nothing else in life for him.

He works so much because the woman he loves doesn't love him. He doesn't break it off with her, because some part of him believes he deserves very little. He is waiting for crumbs.

Raised to Hide

Norma's mother Lillie demanded she not exist as an intelligent reporter, one who knew what she was seeing. Lillie was an egotistical person who had suffered a lot of hardship in the Old Country. She had to babysit for the younger ones while her mother was out buying and selling used stuff, clothing, furniture—whatever came and went from the back of a wagon with the help of a large Polish man. Her siblings had more schooling than she did in her mother-substitute position. She felt plenty of resentment for that. Her father was in the United States attempting to make enough money to send for them.

Dad was away for years. She felt very deprived due to all she had to surrender taking care of younger siblings. But more important than her burden of work was the fact that her mother did not appreciate it. No thank-you was given, no "Well done." Her mother was an arrogant person who saw herself as married to someone who was intellectually beneath her. It was an arranged marriage and not one to the Bible scholar she loved. Wrapped up in her vanity and dissatisfaction, she lacked empathy for her daughter's travail.

Her daughter Lillie developed a philosophy of "Once I'm out of my mother's clutches, I should get what I want." Mom had been all about rules and nothing about sympathy and appreciation. Lillie decided that she need not follow rules when it came to her own desires. This attitude was modeled after her mother's taking from her without a thank-you. You take what you want and overlook the giver; also, you overlook the loser who doesn't get it. People think that selfishness is a child's view of life. It also is a philosophy learned from a parent who enacts "me first." You could say that all deprived and mistreated people remain children. They regard developing empathy as improperly sacrificial and stupid.

This philosophy came with her when the family finally emigrated to the United States. She met a man who wrote in Yiddish and was famous for his *shtetl* stories of Jews living in small isolated communities. In his mind, he still lived in Poland. He didn't want to be bothered with everyday things … like earning money, like reacting to the filthy New York streets, especially after garbage strikes. The United States was not better than their homeland, but since he lived in his mind, anywhere was home.

Lillie took care of things, so he was content. She remained the worker. They had twins, a boy and a girl, and that was mostly that for sex. He felt that he owned his wife, which was a self-serving distortion, since he totally depended on her. Lillie was a factory worker with little income, and her husband made far less. He sometimes worked in a factory but didn't acquire skills to use a sewing machine, and he couldn't keep his mind on the job. He was more interested in the story he was writing—to the point of sweeping and gathering scraps within the time his job allotted. Time meant nothing to him. He frequently lost his job.

Lillie remained on the job, where she met and began an affair with Morey, her boss who met her on the sly. She could not afford a babysitter. In those days, lower-class people did not have sitters. They relied on family members who lived nearby or in the same apartment, but she could not tell them the details of her assignation.

So instead she took her daughter with her on an "important" date. It was a date arranged to please the child without any recognition of the child's ability to tell a story. She was a very smart little girl who was in the first grade. She had already learned to read and write, since an older friend in a higher grade had showed her and she immediately caught on. Her mother said they were going to the circus, and the child did know a little about clowns and elephants and trapeze acts. She yelled, "Yes!"

So off they went to the circus after meeting Morey. The little girl saw that Mom and Morey held hands when they were walking, but she mainly was transfixed by the circus. When they got home, the little girl followed her father's model by writing about her day at the circus. On the next day, she gave the essay to her teacher. The teacher saw the presence of the other man and undoubtedly figured the situation out. But she claimed that she was so proud of the little girl's writing ability that she sent her from class to class to read it. One wonders about the teacher's real motivation. Was she jealous of a child with such ability? Did she hate the sexually wandering mother, wanting to expose and punish her? The unconscious acts as a powerful tool, frequently moving us to do things we do not understand—nor would we do them if we knew our actual motives.

Some of the kids went home for lunch, and her friend Jane told her mother the story. The woman was a jealous and spiteful person who saw her daughter's friend's mother as attractive to all men, including to her husband. She ran to tell her "rival" about her daughter's writing, which revealed Mom's sexual contact.

Even before she left school, alarm bells were ringing in the child's head. She must have felt her mother's secrecy but overruled it in her excitement about writing about the circus. She concealed the essay in her underpants, knowing that something terrible connected with it was about to happen.

Her mother arrived at the school in a rage. She banged her daughter's head against the schoolhouse wall and called her a liar. Liar about what? Telling the truth was a lie and an offense? Liar! It didn't end there. Her mother convinced her head-in-the-books husband that his daughter was a liar and that he shouldn't speak to her anymore. Not wanting to be disturbed, he followed orders. It was easier to go along with her. The child lost her potential protector via his withdrawal. A protector helps a child when under parental fire retain its sense of self and not to create an internal "frozen child." The girl's twin brother, who was framed by Mom as the family genius, rejected her on general terms. "Family genius" was his mother's goal, and his sister was a competitor. It was better to reject his sister and push her away.

The mother stated that a girl of her intelligence needed to be in a better school and transferred her to a school where no one had heard her read the story. Her mother's cloud of disapproval smothered her daughter's abilities in danger and distrust. Rather than remain the brightest, she became one of the slowest students. Her mother continued to glare at her with hateful eyes when they met at meals. Nothing was said. The message was, Keep your mouth shut. Don't notice anything. Don't exist. It was understood.

Her need to be uninformed as well as unseen and unheard showed up in adulthood, when she was always reading but never completed a book. Books were strewn about the apartment on the table, in the bathroom, in her purse. She could never really tell you the plot. She married a man whose whole emphasis in life was making money. In a sense, he was lost the same way as her father was. He had been raised by an extremely poor, bitter, and disturbed father who cowed his mother and raped his sisters. His mother died from a head-in-the-stove suicide. The son blamed the whole thing on their being poor, something he was going to avoid.

He made a lot of money in the business he and his wife opened. He treated his wife as slave labor and barely paid her for her work. Every penny had to be saved. Their savings went up and up, but basically he considered himself poor. Poverty was in his soul.

The marriage was not a bad one for two people who lacked boundaries and were terribly fearful of mistreatment. He established who he was through cleanliness and money. When she invited people to visit, he couldn't wait to start cleaning up. If they had a fire in the fireplace in their country home, it would barely be cold before he swept away the embers. He was terribly fearful of anything getting out of hand, especially his feelings. Did he love her? In his way he did. His obsessive cleanliness distracted him. He would not invade her mind with accusations as did her mother, or at least not with accusations that mattered. He had too much grief and shame of his own to dig too deep.

Her own stigmatized childhood continued. She tried to write about the family. She wrote and wrote but never finished anything. She didn't say so and probably didn't recognize that she still lived in the past, a time when finishing an essay subjected her to her mother's rage.

She spoke disparagingly of her husband but never left him. They were like two children abandoned on a raft. You could say that their lack of ego boundaries, combined with the fear of harm, made them excellent partners. The gulf between them worked just fine. The missing shared emotions—about which she complained to her friends—was similar to the space she had inhabited in her childhood home, with a hateful, rejecting mother and a father who stayed out of reach. Her father's life was in his book; her husband's life was in the office, from which he rarely returned.

It is interesting how a person can get used to receiving very little and eventually, after being confronted by direct brutality, find it to be a comforting perch.

Winner Equals Loser

Sean's basic premise is, If people admire me, they've fallen for my act. The very fact that I put on an act convinces me that I have nothing real to give. This is a cart-before-the-horse argument. I think I need to pretend to be someone else because I am so inadequate. That my pretense succeeds proves that I need it. Those I fool include my fellow workers, my friends, my wife, and our kids.

How did Sean become a self-despising phony? It started when his grandfather emigrated from starving Ireland to Chicago, where he did physical labor to survive. His immigrant wife cleaned wealthy people's houses. They lived in a cheap apartment whose few rooms soon were filled with their children. One of these, a boy, was driven by the experience of poverty to make a lot of money. He got a job as a salesman. Every cent not used for rent or food was invested. His small sum grew quite large. Making money became the center of his life. Although he was born a Catholic, money was his religion.

Terribly insecure, fearing that his impoverished Irish past would catch up with him and throw him in the gutter, he used money as his key defense. Sean was born to this man, who inculcated in him the attitude that making money was life's primary objective. His father needed his sons to climb the money tree. His daughters also could climb the tree or marry it.

Sean's father was totally self-involved. He married a woman who shared his values and devoted herself to supporting his faltering self-esteem. She was the family's denier, exaggerator, and peacemaker. Mom helped Dad cover his feelings of inferiority by supporting his inflated image. They had four children. Their father had little to say to any of them. He spoke only about doing business, about how much money he or someone else was making. If Sean showed him something he had done in school, his father denied its value and made humiliating statements. Dad was in competition with his children. He felt that he gained stature by putting them down.

Mom was the family's social outreach person. She enacted the role of a divinely happy parent but was interested only in external things like her children's test scores, the money they earned, the restaurants they frequented, and the famous people they saw there. She was always looking for status and did things she thought would give her points—like having a seasonal room at a country club with tennis courts, a swimming pool, a stable and riding trails, a golf course, and hiking trails. She rarely did anything there but take a dip in the pool. She would get dolled up for dinner in the dining hall, where people could see her, and she counted the minutes until she could return to the city.

Mom used her children's achievements to boast about. What was unusual about her reactions to most of the features in her life was that everything was assessed some kind of monetary value. Working hard and doing well were not good in themselves. There had to be a money tag attached. Experience meant nothing without its dollar value.

She related to her children as though they were robots that eventually would make money. Of course, the parents saw themselves as robots too. A parent cannot respond to another person's qualities if he or she lacks them. Their children saw themselves accordingly, having accepted their parents' view, as most children do. If the only thing worth doing is making money, if your worth is connected to a number, it means that you as a person are worthless. This value also applies to Dad. It is like Dante's view of hell, with one level of hollow people with numbers carved on their backs.

Sometimes her children expressed negative feelings, which Mom attempted to address. But her insight had extremely narrow gates. She usually encouraged the child to think that making money was a solution. If their issue was Dad's coldness, she thought that if they earned enough, Dad would appreciate them more.

The sadness of this perspective was that no matter how much Sean made, it never was enough, given the ongoing economic this and that which reduce money's value and most of all, given his father's scorn. Sean was deeply stricken by the notion of insufficiency. He saw life in money terms with an ever-diminishing return. He was keenly aware of his losses and never appreciated his gains. He spoke the money language. Even though his adult self found his father boring and rejecting, his internal child believed that he made too little money to win his father's love. It follows that he was unable to love himself. He saw his *un-lovability* in terms of dollars and cents.

At a certain point, Sean accepted the mandate to get married, since that was part of his image, although some very obscure part of his person really needed to have a mate. That part of self was very obscure because he is so little in touch with his self. He found an ideal woman, one who loved without restraint and imposed very few restrictions. Maria had a relatively secure Italian family—noisy, affectionate people who happily ate endless meals together. They enjoyed salad, spaghetti, wine, talk, and laughter. They lacked self-consciousness and shame. Sean didn't have to prove that he was superior to these people.

He was astonished when one time, Maria fell asleep leaning back on the soft couch, while sitting among her friends. No one bothered to awaken her. They accepted her too. When she woke up, she wasn't worried about their feelings. He couldn't imagine anyone being so relaxed. She didn't seem to be on trial.

She wanted a home, a family to care for, and a husband. He fully provided the first two, but not much of number three. He worked very late weekday nights, and on the weekends he was around without being fully available, doing paperwork and making phone calls to attract new customers.

Children did come, three in almost as many years. The children—two boys and a girl—were dark like their mother, not reddish-haired and freckled like their dad. He took this to mean that his appearance was weak (not that red hair is a recessive gene). The acquired finger of blame points to every part of you. He would surely find it.

He even competed for the affection of their dog, a black Lab nicknamed Sully—short for Sullivan to commemorate Sean's Irish roots. Sully was an "I love you" kind of dog that threw herself into everything ... romped with the kids, fetched balls, and rolled in a heap with them. She was reasonably indestructible and didn't mind being on the bottom.

She loved to have physical contact and would lean up against people who were seated, eventually sitting on their feet. After achieving her considerable weight, she had been discouraged from climbing into their laps. Sully slept with the kids, alternating beds so that all of them got their turn. She was a sensitive dog who aimed to please.

Sean was always competing with everyone for their share of attention. He labeled it love, of which there never was enough, and he felt he lost Sully to the kids. He was unable to share their pleasure because of his lack of contact with his self. It is the self that empathizes with a loved one's grief, joy, or excitement. It was his brain that calculated his respective points. It was his brain that endlessly climbed Dad's money tree and decided he was never high enough. It was his brain that labeled himself a loser.

Insecurity about how much one is appreciated never stays outside your door. Even his dog's love for his children was used to give him a negative score. He was running for office all the time and had to come out first. This behavior reflects his internal child's struggle to win Dad's love. To Sean, Sully represents his father. To the extent that the dog chose to be with the kids rather than at Sean's heels, it underscores Sean's worthlessness.

He was always happily greeted by his children—when he got home early enough that they weren't already in bed. He eked out a negative view of their love for him using a trumped-up charge. His wife examined their homework and helped them read and write. She read them stories at bedtime. The children associated her with things connected to school as well as the wonders of the imagination.

When Sean was around on weekends, the boys wanted to play games with him, to swing their bats at balls he carefully pitched. They would wrap their arms around him in affectionate play, and would wrestle with him and shout with glee. The boys loved the rough stuff. His daughter took more of an "admire me" posture with her clothing and piano playing. How did Sean relate to all of this? He looked at what he didn't do instead of what he did. Why didn't they want him to look at their math and writing? He decided that what he did with them counted little and therefore branded him as inferior compared to Mom. All his thinking underscores his father's poor opinion of him.

As an adult, you carry the negative image assigned you by your parents unless you reveal the image to yourself. It is a struggle to reach this realization, since often you don't want to admit the very hateful idea you have already accepted—to understand its origin and then reject it.

Another serious obstacle in the path of change is your negative connection with your parents. It is a battle to free yourself, since the negative image is part of your tie to them. Hatred is what they mostly sent your way. Hatred therefore is equated by you with their "love." To give up their negative viewpoint is to sever the tie. But separation must occur if you are to have reasonable self-esteem and loving relationships, especially with your children.

Sean was not in touch with the emotional self-abandonment connected to equating the value of everything with money. His focus was only on failing to make "enough" of it. His view of love was confused. There was so little of it in his childhood that he did not clearly know its face. It is true that he and his wife and children lived in a middle-class village in their own house, with professionally landscaped grounds. Did his wife love him for that? He did not know the answer, but given his parents' preoccupation with it, he imagined the answer was yes. He noted that his car was not the most expensive on his street and his house was not the biggest. He paid attention to such things. Nothing was big enough, expensive enough to "win."

Aside from beautifying his house and grounds, which was needed to support his image, he was stingy. His stinginess, which was exaggerated to an outlandish degree when it came to the small things, shriveled him into a Scrooge. He had his children eat at McDonald's and resented paying for the babysitter's lunch. How much did it cost him? Four dollars was seen as four dollars removed from his savings, part of the infinite stairway he was climbing to win his father's love. Perhaps the four dollars he spent for her lunch would have gotten him his father's love at last. But he did not know that this idea was behind his resentment. He knew only to hold on to your money and claw your way up, like Dad.

For Sean's father, you were at either the top or the bottom in everything, and his mother followed suit. Instead of seeing his parents as hopelessly shallow, instead of abandoning his quest for their appreciation—which spread to everyone he met—he made it central to his life. He set out to be the person they all adored. Since new people were always entering his space, his quest had no point of resolution.

Of course his quest for strangers' love took him away from his children and wife. Popularity became an obsession for him, a behavioral compulsion. If he perceived a lack of interest, he felt a sense of panic, which spurred him on. He feared then that people were becoming aware of the "truth," that he actually was a failure.

With his friendly, extroverted speech and lots of hard work, he ascended to the top rung of his company. Nevertheless, he believed that he was only fooling his colleagues. He waited for his boss to come to his senses and boot him out. He analyzed the man's every gesture, every tic. Life was hell. His entire self-worth and self-image were outer-directed. He had no real faith in himself. Every moment was a win-or-lose experience. He knew no other course.

His criteria of popularity were very superficial. He had no better judgment of this than anyone who was raised to jump through hoops. For example, at a party, if someone spoke to someone else and not to him, he assumed he was unpopular. He would fall apart if anyone seemed to not like him. But how did he assess it? He barely skidded away from the negative finish line in all his real and imagined interactions. He was pursued by his negative self-image.

Loud talking and smiling almost always worked. He was a compulsive talker. His speech had a seductive edge. He always smiled with great sincerity, peering out from under his mop of red-gray hair and bushy reddish eyebrows, while looking around for the one he needed to seduce next. He would say whatever he thought was most pleasing or impressive. Acting manipulative made him feel worthless. You undermine your self-respect the more you pretend to be who you are not.

Making money had to do with improving his disguise. To believe you need a disguise undermines your self-esteem. As a result, the more money he made, the more worthless he felt. He followed his mother's approach to life as a successful phony. He viewed his wife as different from him, but he was incapable of thinking that she was okay. He was guarded. How could her relaxed state represent anything but incompetence? He associated her lack of anxiety with her being faulty.

He decided that she couldn't be superior to anyone in any way, since she had married him. She had to be stupid, psychotic, misguided, or a secret failure like himself. People who didn't come to their senses and reject him belonged on his psychological rubbish heap, a pile of discarded people that included him.

He waited for her to recover from her blindness and reject him. He expected rejection from his children. He tried to do the best for them, to be available in the way his parents never had been, but he couldn't take credit for it. Not taking credit is a viewpoint that attached him to his father. When the parent hates you and you hate yourself in like fashion, you feel a bond between you, a self-destructive form of attachment.

That his kids went to Mom for reading and played games with him when he came home proved that they thought less of him. Asked why he couldn't take credit for what they appreciated, he had no answer. He is too immersed in the unconscious patterns that attach him to his unloving parents to see his children's love.

One aspect of love is identification. He is both proud and horrified that his older son is beginning to covet money. People think that their children learn the most from what the parent tells them. This is pretty much untrue. The child learns from what the parent does (and says) when it is frequently repeated.

What the oldest learned from his father was to always think about money—how to make it and how to hold on to it. Dad paid for luxury items in the home but always with a sense of pain, as if the money so unwillingly given was a loss that would destroy him. His son speaks about how much money he has. He charges Mom for doing chores, for putting his toys away, and for hanging up his coat. He lies about his savings, pretending that he has more. He is falling into Dad's trap of hiding a worthless sense of self in the garb of money. Dad's obsession with money has made the child question his intrinsic value—hence his movement into Dad's primary defensive operation, that of hoarding the buck. A parent's sense of worthlessness and defensive cover-up is passed on.

His father is horrified by the child's stubborn imposition of this requirement on Mom, but he doesn't see how the behavior comes from him. It is hard work to uncover one's defenses rather than automatically express them, since their purpose is to shield one from anxiety.

Sean needs to get out of this hideous experience of starving his self-esteem by pretending to be someone else. He needs to surrender his hope of receiving his father's affection by earning more money. There is no point of arrival for this endeavor. He needs to stop trying to charm and seduce people to prove that he is lovable.

The idea of giving up his act frightens him. He assumes that there will be terrible consequences. He believes that there is no real person behind his charade, and he will increasingly believe this the longer he keeps it up. Even at work, he assumes that it is his phony self that succeeds, not the part that understands investing. It was his loud, smiling chatter that kept people's attention. No one would want to hear his quiet speech.

Sean listened to his parents' statement about taking his children to a $400 lunch. Imagine that. His parents said they were teaching the kids to enjoy something great. Did the kids really enjoy the food? Would they have been happier at McDonald's? His parents wouldn't know it. What could Sean say to such parents about his children or about the child inside himself?

Fearing you are a worthless person keeps you playing a phony role. Having to maintain this behavior causes anxiety and stress, but to your neurotic self-perception, being who you are is worse. His internal "frozen child" is in a panic about giving up the act. The internal "freezing parent," ever ready to attack, forces him to do it. The adult part of his mind isn't sure it is able to stop or whether it should. The thoughts of his "child" and "parent" bubble through his mind's attempts to be objective. Terror and demand generated by the pair are too powerful to ignore. The more you listen to these voices, the more believable they seem. You reduce their power by ignoring them.

Marked by his actual parents' unloving treatment, which shows his inadequacy, he cannot believe that anyone loves him. The wife stays with him because she needs a provider. His kids' feelings are just the same for anyone. Anyone who falls for him is doing it for the wrong reasons, so their affection is without value. He is convinced that what gets him ahead in everything and with everyone is that they have fallen for his falsehood. He can't experience that he is loved by those he admires; he can't experience those who love him as worthy of respect. Metaphorically speaking, in his mind, shit attracts shit.

There is a hint of arrogance in seeing himself as a successful fake, since he deems people stupid enough to fall for his act. Only among his wife's family, a happy noncompetitive group, does he think he doesn't have to lead the discussion. He doesn't have to know all the facts and come out on top. With them, it is a different kind of life, a good life. It allows him to simply be himself.

Phony people never believe that anyone can love them. Their partners don't know the real person, so whom do they love? This man has so long played a starring role that he isn't sure there is anyone to be known. He sexually plays around to prove his masculine worth, even more to prove his worthlessness. Worthlessness attaches him to the unloving internal "parent." Women go to married men for what they will spend on them. He knows it and they know it, regardless of what they say. If they're attracted by his charm, his image of I care for you (right now in bed), and by his sexual technique, this situation equally undercuts his self-esteem. He is merely a sex machine who is betraying his wife's trust that he is off working and not screwing around. The popularity contest is at all times a losing game. If you don't respect yourself, how can the applause matter? Feeling worthless fits in with why his father doesn't love him. It invalidates his wife's love for him. The experience of being unlovable is supported by his actions. To the internal "child" I am rightly punished by my angry "parent" for doing wrong.

Sex with his wife doesn't count, since he has written her off as inferior for having selected him and doesn't much seek it. Even the sex act is conscripted by his need to create an image. Having outside sexual contacts sullies his relationship with her. It offers him more evidence that she was stupid enough to fall for him. A person who so much despises his self will behave in despicable ways that support this attitude. The wife complains a bit and withdraws into herself a lot. She tells herself to be happy with her home and children, and to some extent she is. But behind it all, colored by her partner's unavailability, she feels deprived.

Sean needs to stop pretending to be who he is not, to speak his mind, to do his job, to act loving, and to be committed to his wife. He needs to receive his children's love. He has to shuck the hated self-image created by his parents' lack of care and act like a butterfly emerging from its cocoon to fill and spread its wings. His role is not only to be that of a giver, which represents his vanquished "frozen child." He needs to be in touch with love received. It is hard for a person raised to hate self to believe that he or she is loved. What if you think you are loved but are wrong? What if you are loved and then the person decides not to love you anymore? What if after people get close to you, they realize you are unlovable and withdraw? People raised without love have great fear of allowing themselves to believe they are loved and then to lose it. It is easier to put on a show of acceptance and beneath it to be detached. It is easier to say no than yes.

Does he need to hear rave reviews to sustain his ego? Or is it just the opposite? Do rave reviews alarm him about being discovered as not good enough, and therefore propel him into continuing his phony act? People with serious self-doubt feel the terror of discovery when they are raised above the crowd. He needs to see that receiving praise means that his work is good enough and then forget it. He can learn that he is an acceptable human being only by being genuine with them all. And most of all he needs to send and receive love. Only by doing this will he keep his children from turning into self-rejecting money-obsessed people like himself.

Ever-Deserted Victim

It is extraordinary how a person raised to be rejected by her parents carries that as a parental "curse" that will cause its reoccurrence. She verbally reiterates this point of view with those whom she holds dear and thinks it with everyone else. Her verbalizing the expectation makes one think that she is determined to make it happen. How many times can a lover hear "I know you are going to leave me" before he picks up his hat and departs to find a lover who believes in his loving commitment?

It is worse when she bemoans her fate with her child. There is no "negative" in a child's unconscious. "You will leave me" repeated over and over again—even while pleading with the child to remain—is heard by the child as "I want you to leave." Whatever is endlessly repeated to a child is taken as an expectation, if not an order.

You could say that the child's leaving her is against its mother's wishes, but this is not entirely so. Her self speaks for the union of mother and child, and her internal "parent" speaks against it. The internal "parent," like the actual parent, wants to punish the woman for divorcing the man her parents approved of—and who wanted to live down the block from them—and marrying a man who chose to live in a different city.

Here is the mother's story:

Judy lives in a fog of fear. Her face is all scrunched together, lined with worry and tension. Even her smile is anxious. She continually repeats that her husband will leave her, although there are no signs of it. She tells him, "I did something you don't like, and you are angry at me." The husband says he isn't angry at her or that he is angry at her for playing victim, more than for anything else.

She adores her three-year-old girl, who talks a lot, crawls into her lap for a hug, and then goes back to drawing, playing with dolls, or exploring. She says, "It is inevitable my daughter will leave me. Everyone—my friends, my husband and child, all of them—will abandon me the way my parents did, especially my father."

To make a double disaster out of her rejecting childhood, she attributes abandonment to the person she loves most, her daughter. Her husband is not so easily pulled into enacting her prediction, but the daughter can be a different story. If Mom tells the child for years that she is going to desert her, the child's unconscious mind will cause compliance. The child will perform the parent-predicted action even if it is told to her as a warning, because the unconscious mind hears Mom's statement as a "do it" even if it is presented as a "don't." The unconscious mind lacks nos.

Fear and negative expectations come from childhood. She comes from an upper-class WASP family living in Grosse Point, Michigan. Her parents were close-knit in the negative sense. Any independent action got their ire up. They were great grudge bearers and had no idea of how to discuss disagreements or different opinions. Theirs was the right way, and that was that. There was only anger, yelling, silence, withdrawal, and sometimes drinking. You were either with them, which meant you agreed with them, or you disagreed with them, which meant you were against them so they discarded you.

Despite years of psychotherapy, no one has seen Judy's post-home experiences of "You reject me, or I reject you first" as self-generated. The psychotherapists were pulled into a sympathetic stance due to all her stated pain. But Judy doesn't need sympathy. She needs to be asked why she is creating her negative expectations, in order for her to develop the ability to stop. She is no helpless victim.

If the parents are cold, distant, unavailable, and attacking, that becomes the child's view of the world. If the parents rejected the child or young adult for the least infringement of rules, for disappointing them by doing something unacceptable to them (such as "You can't have a friend like that"), very hateful parents—the ones who feel directly attacked by any diversion from their rules—won't speak to their child for a day, a month, a year. There's hell to pay for having an independent existence. They hated Judy for ending her first marriage to a man of whom they approved, including the fact he chose to live nearby.

A child raised this way, grown to adulthood, is always waiting for the axe to fall. Judy believes that anyone who claims to love her will reject her at some unexpected time and with little warning. This expectation extends to all people—spouse, child, friends. No one will remain. Such a person is schooled to be a victim. She is always looking for "I am being rejected now," which is very exasperating for the nonabusive spouse or child or friend; the expectation often leads to her being rejected just for that. The self-proclaimed victim trains the would-be rejecter to reject.

It is a big step forward for a person raised to be a victim to recognize that it is learned behavior and therefore changeable. Mind-created illusions have to be discovered over and over again. Humans are rarely one-time learners when the perception to be changed has been long rehearsed. That an idea makes you fearful does not make it true. Do not worship terror. Many people take their feelings as closer to reality than their logical thinking, although thought always precedes feeling. Even if it is out of memory or awareness, it is thinking that determines what we feel.

If our thinking is outside of our awareness, a defense that many use, we do not know why we feel what we do. The fact that our thinking is largely unconscious does not mean it does not exist. We need to track it down. Thinking in the unconscious mind is very powerful precisely for that reason. It is not readily available to analyze. We are carried away by urges to act in a certain way, but we don't know why.

There are many paths to the unconscious. One of them is by free-associating to what you dream. You allow your mind to drift on the dream imagery. See what comes up, and associate to that. A dream represents an activity of the mind around something important to you, when the defensive strategy is less effective. Eventually, you will have a notion of what is going on.

Another way to track down unconscious thinking is through your slips of the tongue and fantasies. It is any place where the horse of the mind runs free. You find the presence of the unconscious when you make the same so-called "mistakes" over and over again and seem unable to stop. What is the personal force that calls them? What seems to be their message? Let your mind play with that.

Some call the actions of the unconscious a simple "habit," but that word barely explains their persistence. You have trouble attributing the idea "habit" to actions that lead to constant loss, to severe mistreatment, or even to catastrophe. You need to ask, "What do I get out of doing this? Whom am I trying to please?" Ask, "Why does subjecting myself to another's mistreatment and abandonment, or to dropping a relationship without good reason, feel like the safest road to follow?" Without the workings of the unconscious, none of this makes sense.

You cannot change the mind of your internal "child" or "parent." As they were created during childhood, so they will remain. It is how you, the adult, relate to their ideas and emotional signals that counts. Say the "child" is fearful of being close to someone, but you are interested in getting to know that person. You must ignore your "child's" fearful messages. If the "parent" castigates you for your interest, you still investigate in order to know if what the "parent" thinks or fears about that person has validity. It is the victim's role not to investigate and find out. The potential victim either submits or runs. "Normal" people take their time entering a relationship. They do not jump into it with their eyes closed.

Say the person you desire as a lover, friend, or partner isn't interested in you. The internal "parent" wants to attack that person for rejecting you, and it also wants you to feel ashamed of your desire. The adult has to tell himself or herself, "Win a few. Lose a few." The adult has to call it "wrong chemistry" and let it go. Not all people like all people. To cling to one who rejects you is taking the position of a victim. The adult must forbid himself or herself from clinging to anyone who is disinterested or obviously ambivalent. To hold on to such a person guarantees feeling pain. Every relationship has its tough spots, but not knowing if you are wanted should not be one of them.

The adult mind has to regard hateful messages sent by their "freezing parent" and submissive messages sent by their "frozen child" as inappropriate in the now. They must not to automatically believe everything they think and feel. The more they study their history, the more they will recognize the part of their mind that was formed by childhood experience. They need to see if their view of life and how to survive its difficulties remains stalled in a past approach.

Adults need to learn their history in order to become less puzzled about their compulsions and constraints. You need to understand how you learned compliance or self-destructive rebellion. The more you give in to past perceptions and defenses, the more you believe in your expected negative consequences.

You need to remind yourself that what is expected hasn't happened. Testing for danger and studying outcomes needs to be repeated until the adult mind separates from its internal "child" and "parent." Your "child" and "parent" will not stop talking to you. It is how you respond to what they say that counts. You need to relate to your hateful "parent" as a frequently misguided bully and to your submissive "child" as a part of you that is arrested in a fearful childhood. You, the adult, need to treat them as relics of another era and move on.

Afraid to Be Seen and Known

Hiding is an issue for many of the people who fail to find love. The fear of rejection, of being physically, mentally, or in some other way harmed, leads them to use the defenses of acting invisible or of developing a false identity to hide behind. In the realm of love, these defenses lead to receiving none. To be loved for what you are not or who you pretend to be is a vote of no confidence by you against your self. That is why the defense of invisibility often leads to other kinds of self-destructive behavior. You further attack yourself because you believe that you are worthless. In the internal "child's" mind, it is hoped that self-attack will win the rejecting "parent's" love. The more you enact this cycle of pretending to be different followed by self-attack, the more you believe you need it.

The only way out of this self-destructive cycle is to live the truth. This does not mean to parade your faults and weaknesses. Parading weaknesses is another form of defense—I show you what is wrong with me so you can reject me right away.

In the development of love, we find strengths and weaknesses in our partners—things they do that bother us, so we ask them to change, but also behaviors we care little about or even enjoy as a first-time experience. We love a person who is different. It is not a marriage of clones, essentially self to self. This is part of the fun as well as the difficulty in creating union. The essence of love is taking the good with the bad. It is a level of commitment flowing between us that allows us to be who we are together, to smile and breathe.

Take Oscar's situation.

Oscar is a West Coast black man whose early intellectual gifts led to training that set him way above his father's accomplishments and aspirations. His ability to read and write in grade school led to his receiving a scholarship to a private school. Usually he was the only black in the class, and this was also sometimes true in the school whose scholarships funded him through graduate school.

His attraction to ancient cultures probably is the result of his personal history, which goes back to the experience of his great-, great-, great- … grandparents, who were captured and hauled from Africa on slave ships. Then they were separated from African tribal neighbors who spoke the same language and had a common culture. The diffusion of cultures by slave owners was done deliberately so that the captives could not talk to each other about resisting, attacking, and escaping. Their culture was deliberately erased. Slaves were supposed to remain ignorant of their past. Even learning to read was forbidden. They were schooled to be Christian laborers and were beaten for any insubordination; their women were raped, and their children were sold. The absence of a historical past inflamed Oscar's interest in buried ruins, particularly in Africa. He needed this information for the development of his self-image. He needed to fill the emptiness, both personal resulting from a rejecting home and historical resulting from an empty past.

To some parents, that their child is a precocious and inspired scholar would be a cause for celebration. But it was not for Oscar's dad. He hated every step his son took out of the morass of poverty and ignorance in which the family dwelled. His mother was too frightened to represent an opposing view. Oscar was terrified of his violent and vituperative father as well. The support of his teachers gave him a ledge of emotional safety so that his intellectual interests could draw him away. The conflict between being seen and being invisible, between doing and not doing something that was important to the world, started then and continued throughout his life.

Oscar is famous to people who know about such things, and he is about to become much more so via his study of ancient kingdoms, particularly those buried one beneath the other as a consequence of war. It's interesting that the consequences of war should pay off for him, since he was raised in a warring household. Home life was less a war between matched sides than a rout and subsequent occupation. His father terrified them all.

Dad was also a digger but not into ancient civilizations. He was a worker who repaired sewer systems in a large city. He went down into the bowels of the earth with a pickax. He may have felt he ruled the city from below, but more likely he felt like a mole. The only place he had real power was at home, over his wife and children.

He was enormous, a very strong man, with huge biceps, enormous calves, and large fists. He wore work boots, lace-ups with metallic toes, even at home. You could hear him tramping through the house. When he lost his temper, which was almost constantly, he would attack with his fists or feet. He put his foot through many a wall. No one in the family ever contradicted him or took him on.

Oscar was his youngest child, a position that had advantages and disadvantages. As the youngest by some seven years, he was the "baby" whom everyone but his father spoiled. He got a lot of negative attention from his father, who projected self-hatred onto the child he labeled a weakling. Probably, his father's father had done the same to him. The image of inadequacy is denied by passing it down from bullying parent to helpless child. Probably all serious bullies feel like weaklings. They attack those who will put up with it. Unconsciously, those mistreated by them are actually themselves. By attacking another as weak, the bully declares, I am the strong one.

Oscar grew up in terror. His mother did not defend him. She too much feared for her own life. He was earmarked by his father as a coward. While absorbing this label into his self-image, he took up running and gym to build his body. He became lean and strong but had his mother's angular frame, not his father's bulk. Even Oscar's exercising himself into good tone did not please Dad. Perhaps the only way to put a halt to his father's projection of weakness onto Oscar would have been to beat the man to a pulp.

The son showed himself to be a homosexual, which infuriated and secretly pleased his bigoted father, since the son now carried Dad's projected sexually inept image. The father assumed homosexuality represented weakness rather than a natural choice of sexual partners. The son wasn't into roughhouse sports and had girls as friends. Again to his father, how shameful! The son was reading about ancient cultures and imagined dwelling among them. He did nothing his father could appreciate. The ancient cultures were too complicated and erudite for the man to hate. Their foreignness gave his son an out. It is interesting how sometimes a profession is chosen because the attacking parent can't go there.

Oscar went to college, where he majored in archaeology. He got into summer digging while still an undergraduate. After graduating, he joined ongoing projects and dug full-time. Eventually, he made discoveries. He found ancient artworks, armaments, and temples; he was noticed by the world of archaeology. That's when his antiaccomplishing behavior first appeared. He discovered porn sites on the Internet. He would turn on the computer and remain entranced for hours. Hour after hour was lost to porn. As his reputation in archaeology grew, he spent more time watching.

He had a lover who deeply loved him. They embraced each other in every way. Then his lover caught AIDS and died. Oscar felt that he died beside him. He had put his life in this man's arms, an older, stronger person. He mourned his lover's death for years. His apartment had photos of his lover smiling from every wall. Still, he felt alone.

Finally, he got a new lover. He loved this man but kept the photos up. The message to his new lover was, You're not that important to me. His lover was hurt by his second-class status. Hearing about this, Oscar felt regret, focused on his new partner, and took the photos down.

Seriously declaring himself as a lover, he felt more exposed again. Oscar had loved the other man and lost him. He felt that loving anyone now was taking a huge risk. It portended loss due to death. The risk of intimacy haunted him throughout childhood with an abusive father. As an adult, AIDS was like his father, ready to slam him into oblivion. Having sex with strangers, which he did on the sly, also played into his fear of oblivion. You court and do the thing you fear most in order to suppress your fear of it.

Having a reputation as an archaeologist made Oscar visible, which led to a childhood fear of his father's rage. Invisibility was preferred. Taking outside strangers as sex partners also threatened him with death by AIDS. He ran from his preoccupation with death and the fear of losing a lover, into Internet porn. This solitary engagement seemed to have no threat. But that isn't so. His habit of watching porn got far worse as his archaeological reputation grew. He was asked to join the dig of a newly discovered kingdom in Turkey in North Africa, in Burma. They were waiting for him to find time, to lend his wisdom and energy to their work. The only thing he needed to do was find the time.

But he didn't find time; he wasted it. He didn't know why he was compelled to sit before his computer looking at porn. He dabbled his time away. He unconsciously felt that this behavior was saving his life. His now-dead father lived on inside his mind. Ever threatening, his internal "freezing parent" would not let him climb onto the world's stage. After the living parent died, the threatening "parent" lives on inside his mind.

He wasn't aware of the origin of his fear. Oscar distracted and protected himself with his porn site fascination. He ran through the city streets to strengthen his body. Then he compulsively ate sweet and fatty foods to undo the gains he'd made, which made him weak and fat again. He was constantly doing and undoing his progress. He was afraid of becoming "too" strong and "too" successful. But he didn't understand this. He thought that watching porn on the Internet was taking a break.

The more famous he got, the more he enacted the role of weakling, even in his sexual life. It is as if the internal "freezing parent" so threatened the internal "frozen child" that enacting the role of victim was felt to be protective. It is like an animal that, unable to get away from an attacking creature, will fall on its back and expose its neck to the predator in order to engender a kind of sympathy.

He found outside lovers, strangers whom he sucked off, taking the baby, passive role. It is not unusual for grown children of assaulting parents to become terrified when success arrives or is on the verge of arriving should they continue doing their outstanding acts. The internal "parent" threatens. The mind of the conscious man is invaded by the mind of his internal "freezing parent" and "frozen child," which together tell him to slack off. Slacking off is imagined to save him from his internal "father's" fists. We learn psychological defenses as young children and unconsciously repeat them for the rest of our adult lives.

He was afraid his lover would find out about his outside sex with strangers, afraid that the lover would learn about his compulsive viewing of porn sites. His lover would see him as unfaithful, which in many ways he was. A person who can't be faithful to himself can't be faithful to another. A person who betrays his health and his profession hasn't the strength to be loyal to anyone.

He felt the danger he was bringing to his career and to his love life. He was confused about his habits. He didn't understand that he unconsciously used self-betrayal to save his life. Only by uncovering and knowing his great fear of his father will Oscar be able to stop living this way. He will be able to see his fear as part of an ancient experience with a virulent father that no longer applies. He will be able to stop viewing porn sites as a way to kill time so he can't become too famous at his work, lest his internal "parent" hear of his fame and kill him. He will be less driven to act the role of a needy baby drinking the semen of strangers in order to protect his adult self. He can be successful, famous, and loved. He can be a self-respecting adult man who loves his lover, is true to the man, and does his chosen work.

Sometimes He Does What He Wants and Still Loves You

People raised by extremely self-centered people frequently misunderstand the concept of autonomy and take what their lovers do to please themselves as attacks and rejections of them, when nothing of the sort is happening. It is hard to find the middle of the road, an objective and neutral way of seeing, when your mind is fixed on the pain of not receiving. Demanding complete and continuous service is abusive to your mate. There is bound to be negative feedback.

The pain of rejection, of never counting for much with your parents, cannot be denied. You need to recover from this experience. Your feelings and what you should do about early abuse remain unresolved issues. But feelings engendered by your being unloved as a child should not turn into accusations against your mate. You have to distinguish between past and present, to separate then from now. If you do not, there will be endless pain and demands for retribution. There will be unwilling service by your partner or hateful refusal, both of which can destroy your relationship.

Take the story of Monica:

Monica was raised in an immigrant family that came from Sardinia. She was one of many children who were born over an extended period of time. According to her mother, all of them were "accidents." There was far too little parental caring. Dad was off drinking, especially after he opened a bar. Mom stayed away from the household to avoid seeing Dad. She was hanging out with her friends. Her children were on their own and taking care of themselves. They had to.

There were much spite and rivalry between the siblings, especially towards the girl who was designated this week's mother substitute and had the power to please. For example, if Monica ever asked for her favorite breakfast cereal, banana chips, the child who was saddled with the shopping ran up and down the grocery aisles until she found the cereal that she liked. It wasn't banana chips.

Dad was worse than the absentee Mom. He frequently exploded into alcoholic rages, when he wasn't moaning in the corner of their living room, treating his latest hangover with a "hair of the dog." To survive in such a setting, Monica became fiercely independent. She was able to meet all her basic needs. She could cook, sew, iron, and fold her clothes, which she neatly put away, and she could wash her hair and style it, all from a very young age. She went through a lot of schooling and received high grades. She got a work scholarship to college. Having learned to repair almost anything, she put many of these abilities together and made a living.

Monica married a man whose mother had been a hysterical submissive, a woman who played the victim card. His father was a self-centered bully, a well-educated and brilliant egomaniac who switched from one "important" job to another. He was a minister who couldn't get along with the congregation or anyone with else with whom he was supposed to work. He would get fed up with whatever job was at hand and would use explosive language so that his employer and congregation reacted against him. He had no commitment to anything outside his feelings at the moment, and he took up drinking to ease his pain. Drinking increased his temper and mean behavior, as well as his demands. It emphasized his negative aspects.

His towering egotism made him think that his children were supposed to read his mind. Things had to be done "just right," which meant that they met the requirements only he could know. He believed that they should know what he needed, so he stubbornly and provocatively wouldn't spell them out. Many people with grandiosity demand mindreading from their children and their spouse, who are seen as servants. Dad felt that having to ask demeaned him. A king needs only to imagine his requests, and his servants will comply. He needed to substitute them for himself as life's victim, to carry away his pain. He needed them to be a target for his rage.

There was no way to please this man. A person who needs to be idealized but is treated by the world as an ordinary fellow has great feelings of pain and rage. He disgorges these feelings against those who are closest and lack defenses. First he attacks his wife and kids. He brings them up on charges—sometimes meaningful, often ridiculous. He insists that they not talk back. His index of rage ascends if they argue.

Monica married this attacking man's younger son. She was attracted to him because of how helpful and considerate he was. He had been a victim to his imperial father and to his older brother, who was a bully just like Dad. He also had been victimized by his mother, who featured helplessness to control her children. Weakness can be used as a mode of manipulating those who sympathize. The man's freedom had been taken away by all of them.

This younger son loved Monica, and she loved him back. Since her background had to do with having her needs ignored, she pressured him to do everything she wanted, even if it interfered with his own intentions. She railed at him if he planned to do something alone. Being left out stimulated her memory of a childhood with virtually nonexistent parents.

She fell into the habit of saying, "If you love me, you'll do what I ask," quite like what his mother always said. They brought to each other needs that were never met by their parents, as well as behaviors that were used by each parent to control. Each one is looking for a certain kind of love that was never given. They both found in the autonomy of their partner the selfishness of their parent.

He countered her demands with stubborn resistance. He growled, "I need to do this for myself. I've always done so much for you." When she further pushed him, he felt his hatred for both parents, his hysterical mother and his tyrannical father. It was his mother's "Do what I say, because you'll hurt me if you don't." It was his Dad's "Do what I say, because I demand it and will hurt you if you don't." He felt unloved by his wife because of her self-centered behavior, and she felt unloved by him for the same reason. They saddled each other with the image of their unloving parents.

This is an aspect of the repetition compulsion: not finding in the one you love what was seriously missing in your parents. Finding these negative behaviors in your partner doesn't mean that extreme selfishness exists. That neither partner is a self-centered egomaniac gives them a chance to work it out. Neither is an exact match to the other's parent. Both are overly submissive and deprived grown children, attempting to create love. Both are angry at the repetition of an unloved past they imagine or exaggerate.

They need to learn that each has the right to sometimes put self first, not to be a slave to the other person's needs. Love is not a serve-all-the-time requirement. They need to learn about each other's childhood injuries, and about their own. This way, despite being driven to ask for too much, they will see their exaggerated demands and not be so reactive when their partner sometimes cannot or will not do it. With understanding, childhood hurricanes turn into passing adult showers.

Understanding will keep each from seeing the other as a selfish beast, an idea that could destroy their marriage. They did not marry their parents, but there may be a little of their parents operating in each. Children frequently identify with the stronger parent and pick up some of his or her objectionable traits. It is up to us as adults to know these traits and reject them. We hold on to our parent's bullying and other dysfunctions only because we see ourselves as helpless. Imitation can represent a child's defense. Stating our needs and setting limits proves this isn't so.

There is room for each to grow out of childhood isolation and deprivation so that their marriage can be happy. They need to understand that their mind remembers unmet needs. It holds on to traumatic experiences despite their desire to forget.

In a marriage, the couple feel as if they are living a replay of the past. The past is there between them but calls for a different response. When hearing their request rejected, they may take this as a sign they aren't cared for. Around the problem of rejection, each fears having to ask for something, feels a compulsion to agree, and fears the consequences of saying no. They need to see that sometimes their partner does not want to deliver what is requested (at least at this moment and sometimes always) but still loves them.

This is an early lesson learned by children of loving parents. The parents are not always able to give what is asked for but still love them. A lover who can't comply with a request, after stating this and seeing the partner's hurt expression, can say, "I'll do it later." Giving a time and date will help. So does softening the negative stance by saying, "I love you," if they feel it, since love is not a thing to be falsely declared. Giving a hug doesn't undermine one's autonomy.

If individuals hold on to demands that are not of an emergency nature but simply a wish to have it *now*, they can be asked to explain why they have to have their way at this time. Understanding their reasoning does not imply obedience. Understanding has to do with learning others' history and developing empathy for what they are going through.

Partners might weep about what they never received in childhood, which helps others to understand without forcing them to comply. It remains a sometimes yes and a sometimes no, depending on their own needs. Understanding does not imply forced acceptance. Empathy is not subservience. Partners have the right to make up their own minds.

Life goes on as a partnership of two separate beings. Neither is to become the other's slave or ignored offspring, as occurred with their parents. They attempt to help each other recover from their unloved past, but it is not required that they make up for all that was not given. Some of what was never received will have to be mourned as forever missing. Mourning is a healer.

A loving life occurs as they grow into adulthood together. Adulthood implies the ability to take reality as it is and enjoy it. This is the only life you've got, so what's your choice? You will become a stronger person if you don't take your loved one's behavior in a self-referential way. What he or she does, doesn't have to refer to you. Most interpersonal mistreatment given or received has to do with pain, anger, and needs carried over from childhood. As they learn each other's history, it makes them happy to learn that their partner increasingly knows and chooses to be with them. Intimacy is scary and wonderful. It is scary because you always have a bit (or a lot) of fear that once known, you will be abandoned, and the ever more wonderful experience that it doesn't happen.

Exploitation as Love

If your childhood combines an excessive amount of being ignored and criticized by your parents—whose demands you met with little thanks and who subjected you to all kinds of mistreatment, combined with frequent statements about how much they loved you—you are confused about what you are supposed to give and to expect, as well as how to handle your eventual partner's needs.

Once you are grown, you are a patsy, which means that whatever partners give or take from you, whether or not you ask for it, creates a debt for which they require payment. Their demands go way beyond what you would like to do and are able to give without robbing your self of money, strength, and time. The partner masquerades as a "giver." He or she assumes a position of honor, but there is little honor earned.

She met a guy, an environmental photographer who was one of these types. Mike was trying to use his photographic work to aid the environmental movement and was quite good in bed as well. He introduced her to postures she never had done before, but he was able to function only in the wee hours when she would rather sleep. His waking her up at three in the morning for sex is an example of "I give you some but take back more."

When her friends visited, Mike dominated the conversation. He had flashing dark eyes and a very loud voice, and he almost always interrupted her. He always dressed all in black, some kind of quasi-outlaw image. His voice boomed out over her shy speech. She felt humiliated and ignored by him, especially when he flirted with her cousin's showy wife, but then she argued with herself about it. Hadn't he given her a photo of elephants standing beside a watering hole? His flirtation didn't really matter, did it?

Her very good friend Connie later pointed out that Mike and her two female friends all tried to give her orders. They told her when and how to serve. Connie said, "It is your house and your food, so you need to make the decision. If they don't like it, let them remove themselves."

She knew her friend was right. Connie was a strong and much-respected person, and was almost always loved. But having been raised by very controlling and threatening parents, not only did she not know how to assert herself, but she was plagued by the notion that no one would befriend her if she did. The reality of Connie, who loved her and said she was inappropriately obedient, did not stop her from submitting.

This notion came from parents who frequently announced that she was loved only by them and could be loved only by them, in order to keep their hold on her. Why did she believe this? All children believe in their parents' love, even if the children tell the parents "I hate you"; sustaining a child's life depends on the parents' love, and the child has to believe in it. Children cannot accept that their parents would deliberately deceive them. To believe that they live under an indifferent or hostile roof while being totally dependent courts madness, a state of rejecting reality. Where else are small children to go in the world or in their minds? The parents must be assumed to love, that they are your friends and mean the best for you, even if they seem to hate you and you hate them back.

So she tolerated the man and supported him and let him live in her house. She served her visiting boyfriend's needs despite her body's fatigue and her mind's frustration at not listening to her self. She allowed him to use her up.

Mike told her of the wife he had abandoned, along with their three children, in Mexico when he was gone over a one-year photography trip. He found that his wife had sold their farm. How dare she! He spoke of his children, who were now living in a Mexican city, the daughter married with children but still close to him. They smoked pot when they got together and ignored the years of his absence. Mike's daughter sustained his image as a decent parent by accepting that his absence was due to work. His sons were less willing—more loyal to Mom, more loyal to self. They were not so easily bought.

She saw that this man expected her to be his ongoing contact, the one he would live with whenever he was around. She was like an on-location wife in a third-rate movie. Was there a you-live-with-me hostess when he was in Africa? He did not regale her ears with such information. He was too smart for that.

She finally called a halt to all of this after he got her to drive him to San Francisco in the middle of the week to show his photos to a gallery owner in hope of getting a show. She had to take time off from work. They were on a tight driving schedule. The gas was expensive. She was exhausted leading two lives, working for herself and serving him. A thought penetrated the fog of her so-called love, one that affirmed her autonomy. She didn't want to continue anymore. She told him to move out. She said it in a hurry.

He was very hurt and said he felt betrayed. After all, look at all the good he was doing for the world. He tried to make her feel that supporting him was an offering to the environmental movement. She said she was too exhausted to continue, which took her off the hook of obligation. Sickness, exhaustion, and inability to function seemed to be her only excuses. If she had not been so tired, she could not have stood behind her no.

Where did the personal side of this obligation come from? It was concocted by self-serving arithmetic that he imposed on her. He cut some of her firewood and stacked it. In return he lived in her house and had her drive him where he needed to go. Also, he pointed out that he had a fire going in the living room when she returned on the weekends. She was able to create her own fire, thank you. She said that he had to leave, and he did.

After he had been gone for a while, she recovered her strength and found a new boyfriend. When Mike came back from Africa, he called her and said, "Why don't we get together?" She said she had a boyfriend. Mike said that her boyfriend needn't know about it. He used sex as his calling card. She said she was loyal to her new partner and wouldn't do it. He argued with her about her decision, but she was firm.

Loyalty to the one you love is one aspect of the boundary she established, and of which she now is proud. Boundary elements should not only consist of what you fear will happen to you if you don't follow your lover's rules, which can be negative and childish. You need to be proud of how you act for your own self, because it represents your *being-ness.* Honoring your boundary creates a person who is worthy of self-love.

Otherwise, your boundary will be porous, since you cannot fully align yourself against what you dislike, do not want to do, or are morally set against doing. Every time you sacrifice what represents your higher self to a person who demands it, your boundary line grows cloudy. The more you sacrifice, the easier it is to sacrifice again, because you are losing the sense of who you are.

You can recover or even create a boundary line by recognizing the elements that give your life meaning. Fearful of doing it, especially if you were raised by people who did not respect your boundaries, you first take little steps to discover sensitivity, and you feel aha! So that's what it's about, musing and wondering where this will take you. After a while, this approach of discovery will be honed into a method you use all the time. Metaphorically speaking, you are putting bricks into the boundary of your self.

Loving from Behind Walls of Hate

This is a marriage of black and white; he's dark and she's light. Beneath the color of their skins, they are very much alike, two people out to defeat the rejecting world—and frequently to defeat each other. They frequently shift back and forth between perceived enemy and friend.

Mandy and Horace live about fifty miles from a large city. They are close enough to do business there and far enough away to forget it. Neither of them is able to trust anyone else, and possibly not even to trust themselves. They are perpetually on guard. They live in a state of warfare in which they have to fight for every inch of territory in order to survive. Their philosophy is to win, and they are not above dirty fighting.

Each one is struggling for autonomy but not the kind in which they can coexist. Rather, one has to be on top. They use shouting as a weapon. The husband can turn a deaf ear to his wife and sink inside himself while his wife screams to penetrate his baffle. He is reasonably verbal, but her quantity of words and volume drowns him. They have screaming fights, sometimes through the window with one of them standing on the deck outside. Neighbors are familiar with their vociferous accusations.

Their loyalty is shadowed by antagonism. The wife has cynically stated that getting a divorce is too much trouble. Behind all the abuse, when they get in touch, they feel love. They have to feel very safe to drop their guard. Love requires descending from the battlements.

Mandy's mother was raised in a very hot climate. She was fifth-generation British who came with guns to take over native areas. It was the time when "The sun never sets on ..." Her family has a sizable farm on the *velt*, a huge grassy plain. All the farm work was done by black laborers who lived on the property in a semislave condition. Not mentioned was the fact that this land once belonged to them.

Mandy's mother involved herself with what needed to be done around the kitchen and gave the workers endless orders. Mandy learn how to command by observing. She also learned subservience from being bossed around by Mom. The child of white colonizers was severely restricted by what she was allowed to do, wear, and say, and by what was forbidden. A lot of it had to do with maintaining her appearance. She had to be clean and well fed, with gimlet eyes for workers who strayed from their tasks. There was not much room for back-slapping fun, for letting down one's hair. It was all about looking like a rightful owner.

A lot of the colonizers' lives were ruled by their fear of a negative black reaction. Many owners slept with guns beneath their pillows. The owners needed the work of their laborers to survive, but they were unwilling to pay a reasonable wage to the black workers, who raised and harvested and stored their food. The workers made their own tools and tended their small private gardens after work hours to have enough to eat.

Living dependent on the work of others makes you a dependent being, a kind of slave yourself. Mandy's grandparents wanted her mother to remain in Africa and live like they did—without becoming a material part of the land by working it with their hands. She hated their helplessness and distance from the earth. She identified more with the workers than with her forbears. At the same time, she learned to step on people in order to survive. The conflict between these principles remained.

On the sly she moved away from her mother's "keep your hands clean" position. She observed and learned to cook and to bake from the cook as well as from reading cookbooks; in like manner she learned to use a foot-pedal sewing machine to design and mend her clothing. She learned to raise vegetables. She observed the native healer and was happy to be taught the art of healing by using native herbs. She secretly learned hands-on skills because she planned to escape and to have abilities that could support her once she was away.

Rather than marry a local man and carry on the family tradition of giving orders and sitting around drinking the local yellow gin, she looked at American newspapers until she found an au pair job. Then she fled. One job led to another until she met a successful businessman who fell for her blond hair, blue eyes, and incredible competence. They married and had children. One of them was Mandy. Her mother had rebelled against her family's excessive control, particularly of women. She then imposed it on her children, particularly on her daughters, which shows how identification with the aggressor continues despite one's intention to do otherwise.

She was a harsh, punitive, and distant figure who had acquired her mother's need to rule. Injustice done to a child is injustice learned by the child—either that or to be its victim. Often, the child learns to do both, sometimes acting as the victim and sometimes acting as the abuser.

This situation was exacerbated by an experience in which a close friend unjustly turned against Mandy at a party. Lots of young folks were scattered around. A visiting guy joined Mandy in an athletic prank, which she and her friends did all the time. She did not know that he had been drinking and was athletically ill-equipped when he fell and hurt himself. She tried to help him respond and stand up, but he remained lying on the ground. They took him away on a stretcher. Her friends accused her of leading him on and causing the accident. People who felt the need to blame someone made it all her fault. Among those who subsequently shunned her was her "best friend."

That everyone blamed her hurt her deeply. Her best friend's rejection stimulated helpless rage. Had the woman really been her friend? Can she trust a "friend"? Is there such a thing as a "friend"? These questions were never resolved and undermine all closeness. She is always ready to attack the enemy, and also to point to their stupidity. After this accident, Mandy took a social position of being charming, talkative, and seemingly friendly; she showed all kinds of social skills but trusted no one.

She decided to do everything her way. She got extremely thin, modeled, wore black leather miniskirts and black nail polish, and did drugs, each of them to the point "that it was enough." She also became good at earning and saving money. She met and married Horace, a man who shared her skepticism about people and with whom she developed a business. The fact he was black, aside from being a person she admired, may have to do with rebelling against her mother. Mom had black men (and women) to boss around, and then her daughter married one.

Horace was an ambitious person who defied the rules. She felt she could learn a lot from him about how to stand your ground. At that time, and possibly into the present, she sees herself as a weakling. This self-concept may account for how demanding she is of others and of herself, and also for her tendency to put people down. She had learned the art of vicious speech.

Horace states that more than fifty percent of boys are bad. Where did he get this figure? He comes from a black family that is ambitious. However, no matter how high they rise, their sense of vulnerability and feelings of inferiority remain. Horace's brother has an anger management problem. He eats to stuff his anger down.

Horace said that he had been a bad kid who got into many fights. He beat up his younger, smaller brothers. His father warned him to stop hitting them … once, twice, and then a third time, before punishing him with a beating. After beatings seven, eight, and nine, the son stopped directly venting his aggression. Beating him into acquiescence showed that Dad was stronger. Morality, ethics, and empathy had nothing to do with Dad's edict. It was based on might makes right. By beating him into submission, Dad exemplified hitting a smaller kid to get him to obey.

Horace saw his father's behavior as unfair. He wanted to defeat the man and anyone else who threw their weight around. He sought new ways to break the law. He drove the family car when no adult was there to stop him. He was so short at the time that his nose was just above the dashboard. He robbed his mother's purse to replace the gas.

As an adult in business, he once boarded a plane close to takeoff time, but his workers had not yet arrived. The stewardess refused to delay departure despite his pleading, so he threw himself down on the platform atop the boarding stairs and clutched his ankle as if it had been sprained. There was a lot of fussing around him while he held onto the railing and moaned. When his men came running across the field to board, he hauled himself to his feet and entered. To Mandy, this act represented a level of daring of which she had never dreamed. He had pretended to be injured in order to take control. He had no guilt about doing it. It made him feel quite powerful. She fell in love with the man.

She fell in love with his defiant behavior. She is always studying people and especially animals to see how some stand their ground and push away rivals. She sees how the blue jays take over her bird feeder and scare off the other birds with loud cries and fluttering wings; she sees how her cats are wholly concerned with getting what they want. She loves them for being demandingly self-centered. They will eat only this and not that. They cannot be persuaded to do otherwise.

She has learned from these creatures how to be underhanded in her pursuits as well as how to be directly aggressive. The main thing is to get your way. She is trying to eradicate years of being forced to cater to her mother. Her husband's behavior exemplifies "I will pursue my goals no matter what you say. I will fool and override you." The "love" they share is not one of peace.

Horace is a pull-yourself-up-by-your-bootstraps kind of guy married to a woman who has to have her own way. She learned the art of seduction and especially of using accusations and tears to influence his actions. "How can you hurt me by doing *that*?" She uses distracting talk and heartfelt excuses to bamboozle her opponent, and worst of all, she threatens to withhold affection to "persuade" him to comply. They are a well-matched pair of below-the-belt fighters.

The more he loves her, the more he feels anxious about her attacking him and withholding her affection. He may yell back but still finds her words disturbing. She is good at arousing guilt and passing blame. He anticipates the coming attack and feels afraid. She enacts the role of her bullying mother to his enactment of a defiant child. He sees in her abuse his unfair father, whom he fights to overcome. Each attacks the unfair parent in the other. Warfare is always throbbing beneath the surface. To the extent that he can ignore her threats, he fights to have his way. To the extent that he absorbs her pain, he is beaten.

Behind all of this fighting to the finish, which never happens, there is a history of deprivation of love in childhood. He needs to prove his father's beating him was justified, which means that his father loved him. She needs to feel that her controlling, verbally abusive, and unaffectionate mother loved her and that Mom's coldness concealed love.

Denial rules their mutual abuse. He needs to accept his father's beating him for "crimes" against the family signified Dad's love. She needs to work tirelessly for their business and receive little gratitude for doing it, which means that her mother's restraint signified love. In their mutual punishment and deprivation, they both have to think that they are working for the approval of their internal "freezing parent."

The repetition compulsion is doing its work. Each one is enacting the role of an unloving parent to the other. Each is the other's beaten child. Each one is translating the other's coldness, screaming, forgetting obligations, and self-centered perfectionism into love.

Chapter 2

Developing Your Sense of Love

The Freezing Parent and the Frozen Child

A parent's behavior can freeze his or her child. The parent expresses burning rage toward the child for petty misbehaviors, or even for those the parent imagines or projects from his or her own impulses, needs, and behaviors. The parent simmers for a while and then explodes, hating the child for every kind of shortcoming, including those that are imagined.

Such parents have a storehouse of hatred to call on, most of it sent by their parents. They call the children names. They attack with words, hands, or fists; remove the children's allowance; and take away other privileges. Frightened children who are subjected to such a barrage seek anesthesia by inhabiting an emotional world of ice. They get away from it all. An icy state reduces the potency of feelings that cannot be expressed. No sympathy is forthcoming. The children soon learn that if they fight back, the mistreatment will be worse. The parents' finger of blame can point in only one direction. If the rage-filled parents try to curb their angry feelings by acting detached or indifferent, they too seek emotionally freezing ice. The children find no agreeable warmth in their interactions. There is no period of "excuse me" and forgiveness.

The parent's icy behavior is a model for survival in an unloved state. The freezing/frozen parent creates a frozen child. The actual parent—whose emotions swing from cold to hot, from indifference to love—is responded to by the child in terror. The parent drives the child into icy compliance because the child cannot stand waiting for the next explosion. Warm to cold to warm gives the child no resting place. It is like walking on a lake of ice knowing you will fall in.

The children do not know what to do to please their parents. The parents are confused about it too. They do not understand why they do what they do, why they are subject to attacks of rage; they only know they cannot stop. The answer for everyone lies in history.

The parent had parents who were harmfully changeable, enraged and attacking, ignoring, using, loving, and then hating. What is the parent to do with feelings of helplessness, unworthiness, and rage? The parent's hatred, confusion, and helplessness are rained down upon the child. One often tends to attack what is easiest and nearest.

Each child is treated as the parent's parent or as a representative of the parent's hated self. Each offspring receives hatred generated by the self-hating parent … which was caused by the self-hating parent before. It is as if there is a huge pipeline carrying destructive feelings from one generation to the next. Each once-hated child becomes a parent who passes hatred on rather than deal with the necessity of separating from his or her own parent and rejecting the offered hatred.

It is a peculiar combination of love and fear that leads to the acceptance of hate. I will be killed if I don't accept hatred as justified. I will be devoid of love if I don't see parental hatred as acts of love. Lying to the self has a role here. Each child does not set boundaries and achieve understanding that replaces absorption of and playing the parent-assigned role. Each child remains hate's carrier to stay bonded with the hating parent rather than leave the parent behind.

The experiences of childhood are internalized by the child as a fixed representation in the mind. If the parent is cold and rejecting, the child shrinks and freezes beneath his or her blows. The internal representation of this experience becomes a "frozen child."

The internal "freezing parent" is a copy of the actual parent who demeaned, obstructed, rejected, and attacked the child. The "freezing parent" is taken into the mind unchanged. It is part of a defensive identification with what threatens. The internal "freezing parent" stimulates the experience of helplessness in the internal "child" as well as in the mind of the adult self, which receives its messages and does not reject them.

After the person grows into adulthood, his or her internal "freezing parent" directs the person to seek and adore mistreating lovers. It directs the adult to succumb to the lover's mistreatment and take the blame.

The "freezing parent" threatens the person for daring to think of venturing away from its "parent" -directed activities. It keeps the adult from dealing with the present life rather than relive the past. The "parent" says, "Danger. Don't go there. You will be hurt or overwhelmed." The "parent" says, "That person is not good enough for you" or "You are not good enough for him or her." It tells the person to strike first: "Say you are unlovable. Get out and give up." It tells him or her to surrender to the partner's hatred, which is labeled as love.

If the child had an attacking parent with whom the child identifies, an internal "freezing parent" develops that tells the adult to act abusive, to be the one who mistreats and enslaves. The attacking adult is welcomed by the "parent," who sees him or her as a "parent" clone.

To the mind of the basically fragile but operationally brutal parent, a mirror image enforces the power and importance of his or her enacted phony powerful self.

The Warming Parent and the Warmed Child

A warming parent supports a child's getting into the mystery of what is out there. A small child is often daring, wanting to explore the world, to seek, feel, see, and touch—often panicking the parents when they see what their little adventurer is getting into. The warm parent applauds a child's exploits and comforts the child after he or she has received minor injuries or disappointments. The warm parent says, "It's not such a big deal. You're okay in my book."

A warm parent is the model for the child's development of an internal "warming parent." The "warming parent" reassures the child that he or she is not alone. The "warming parent," like the original parent, tells the child that everyone makes mistakes. It says that there is no better way, and possibly no other way, to learn something." The internal "parent," like the original parent, says, "I love you," to the child, who eventually will hear this from and offer it to his friends and lovers. The "parent" gives the child a lot of love, which causes the eventual adult to set high love "standards."

There is security in knowing love through direct experience. People raised by critical and cold parents develop an internal "freezing parent," which constantly creates a din of "You are unlovable" in their brain. The internal "freezing parent" later blames the adult for interpersonal difficulties that are part of every growing relationship or are the result of choosing as a partner one who can't love. Heeding the internal blamer, the adult loses the ability to judge whether or not he or she is loved.

The "warming parent" does not mislead the child then, and later when the child has grown into adulthood. It gives appropriate warnings when needed, such as "Watch out for that driver who is careening out of his lane." It is not prone to exaggerating or ignoring the facts, whether they are emotional or physical. The "parent" acts as a supportive coach whose counsel creates resilience and persistence.

The internal "warmed child" is simpatico with the internal "warming parent." The "parent" encourages the "child" to persevere. The "warmed child" absorbs this and later tells the actual child not to focus on whether he or she is a success or a failure at doing things; rather that he or she should learn from mistakes, focus on acquiring new skills, and have fun while doing it. The "warming" parent shouts words of encouragement.

The "warming parent" vibrates into the child's mind the experience and expectation of being loved. The actual child who is so directed does not attempt to win love from one who does not offer it. The "warmed child" does not confuse love and hate, does not think that love underlies abuse, and does not think that "less is more," an architectural terms used for planning on a mechanical "grid" rather than designing free-form and expressively. Human thinking and feeling is not on a predesignated grid. It unfolds in a natural way in response to its needs and to what the environment sends its way. People are far more complex and interesting.

A person who has a "warm parent" does not see accepting abuse as the price of admission to the show of life. The "warming parent" directs the child grown into adulthood, to go where love is freely offered. An adult with a "warming parent" finds it easy to do.

Janus Faced: Presenting a False Image

Are you acting like Janus, a Roman god who was depicted with one head facing left toward the beginning of things and one head facing right toward endings and transitions? More recently, the two-headed Janus has come to mean deceit. Are we Janus thinkers, looking only at our past or peering only into the distant future? Neither face is in the now. The person we are deceiving is ourselves, since now is the real place to be. We exist only in the present, not in the past or future.

How does a Janus fixation apply to love? People oriented only to past or future rarely show their present face. Neuroses that originate in childhood trauma of parental rejection result in emotional injuries and a defensive orientation, which includes self-contempt, an attitude accepted and believed for life. To call the self inadequate and wrong instead of blaming the parent for his or her mistreatment is a mental operation that keeps hope alive of receiving the parent's love someday, if you only fix what is wrong with you and do it "right" this time. Self-condemnation keeps adults from openly relating to current could-be lovers. When seeking to court a lover, they hide their present face, which is assumed to fail.

The necessity of hiding their present face comes from living with rejecting parents who did not like them as a child. That's when your self-image is created. For example, parents who respect their children allow them to develop boundaries, to choose to play with the toys chosen now—not the ones the parents like best—and to have the right to keep a secret. This is not so with children who have to hide their faces. Their natural selves are so unacceptable to their parents that it becomes internally forbidden. The children adapt almost exclusively to outside requirements, expressing their parents' required action at activities they endorse and avoiding or failing at those they hate. The children fail when expected to fail and succeed when it is required. The children stay exactly where the parents place them. Most important, they act appreciative of their presumed and often-stated love although they do not feel it. A false love life proceeds from this situation.

When the children have become adults, their minds remain corralled by anxiety, which makes accessing the true self very difficult. The "Janus division" continues. They cannot achieve closeness with another person, since intimacy means dropping one's defenses. Where the sense of self should be felt, they feel emptiness and hatred, which is directed mostly at the self. The parent hates you. Then you hate yourself. Then you find lovers who hate you. The circle of antilove is completed.

People who say that you have to love someone who resembles your parents, even if they were abusive, have not experienced the necessary transformation. They do not know that you are not inexorably bound to the defenses that connect you to your past. They do not know this, because they have not experienced it themselves. Most basic truths have to be experienced for one to know and accept their reality. Theory is made only of words.

Change involves knowing and then rejecting the internal "frozen child's" fear of being destroyed by the "parent" for not fitting in to the "parent's" projections. Change comes after you strengthen your sense of self so that you can focus on what you feel right now. It is immensely rewarding to give up the internal baggage of threats and fear, to separate from unloving connections. One might characterize it mythologically as descending from the throne of Janus and saying good-bye to a split and false identity.

Love is about being together with your self as a unit of body, mind, and feeling. When sharing love, you feel the great pleasure of sharing. You have to be together with yourself in order to lose yourself that way. Love is going home.

Slavery Continues

Slavery, the act of holding, owning, having one work sans payment, denigrating, and mistreating another human being, sometimes translates into a power reversal; this reversal moves back and forth within a person who is part of a couple, as well as in offspring through the generations. The slave owner's child, or the child's child, acts like a slave to the child or to a mate; or he or she becomes a master who treats children and/or a mate like a slave. Confused and alternating identities of slave and master keep appearing.

How did this sequence of events begin, and how does it apply to people who are not descendants of a literal slave culture but were emotionally raised as slaves? It becomes clear if we examine how it works in an actual slave-owning society.

Starting with the owner generation, when you were a child, one female slave was your caretaker. This parent substitute loved and became a part of your sense of self, which means that you identified with her. In the United States, the black slave was a caretaker (usually) of a white man's children, who typically called her "Mammy." She is a trusted member of the family, although simultaneously despised for her race. Seeing the slave as "less than a person," was the way self-respecting people justified using a person without recompense. Children do not make such distinctions. To them she is more than a servant. She is the person they hold on to and care about. She usually loves them too. A relationship is born.

For her, the contradiction of being respected and disrespected, honored and despised, is there from the start. She receives subsistence—food and shelter, something to wear—but she can be sold at will, as can her black and mulatto children (the consequence of being sexually used by the master, his friends, and kin). As she raises the master's children, she carries them around, feeds, cleans, dresses, and toilet trains them. They spend more time with her in the kitchen, yard, and shop than they do with their parents. She teaches them the beginning of good manners. She is their primary caregiver. They see their mother on occasion but often less than they see Mammy, who is their island of security. The youngsters form a strong attachment to her.

To admit to having deep affection for this woman eliminates the separation of white and black, the separation of user and used, the power inequity on which this society thrives. As the child grows older, the parents introduce a conflict in the child's attitude toward his or her mammy. It is okay as long as the child is unsteady on his or her feet. The child can even share a bed with Mammy's children. They are all together then—best friends. But it is less okay once the child attends school and has external obligations like doing chores and homework. It is increasingly not okay as the child develops a mind of his or her own. Then this allegiance is expected to end. But how can one end a thing that resides in the heart? It is like disconnecting from one's blood and bones.

What are such children to do with their feelings of love for, connection to, and dependency on Mammy? These feelings, versus the demands of the slaveholding society, put the children in a terrible bind. The children eventually have to deny their feelings—disown, deny, and contradict them through a variety of behaviors, many of them cruel to Mammy and all of them cruel to self.

The children are confused about whether to share their accomplishments, joy, and excitement over what they have learned in school, their desire to tell Mammy their latest life adventure. The children have been told that they are not on the same social plane as Mammy, which means she cannot understand them. They have to lie to themselves about what they feel toward her, which is a great loss for the children. If I have to lie about my deepest feelings and relationships, where does the truth lie and what is my self? It is a period of loss without resolution. Mammy is still there before your eyes. She has not died and gone to black heaven. It is your heart that is in prison.

The child learns the art of serious rationalization, which means that his or her feelings of love are not recognized. The child finds ways to deny and misunderstand what he or she feels. This is supremely important for a young adult who is fitting in. I don't feel pain at leaving you. I deny that you and I share feelings. Of course my heart knows better. For the growing child who is forced to do this, there is progressive separation from the sense of self. It has to be that way. The child is putting on an image, one not felt and earned. It is a disguise one has to believe in. It is an image without real feet to stand on.

Mammy swallows her feelings of pain over the loss of their connection. What else can she do? She doesn't dare dispute the child's love being taken from her. That would be too dangerous. As an owned person, she has to be mindful of consequences.

The child being extracted from this essential relationship is robbed of a sense of deep relatedness and of love. It is like tearing away a piece of the sense of self in order to belong, but belong to what? Society is not a loved one. Society does not love. It is a concept to which one attaches. It is an unreal state that calls for ever more violent affirmation to take his or her attention from the loss.

Denying feelings for Mammy is a loss the child cannot face and so from which he or she cannot recover. You have to know from what you suffer from in order to heal it. To deny one's identification and suffering makes the sense of self feel small and unimportant.

The post–Civil War child witnessed the roles of master and Mammy/slave expressed between parents … also from parent to child or from child to parent when the parent put the child in a master position. Identification with the Mammy role or denying it by keeping an arrogant master distance is found in boys and girls. Some exclusively take one role, that of either slave or master. Others switch back and forth, sometimes being slave and sometimes being master with the same or different people. This split self problem is expressed.

How did this racially based emotional disorder, this denial of attachment, get handed down through families that once held slaves? How did they handle the trauma of renouncing their connection to and love for Mammy? Do they reject the dependent side of themselves and cast their lover into a dependent role, which they then revile? Or do they express their connection to Mammy by taking the reviled role as Mammy with an abusive lover?

Parents express their own loss as well as their parents' loss and their parents' parents' loss … and so on. Children absorb their parents' feelings and accept their parents' struggles as their own. Sometimes, exactly as the parent plays it or as inheritor of the role the parent denies but projects onto them, they take on the denied Mammy or the master-as-tyrant role. Children mimic what they've seen and felt. They express what the parents expect of them, even if the parents don't consciously know it. Parents who are so ignorant slap their forehead with an open hand and say, "I don't know how my kid turned out this way."

The parents' conflict between Mammy/slave and master/owner affects the child's self- esteem. The child takes on their parent's own split sense of self. They identify with slave Mammy as a despised and weak but beloved caretaker or with owner master, who is powerful and essentially unloved. Assuming only one role denies the other and so feels incomplete. A potentially whole sense of self that lies behind is in conflict with the split identity. There is an internal struggle between the need for integration and the parent's required rejection of same. External pressure from the parents and society as a whole suppresses the sense of self.

Take the struggle in the family of Rosalie:

Rosalie's mother's family and her father's family once held slaves many generations back. Their behavior remains evidence of this. They carry out the Mammy/slave and/or tyrant master role in their married life as well as toward their children.

The mother and father preyed on those over whom they had power and slaved for those who had power over them. Dad's family required him to do the family profession he detested, which put him in a slave position since slaves lack power to make their own decisions.

Dad hated and despised the children he had to support by the profession imposed upon him. He shoved them out of his consciousness, spent zero time with them, and pushed them aside when he entered or left the house. He gave little financial support to his family while living with them and none at all after he left. In his mind, he was a slave escaping. His lack of respect for his wife and children also represented the master/owner role. Those reared in the latest incarnation of the slave culture emotionally and frequently move from one psychological state to the other.

After Dad abandoned his family, Mom was forced into teaching ballroom dancing to support them. Then Mom pushed her daughter into a mammy role with her younger siblings. The daughter got no praise for fulfilling this role. Slaves are not praised for working any more than you would praise a mule for carrying your packages. They are there to serve. You have fed the child, haven't you? Nothing more is required.

Mom switched from master to slave with her youngest son, whom she treated as her master. He later expressed this identity by marrying a woman who was raised to serve. He became extremely grandiose with a master's guise to cover his helplessness and dependency. She supported him while he fooled around with other women, made art deco furniture he didn't feel compelled to sell, and smoked a lot of grass. She gave him money and turned her eyes away. Her role as a Christian martyr had a mammy/slave connection. She moralized her oppression. At the same time, she put down others who saw her in an unfair state. She stuck out her chest and called herself superior. There is always blindness when one denies one's other half. She had a divided slave/master identity, sometimes expressing the slave side, sometimes the master.

The daughter dealt with the master/slave conflict having been assigned by Mom to the slave role in her adolescence and by becoming a "master person" who pretended to be a slave. She had a fore and aft identity. She had the power of keeping the family going during Mom's absence. She had the helplessness of being assigned to this task and position. She states that she can drop her abusive, parasitic boyfriends any time she chooses to, but she doesn't do it for long periods. Her early love connection to Mom was as a slave, so slavery still remains her strongest calling.

Her men are talented druggies who frequently insult her. She finances their drug purchases and sometimes partakes with them, but never so much that she cannot function as provider. She flirts with physical abuse, and when in her fearful, cowering state she feels an element of excitement and even satisfaction, which shows her mammy/slave identification. She sounds like a frightened child when speaking to her abusive man.

Then there is the split. She plays slave on the surface but secretly is his master, since she is the one with an earned income. When she is ready to get rid of the man, she tells him, "skidoo." She has enacted the role of slave turned into master with a long succession of men. She played slave with a man while he sexually pleased her and turned into the master and kicked him out. There was no emotional connection. Which of these behaviors represents the true person? She probably doesn't know, nor can she. You can only know your true face when nothing is denied.

With her daughter, Mother as Mammy/slave never switched to master. She always felt guilty about not giving enough time to her child, as she worked since the girl's father was financially useless. He covered his inadequacy by acting the role of master, which she as his mammy/slave supported.

It was an immiserated view of self that she never gave enough; and nothing was expected from her child, whose every self-indulgent, irresponsible act was excused and supported. She turned her daughter into her master. The daughter learned to despise and use her denigrated mother. Her mother inculcated the emotional state in which the child despises and dismisses Mammy. She enacts her despised-mother-equals-mammy role as it had been with her dad. She rightly questions her daughter's love, but instead of having a showdown with the now grown child, she gives evermore. Her story about doing this is always one of loss. If she is not endlessly indulgent, her daughter will not let her see her grandchildren.

The man her daughter married had been cast in the role of slave by parents who claimed to be aristocrats and expected him to meet their every need. He felt humiliated and abused by their attitude toward him. By withholding gratitude for his service, they endorsed the "you are a slave" equation. It was no accident that he married a woman who leaned on him and treated him as her slave. She used or ignored him as it pleased her. It did not matter how intelligent he was or how much money he made; she despised him for his willingness to defer to her. Her affection had a heavy price. She found it easier to fight than to love. She was outraged by his desire to spend more time together and labeled it demanding. She did not consider taking a little time off from work and changing her daily plan to heal their conflict. Her thinking focused exclusively on What can *I* achieve outside the marriage? Her self was enclosed by walls of ambition.

This woman cannot see herself and her husband as a mixture of weakness and strength. She can't see that she needs him and that expressing this need does not put her into a slave position, a characterization she fears and probably secretly believes. Both sides of the slave/master identity and love struggle are passed down through generations. She is caught up in a denial of her slave/mammy identification—represented by her mother—by despising the love connection.

Which of her children will be given a slave position, and which ones will be given that of master? Will their roles be exclusive and continuous, or like Grandma, will they play slave until they tire of it and then switch to master? Will any of her children be openly generous and needy, weak and strong with people they love? Will any of them be able to express the spirit of a unified self? One can only do this by dropping the denial of half of one's identity, enacted by the parents and by their parents before them.

CHAPTER 3

Your Defenses Can Hurt You

Your Defenses

Your defenses can act like very strong birds flying you on diaphanous wings to your destination, or like a dense, unsightly wall that nothing can get through. If you have suffered a serious lack of love during childhood, the defenses that developed through this period of mayhem tend to be too weak in certain situations and too strong in others.

Shaped as a reaction to your parents' mistreatment, these defenses act like blinders on a horse—which keep it from seeing what might scare it so that it will take the carriage where the driver needs to go. Rigidly preformed defenses affect your ability to perceive. They make you blind to differences and keep you ill-informed. Your dysfunctional thinking is shaped by other people's stereotypes, people who serve as parent substitutes and require the same kind of unknowing.

You do not know how to trace their cause and effect. You have not learned to do it, because the parents forbade your understanding of their difficulties and harmful ways of coping. Your investigating, asking questions, and drawing your own conclusions threatened them. You had to believe what they presented. As a result, you cannot understand or interpret what does not fit in with your rehearsed and forced preconceptions. You learned not to inquire when you wanted to clear up your blind spots.

Childish thinking prevails. You fall prey to concrete thinking. You make connections between events as if what happened first caused what happened second. Because you jumped when the sun came up, jumping causes the sun to rise. You abused your partner who stays with you, so you conclude that abuse creates a lasting relationship. Your parents beat you and called you bad. Therefore you are bad. You'd be further punished by them if you disagree, so you believe what you are told.

Neurotic responses attach unrelated factors with the glue of superstition. The addition of a punishing parent also enters the mind. The power of superstition based on fear of receiving harm means that you cannot give up doing what you think protected you. Your internal "parent" threatens punishment for questioning its conclusions. Its judgment has to be seen as in accord with the truth "or else." You protect yourself by "believing."

People have a tendency to believe that they have changed the way they do things as circumstances changed, but given the arrival of certain stimuli, they fall into habitual modes of reacting. Even if circumstances get worse, they will repeat these reactions. In order to act in a way that is better suited to reality, you have to become aware of the nature of your defenses, the conditions under which you use them, and whether they are effective. You need to not be controlled by anxiety and fear. You need to look outside your feelings in order to truly see. Then you can stop engaging in ineffective or destructive behavior when circumstances press habitual buttons in your mind.

Are you following Mom's or Dad's orders, or are you simply copying them? You have to tolerate the anxiety that comes from discontinuing what you have always done, and in this way you will break a connection with your real or internal "parent(s)." You need to make decisions based on an analysis of the facts, most importantly focusing on results. You need to ignore the mind that orders you to act a certain way. Do not be swept into ancient patterns of reaction.

The grown-up mind has to be an objective witness rather than pulled into the emotions of its internal "child" and the orders of its internal "parent." You need to become detached from your "freezing parent" and "frozen child." This separation can feel very frightening, since your actual parents required you to bow to their edicts. If you didn't do it, they rejected you. These bad consequences are consolidated in the image of your internal "parent."

Some parents needed you to be wrong in a way that drew their hatred. They needed to hate you instead of hate themselves. You will find neither freedom nor a sense of self in seeking their hatred (and finally their acceptance) as a result of your actions. The sense of self comes from exploring various pathways and making up your own mind. You must become deaf to internal cries of love or hate. You need to practice not listening.

The parents were trying to deal with their own unresolved childhood traumatic events by putting into you the image their parents put into them and then beating it out of you. When the parents hit, scream, deprive, criticize, and ignore, it is your problem now, not their own. When you depart from the parents' defensive projections, they are beset by anxiety. Your separation causes a breakdown in their defenses, and unacceptable self-images come rushing into their minds. It is like a herd of wild horses dashing out of a corral and beyond the gate where everyone can see them. As a child, you learned to control your autonomous and rebellious tendencies in order to calm your parents. You are doing that no more.

Defenses that do not resolve the underlying problem are passed from generation to generation, each one fitting into their parents' unstated and uncomprehended need like a hand fits into a glove. What happens to the internal "freezing parent" when your hand, which means your thinking, no longer fits their glove? The tyrannical "parent" insists that your hand has to fit—that you must make it fit, even if it cripples you.

You may choose to live far from your living parent, but your internal "parent" travels with you. Your actual parents may be dead or distant, but they live on inside your mind, where they attempt to exert the same kind of control they always had. You have to travel a psychological distance from your internal "parent" and "child" to understand that your fears and need to comply pertain to childhood pressures.

The adult self feels the internal "child's" anxiety. If he or she doesn't review and understand the historic context of the "child's" experience, the adult may go along with the "child's" request to comply. There is great suffering for grown-ups who fall in line. Adults need to separate their adult thinking from that of their "child" and "parent." They have to make up their own mind.

A new kind of consciousness needs to develop. Each person has to follow his or her own exploratory path. You find out what you like and what works for you by trying it out. Are you fascinated or bored by what you have done? Does the one you love, love you back? Is there an absence of abuse? Is there joy? You need to explore via trial and error, whether to continue doing it or to stop and change. If people disapprove of what you do, that doesn't make it wrong for you. If they approve, that doesn't make it right. Make sure that the choices you make and the conclusions you draw are exclusively your own.

The Iceberg of Bad Attachment

Because an iceberg is more dense than the water that supports it, only ten percent of its surface is above water. The ratio of the conscious to the unconscious mind represents a similar disproportion. The unconscious mind is a huge mass of material—needs and feelings, biases and hatreds, denials and affirmations—all which can steer the ship of consciousness. This vastness accounts for a lot of the confusion about why you have chosen to love the kind of person who causes you so much misery, and do it over and over again.

People attracted to "lovers" who need to be destructive and require submissive relationships hope to end their need for such people by chipping away at the emotional iceberg of their connection to abusive parent(s). They have embarked upon a losing voyage. The desire to eliminate an iceberg by using the chipping method is a ruse presented by the unconscious mind. You cannot eliminate a huge iceberg floating in frigid water with a knife, even the knife of understanding. It will outlast your efforts by millennia.

When people say, "Why don't you stop submitting to your lover's abuse, eternally hoping and waiting for something better to happen?" they verbalize a commonsense position with which you totally agree, but your behavior remains unchanged. You love/hate/fear/despise and need the same person. For people to say, "Just give him up"; "Stop worrying about what he will do to you if you assert yourself"; or "Start acting in your own defense and on your own behalf," the word *just* does not describe your difficulty. Giving the person up is the hardest thing to do. You do, and you don't. You stop and you start and then stop again. You are moved toward that person by an unconscious force, which is something your advisors do not understand. Nor do you. You think that what attracts you is your essential and true self. But you do not understand what this means, which is the cause of your forced obedience.

To change the part of you that wrongly loves, you have to get into your mental boat and row away from that iceberg of your unconscious needs and fears. You have to turn your back on it. Understand the way you trap yourself by looking at your repetition. Almost in a hypnotic trance, you review and review and review. You are like Sisyphus ever climbing to the top, falling to the base, and then climbing up again. Helplessness is a learned response. You are capable of unlearning it. Turning your back on a fight you cannot win is very wise. The best and only thing you can do is move on.

Swallowing the Bad

Children raised by parents who are self-centered, essentially insecure but superficially grandiose, and as a result can't admit to making mistakes, learn to "swallow the bad." This expression means that they ingest blame for their parents' mistakes, for their selfishness and rage. The children see themselves as guilty rather than their parents.

It becomes a life task to carry the blame. The children sometimes rebel for a while and then give in. As adults, they follow a circular path from acquiescence to rebellion and then back to acquiescence. The pattern of rebellion and submission is, "I hate you. I am sorry. Please forgive me. I am bad … You are bad. I hate you. I am bad. I'm sorry …" There is no resolution. The reason for this is the forever quest for their parents' love.

Since young children tend to think in oral terms, the idea of guilt for abusive events enters their psyche as a poisonous meal. Parents, who find their own behavior shameful, purge themselves by attributing their misdemeanors to their children. The children's tendency to swallow and the parents' need to disgorge achieve a common resolution. They shower the children with their missiles of self-hatred. The children's psychological mouth receives the parents poisonous food and assimilates it as their own.

The older child and then the adult continue the taking-it-into-self tradition. The adult swallows the bad, however it is sent. Often, the mental/emotional quandary is translated into a physical act of gulping down huge portions of food. The adult is in a contradictory struggle, submitting to the hateful "parent" versus establishing his autonomy. He or she does not know that it is the internal "parent" that now causes a compulsive acceptance of unworthiness and blame.

As adults and as love's victims, they convert the symbolic act of swallowing their partner's abuse into literal eating. This is making physical an emotional event. Their compulsive eating represents giving in to the "parent's" control.

Then there is the fight for freedom. The victim who quickly takes in an excess amount of food has little pleasure, since the event flies by too fast to savor. He or she then gets rid of the food by vomiting. Such people may be concerned about gaining weight and often exaggerate their fatness. Vomiting injures the digestive apparatus. Sometimes they become anorexic, and their weight falls so low that death threatens. They do not appreciate how thin they are because every bit of pinchable flesh represents acquiescence to the "parent." The equation is unconscious. They do not know the origin of the habit, only that they have to do it.

You can put an end to taking in the bad by no longer accepting an unexamined guilty position. You have to recognize when your lover or friend is doing something that harms you, like always coming late, breaking appointments, or borrowing money without repayment. You must refuse to continue accepting such behavior. You tell these people that they must stop doing it by a certain date and that if they don't, you will end the relationship. If they still mistreat you, then you must follow through and end it.

It is necessary for you to know when you are mistreated. This knowing is very difficult for a person who has been trained to deny abuse. Do not succumb to a tendency to rationalize your feelings, an approach that interlocks with your taking blame. Do not magnify your real or imagined misdeeds and then hate yourself for doing them. This approach justifies receiving abuse. Exaggerated guilt resonates with your parents' projections. You take in the bad to seek their love and then disgorge it to show you don't accept their judgment. Vomiting can have a self-punishing intention. Vomiting that wounds the body is associated with self-hatred and is itself an offering to the punitive "parent." Swallowing the blame reinforces your connection to abusive lovers or friends. You hurt yourself or they hurt you because you did something "wrong." You justify their horrendous behavior.

But mistreatment is mistreatment regardless of whether or not you made a mistake. Mistreatment is never acceptable. Good teachers, like warming parents, correct behavior by saying, "Do it this way." They do not attack the student's self. Good teachers make little of a student's mistake, even seeing it as a creative approach to a problem that didn't work.

In learning about yourself, you need to see how your parents attacked and blamed you for their faults. You have to see how you accepted their projected self-descriptions followed by their inflicting serious harm. Your definition of love has been corrupted by this experience. By accepting their mistreatment as appropriate, you endorse your own false image. The abuser who projects his or her flaws, real or imagined, onto you does not know who you are and cannot love the real you. Seeing yourself through the abuser's eyes, you cannot know and love your self.

And how does swallowing the bad apply to your love life? Take Ariella, a woman whose parents emigrated from Cuba. Her mother died, and Dad remarried when Ariella was about five. The stepmother hated and tortured her. She was like a semi-insane persecutor who thought that her duty was to humiliate, reduce, and demean her imprisoned charge.

The stepmother would not let Ariella join them at family meals. Ariella was given an egg sandwich to eat in her room. Her meals remained the same while the stepmother and her children feasted on a variety of foods. The stepmother confiscated gifts sent to Ariella by relatives who lived up north and gave them to her own children. She limited the girl's showers to once a week, with the door open, and only with cold water and lasting five minutes, even if her hair was still full of shampoo. The stepmother stood by the door with watch in hand to time them.

The stepmother's torture was endlessly inventive. She seemed to derive pleasure from doing it. She was on a power trip. She forced Ariella to stand in the middle of her room until she returned and released her. All the child's independent actions were stopped for made-up reasons. The stepmother fetched the necklace Ariella was beading from its hiding place above the door jamb and disassembled it because it was made without permission.

If her father, who was a restaurant owner in other states, saw his daughter stranded in her room, his wife said that the girl had crazy habits and he should not concern himself. The father, his wife, and her kids went to Thanksgiving dinner at other people's houses. The reason given by the stepmother for Ariella's exclusion was that she did not ask to be included. Dad accepted this explanation.

Once, the stepmother, descending behind Ariella on the stairs, bent her arm back to punish her for some kind of undefined misbehavior so far that she broke it. Then she claimed that the girl had fallen down the stairs. The girl was too afraid to call her a liar. She did not tell her dad, who long before had surrendered to the stepmom as his guide.

The stepmother forced Ariella to go around naked, although her own kids and their visiting friends were clothed. She bound Ariella to the toilet seat with masking tape and put tape between the door and its frame to show if the girl escaped bondage during the woman's absence. Dad helped tie her down. He was an immature and dependent man who did what he was told, a total coward.

Ariella learned to be excessively conciliatory and easily controlled. When she started dating, she put up with all kinds of mistreatment—which equaled "swallowing the bad." Then she finally expressed a degree of discontent before falling back into submission.

After much serious self-study, she is beginning to seek and know the "good" and has chosen a boyfriend who seems to care for her. Even here, she is too easily led into complicity before knowing the full story. She is afraid if she looks too hard, his love will disappear. For the first time in her life, she is less anxious and more content. She is not swallowing the blame.

Learning to Cover Hate with Love

How do your inability to know true love, and your attraction to mistreatment and deprivation, begin? How did you learn to abuse and despise those who love you? What are the benefits of having such attitudes? To understand, you have to know the past. Attraction to mistreatment and mistreating those who love you started when you were a child with an abusive parent.

Abusive parents who can't face the emotional damage they are causing often blame their children. The parents think their behavior is justified by what the children have done. If they use "improving" the children as a rationalization for abuse, they call the attack "educational," which puts a mask in front of hatred to give it a beneficent face. Less severe but unloving actions may not be obvious to a casual viewer, but they certainly are felt by the children. Cruel behavior may be labeled unimportant by the parent, but the children still feel attacked.

Regardless of the blows received, the children will cling to the parent (or caretaker), who is their most important person. Moments of parental cruelty shake children's security because they need the parents' love to keep them alive and protect them. But who then is the enemy? What if the parents' behavior speaks of hatred or indifference? What if it says that the parents don't care for the children or even hate them and want them dead?

Children cannot live in such a state of mind. They can't bear to fear so much hatred from their parents and their own hatred and fear in return. Killers seeking each other's demise can't cohabit. Children need to be surrounded by love. They can't lie down to sleep with hungry jackals.

A child's unconscious mind reshapes his or her view of what is happening. It creates a cover-up photo that is frozen in time. Such a false reality can't grow and reshape itself through experience, because it is there to cover a dark truth. Depending on the degree of a child's early pain, to that extent the child will need to rewrite history. Children will end up with a myth of parental love that covers hate. The children's memories of parental hatred are suppressed, forgotten, put aside, or rationalized as acts of love, which later binds them to taking hateful lovers. The lie continues. They need to take that ancient, frozen photo and study it, to bring to consciousness what is missing—the disappointment, anger, and fear beyond measure they felt with their parents.

Most people do not attempt to make such a reconstruction. They don't know that a different reality exists inside. Ignorant of what turns them to taking hurtful lovers, they exist in a state of puzzled suffering. Memories of their abusive parents are painted with the brush of love. Hurt-child memories are seen as unrelated. The more they were threatened by their parents, the more powerful is the image of their parents' love. Love projected onto memories of destructive parents serves as a tranquilizer. False memories of the past glue children to a false future.

If some brutality is remembered, children preserve their parents' loving image by saying, "I deserved it." Their self-esteem goes down in proportion to the amount of parental salvaging they need to do. Children cling to their self-generated lies. Their parents lie to the children as well and even to themselves about the love they do not feel.

Damaging parents remain equally important for their children throughout their lives, whether or not the parents are alive. The parents live on in the children's minds as an active force. This happens even if grown children claim to hate their parents—perhaps more so. As the real parents did when they were living, the internal parent rejects, scolds, advises, and sometimes congratulates the adult for being in line with the parent's image and desire.

Grown children seek the internal "parent's" love by following its advice, which may include acting and feeling inadequate the way their parent labeled them. The adults' feelings for the hurtful "parent" are often powerfully positive but also suspiciously full of longing. They have the longing of a starving person looking for something to eat. Their state of emotional need is connected to the love-emptiness of their childhood. Sometimes they claim to hate their parents but unconsciously seek their love.

As a consequence of the severity of the childhood fear of being totally unloved and even physically murdered, grown children continue to reinforce this lie. The adults lie to themselves because in their unconscious mind, the childhood fear lives on. To deny this fear, their behavior offers a testimonial to the parent's love. Even though they may speak about their parent with anger, they will seek a mate who closely resembles the parent in his or her most hurtful ways.

Grown children are disappointed and angered by each new lover, as they were with their childhood parent, but they still choose parent copies. Fear of feeling again the threatened state without disguising it as love rules their choices. They have to keep finding love with a certain kind of person to suppress the memory and experience of parental hate. They suppress awareness by enacting the role of one who deserves abuse. The more they use it to stamp out the memory of being hated, the stronger the defense becomes and the greater is their need for punishment.

The path out of this miserable repetition is to uncover, know, and feel your true past. You need to mourn love's absence in childhood as a consequence of the parent's incapacity to love. You need to face your childhood fear of being left to die by the parent and to know that "now I will survive."

Blind to Your Repetitive Choices

Unlike physically blind people who step aside when people say, "Look out," who allow others to take their arm and monitor them across the street, who get a seeing-eye dog, such people know that that they are blind and are open to receiving help.

People whose unconscious directives fill their minds are blind in a different way and often do not know it. They do not bump into things. Their physical eyes do the trick. It is the emotional self that is blind. They cannot respond to the results of their love choices. They are blind to what is really going on. They do not see that their unhappy affairs are repetitive because the internal "parent" tells them not to observe and know.

When people warn them about their partners, they say it isn't true and tuck their doubts away. If they get to the point where they can't avoid seeing the repetition, they say, "This is the person I love. He [or she] turns me on, and there is nothing I can do about it." Such a person is like a slave at the feet of a punitive master on whom the slave's life depends. He or she can't help loving such a person, because the driving force that had a life-saving purpose in childhood is now unconscious.

There are many who claim there is no way to undo our attraction to the type we loved as children even if—or even especially if—it was to deny their hate. Children first love their parents or caretakers. Those who claim that the choice of first love repeats itself, that the "habit" is unchangeable, have never unconditionally tried to change it. Instead of seeing their own early misery and feeling it in order to empower their struggle, they say, "First love is always loved." They say that the past casts your love life into its permanent shape like a hardened block of cement. It is the fear that blinds them rather than habitual cement.

Others say that "first love" is like a more-primitive animal's bonding, a connection that appears to be programmed by the animal's genes. A flock of newborn geese followed Konrad Lorenz, the famous zoologist, who presented himself instead of their mother to them right after their birth. The goslings related to him as their parent.

But the act of human loving is not a simple S/R (stimulus/response) situation. It is not simply a genetic mechanism. Nor is it uninterruptible from birth to death. There is an O (the organism) rather than S/R, and the human organism is very complex. People who repeat unhappy love choices are full of emotions and ideas that lead to their responses. These are not the consequences of a biological predisposition or a habit formed simply by repetition.

Human love responses are shaped by past experiences, by parental treatment, and by insight or its lack. Human love can be an act that heals a wound or one that denies a terrible truth. Human love has a plus and minus to it. "First love," when positive, has to do with nondefensive union and security. "First love," when negative, has to do with fearing the parent will stop caring or has stopped caring for you, a condition that threatens the baby with death. Loving the provider is a major form of bribery when death is threatened. Fear of dying due to the indifference or hostility of an unloving parent remains in the unconscious and continues to exert the emotional necessity to win the parent's love. This fearful state, if not known and resolved, continues for life.

New kinds of love experiences can occur if we allow them to. These feel like waves of healing that land on the shores of our self-rejecting attitudes and wash them away. We are healed by surrendering to the positive. Our concept of love is shaped by this so cannot remain the same.

A person has the potential for new attitudes and attractions but lacks understanding of the childhood trauma that leads to their repetition. Attempting not to feel the early pain is like placing a huge weight against the fulcrum of change. Change depends on becoming conscious of what hurt you and then making a different choice.

It is fear that keeps a young child clinging to the body/skirt/sleeve/arm of a parent who has the propensity to unlove, abandon, or harm him or her. The child acts charming to placate the parent. He or she clings when nothing else works. The need to establish a reliable connection directs the child's behavior.

As has been stated before, the rejecting, indifferent, or angry parent becomes a construct in the child's mind we call the internal "freezing parent." The terrified child similarly becomes a construct we call the internal "frozen child." These two figures create the repetition compulsion which later directs the adult's love life. The "child" endlessly seeks love from the rejecting "parent" who says, "Thou shall love no one but me or one exactly like me."

The feelings of the "child" as well as the prohibitions of the "parent" are felt and mostly heeded by the adult who feels that his or her "true" self is talking rather than an aspect of the past. The adult needs to recognize that his or her responses are shaped by parental reactions, some of them quite frightening, in order to stop following the "parent/child" directives.

How are people to know and understand what exists behind their mental fog? How are they to get past unconscious barriers to self-knowing? Unconscious motivation with its fears and defenses is like a tidal wave that engulfs and sweeps them along. They can set anchor in the midst of this historic repetition or drift in the shallows, feeling empty, alone, and safe. But that is a nowhere state, neither free nor captured. They escape by paddling like hell to dry land. Once there, they can change the parameters of their game and choose a partner who does not fit into the history of childhood abuse.

Escaping from the past by paddling to shore is an image that means to explore and understand your relationship to your original parents. The defenses that seemed to aid you in reaction to their abuse now hold you back. You discover that these defenses are no longer necessary by not using them despite your fear of harm. Wisdom comes only from experience. All the rest is words.

Adults need to look at what they are afraid of in an emotionally bright light. Starting relationships with people who it turns out do not love them, and then fearing to end them, is a throwback to childhood when parental anger threatened. We need to know our fears in order to reject them. We need to test the consequences of moving out of a poor relationship as well as moving into one of nondefensive loving. We can take small steps or big ones in meeting people. The main thing is to move out of the paralyzed state of our repetition compulsion. We need to speak our need and reach out for love, and only for love, in order to learn that the way to love is possible.

The Need to Destroy Love

Something happens in your love relationship, a very big disappointment but not a new one. You focus on some of your partner's faults and think of him or her with rage. You are roiled by a sense of injustice. Many associate falling in love with denying your lover's flaws, until suddenly your vision returns. Then you focus on the flaw, and everything else disappears.

Humph! This has gone on long enough! You attack your lover for what you declare he or she has done wrong. You make demands, say you will leave him or her, say you feel fed up.

Your lover responds sadly, angrily, or both … sees your viewpoint but has trouble stopping the behavior you object to and doesn't know why. Unconscious needs and impulses rule the lives of all of us. The issue always is to get in touch with what you need to change, to see what underlies it. Your lover claims he or she will try to change. This promise is the truth.

When you say you consider leaving, it strikes fear into his or her heart. You hope that such fear will force him or her to change. Your parent used fear of abandonment to manipulate you. However, the most significant change brought about by the repeated fear of loss is hopelessness.

By talking about having to break up in order to compel your partner to change, you implant an expectation of separation. Such talk desensitizes you to the idea, so both of you are more likely to let it happen. You are like an actor in a play about losing your lover. Your dissociated talking convinces you that what you are talking about has nothing to do with life—until habit takes over. Having rehearsed the loss in your mind makes it easier for you to let love slip away.

Focusing on what is wrong and on the need for a breakup seems to have a life of its own. Rejecting and criticizing is a behavior you learned in childhood. You need your lover to step in and strongly contradict you. He or she has to stop you from being hurtful, since you can't. Your lover has to help restore your sense of being in "a couple." His or her loyalty and sense of love are needed to eradicate the consequences of your destructive urges. Your lover has to bring you to your senses, to do it over and over again. You are happy for a while before once more falling into an angry, rejecting state.

At these times, your destructive internal "freezing parent" has a hold on your mind. Feeling love again is like the fairy tale of a maiden awakened from a deathlike trance by the kiss of a loving knight.

In an actual love affair that is being wrecked by the "parent's" need that he or she attack and reject the lover, the lover's asserting his or her love rescues the person from the "parent's" control, which is experienced as if the adult is in a trance. A lover who can hold on to love by remembering a partner's good side is in the role of prince to a partner who has fallen in line with the "parent's" requirement that love be lost, again.

Why do we need to destroy our love? If we have a long history of attacking our lovers, where is the pleasure and what is the gain? What is the payoff for being unloved and abandoned? We feel great loss even when we are the ones who leave. We have gotten rid of a person we despise, need, and love. After he or she leaves due to our nagging, we feel rejected.

We have reverted to our experience with parents who did not accept us. We identified with them as a defense against feeling their hatred. If we are the rejecting ones, the hurt we feel by their having abandoned us is ignored. Toward our defective lover, first we play the role of a rejecting parent. After our partner is hurt and turns against us, eventually to leave, we play the role of the rejected child. Unstated and probably unconscious in our replay is the question asked by our internal "child.": Mommy/Daddy, do you love me now? Being rejected by the current lover is translated into a childhood act of love. The "child's" sacrifice asks for recompense.

If you are the aggressor, the horrendous things you say may shock your adult mind. You can't believe what is coming out of your mouth. You are acting the role of hateful "parent." Your conscious self feels helpless to intervene and stop you. Due to your lifelong subservience, the internal "parent has a more powerful hold on you than you do on yourself. You hope your lover's mind has not understood you. How can you, the once-tortured child, mistreat the one who loves you?

You are the mouthpiece of your internal "freezing parent." You have reversed the victim position. Now you are the one who causes pain. By doing this, you anesthetize the intolerable pain of an unloved childhood. You soothe your terrified internal "child" by enacting the role of master. Your lover's reactions are less important than your need to rewrite the past. Your current abusive love life revolves around your parent's lack of love for you like planets revolve around the sun.

Why can't you recognize that your parents mistreated you? It is not the adult part of your mind that balks at knowing. It is the internal "child," which feels endlessly vulnerable, weak, and helpless. There was so much fear when your parents turned against you for inconsequential errors. Your child-self could not handle knowing that your parents were ruthless and frequently uncaring. A child could go crazy living with such a reality. Instead, you took blame for what they did or didn't do and ran with it. You are running with it still.

You repeat the lie in your current love life. Your parents didn't really hate you. You caused them to abuse you. You abuse the one you love, as they did you. Adults who hurt their lovers are whitewashing their parents' loveless behavior.

We Hold on to Being Unloved

Loyalty can be a very strange thing when it has to do with our parents. Loyalty can be good or bad, depending on how you define it. If loyalty to another person means being disloyal to yourself, it is bad for you. But what if in your childhood, your parent(s) turned the meaning of loyalty on its head? Loyalty to the needs of certain kinds of parents will have a profoundly negative influence on your life.

Self-centered parents assume that a loyal child will perform self-sacrifice when the parent needs the child to do something that is adverse to the child. The parent may be so self-indulgent that he or she doesn't see the child's surrender as self-harming, or sees but discredits it as a loss. Their thinking paints a rosy picture. If what the child does is good for them, they believe that it "benefits" the child. A submissive child is considered "good."

Insecure parents who need to inflate their self-importance push the children into their cheering squad. Such parents have to be seen as better than everyone else at things they consider important (if not at everything), including those that are done by the children. The children are treated as inferior or as identical so that both of them are "the greatest."

If a parent is an "I am better than you" person, then the child is one of the inferior "others." The child who is treated as a servant, as a failure, as a ne'er-do-well, follows the parent's directives so has trouble acquiring new skills—or the child learns but is unable to show them. One woman, whose father endlessly put her down, failed a typing test for a clerical job although she types like a whiz when alone. She takes no credit for the excellent work she can do, and she quakes in her shoes if she is asked to meet the boss or to receive an award for excellence! Only her father can be the star.

In the social arena, she thinks no man can be interested in her and runs away from those who stop at her desk to say hello. She keeps her eyes down at church, and feels terribly lonely and bereft. She also believes that social isolation is her fate, even that she deserves it.

If you don't understand why you do it, you will be unable to surrender your self-restraint, especially since you are in secret accord with the parent who demands it. Children affiliate how they see themselves and what they do within their parents' system of need, even if they verbally protest it. The issue of surviving shapes their hand.

Many adults dislike the idea of engaging in a deep review, since this includes experiencing their one-time suffering. Why should I suffer these terrible feelings again? They say, I should just move on. If only you could move on that way, but you can't. You have to feel what you felt when your parent abused you in order to develop the motivation to give up your unhealthy adaptation to a victimized relationship. Avoiding feeling historic pain arrests your psychological development.

What is the result of parental jealousy? Say, your mother had to be the only sexually attractive female in the family. While you were young and undeveloped, she didn't feel threatened by you. In high school, your beauty began to draw attention. She increasingly attacked you for your looks, for your pretty sweaters showing your emerging breasts, for smiling at people, and for boys coming around to see you uninvited, all which threatened her supreme position.

She tried to keep you away from the neighborhood boys by finding work for you to do in the barn. You tried to go unnoticed to protect yourself. Your clothing was baggy, your hair tied back in a bun. Invisibility was your goal. But still there was your hair. At the time of your high school graduation and dance, you had a mane of glorious red hair, which she forced you to have cut off. All your friends said not to do it. You begged your mother to leave your hair, said you would confine it in a scarf. No deal. Even the barber objected, but Mom had the power and insisted.

Following Mom's instructions, the barber chopped it off close to the scalp, which made you look mangled in your graduation picture. She called your choppy hairdo "practical." Your hair attracted little attention from strangers and screams of horror from those who knew you. Your mother seemed oblivious to the negative reactions. Secretly she was pleased. Mom was a beauty who would not share the throne.

You absorbed her message to be unattractive, and that is how you remained. Now you don't notice if someone tries to catch your eye. Sexual pleasure is forbidden, although you can't say why. Even if your mother and father ask, "How come you aren't dating?" when you do have a date, they revile the person. How could you be with a lowlife like Mr. "X"? You look away or tell yourself that some guy really wasn't looking at you. You think of yourself as a kind of "leper," which leads you to gain weight and develop a belly. You become homely with only a hint of your beauty showing underneath.

If people come near and touch you, you feel a kind of fury, as if they had climbed over your garden wall and invaded your sacred space. That space belongs to your reigning mother. Your parent claimed you—body, mind, and spirit—even claimed your right to be loved. She wanted to seal you away from fans and lovers. Her spirit of ownership was presented by her as taking care.

You remember how she took care the time she shot all the wild cats living and breeding in the barn. She hadn't spent the effort to have the cats fixed. Care for her equaled death. Even when you are an adult living far from her, Mom's threatening aura rarely leaves your mind.

Sexually and emotionally starved, you are empty to the bone but do nothing to correct it. Your internal "freezing parent" dictates that you must wait for your "parent" to set you free. You lead the life of a princess locked in an ivory tower. Your mind soothes itself with, "Someday my prince will come." Children raised by competitive and jealous parents usually surrender having independent judgment. They stop showing their talents and beauty, stop living for their own pleasure and achievement. They give up spontaneity as too noticeable and therefore dangerous.

Living in a state of emotional deprivation is treated by that person as an act of loyalty to the parents. Take the example of a father who called himself loving for never striking his child with his hands. The child tries to convince herself that a parent who hits only with words must truly love his child, but her heart remains empty. Striking with words or hands is equally abusive. If her arrogant parent had been a physical brute, she would have felt no worse.

Take a mother who called herself loving for doing all your laundry. But she never had any interest in how well you played the piano or what you wrote for the school magazine. Both parents spoke about their work, their pains, their greatness at doing things better than anybody else, including you. The spotlight was on them. You took the message that you were to hide.

All roads have the same destination for a child who is loyal to such a parent. These roads lead to pain that is seen as love or as a justification for its lack. You hear your mother say that you act so miserable, how could anyone love you? Your shed tears and are downcast in the face of their rejection. You feel yourself to be cursed.

You have to be phony to the core to survive their sneering at you without being visibly upset. Many victimized children have smiles plastered on their faces regardless of how they feel. Since a smile indicates to parents that they are successful, offering a false front is the way to get along. The smile has nothing to do with what the child feels, although it sometimes distracts him or her.

Do you know if you are choosing to be unloved? Are you uncomfortable, even frightened, if someone admires you? Do you think that an offer of unadulterated love is false and that you should run away from it or angrily reject it? Do you mistrust love that is openhanded? Must you seek love buried in a concatenation of confusion and mistreatment so that no one can know what happened and hold the receipt of love against you? Is the possessive internal "parent" lurking in the back of your mind ever ready to pounce on you for looking for another?

Are you attracted to people who lack feelings, like the Tin Man who had no heart in *The Wizard of Oz*? Do you spend great energy trying to get such a person to love you? If the one whose love you seek doesn't offer it, do you take the blame? Are you glad that your lover hogs all the listening time so that you can't speak and manifest your stupidity? Can you fall only for people others call abusive? Do you have lovers and friends who put you down and have cruel ways of describing your mistakes? Do you magnify the importance of your errors? Is your mind focused on how to deal with the next attack?

You feel strangely reassured by people telling you what you need to change in order to be okay. It is like returning you to your torturing childhood home. The pain you feel with critical friends and lovers reinforces the tie you have with your parents. Choosing to love these people is propelled by your need to re-experience childhood abuse, which by your habitual denial is labeled love. Tolerating, even seeking, this is what you call loyalty to them all.

Fear Keeps You Holding On

People repeat what they hear about love. They tend to assume the truth of the crowd, rather than struggle to understand what they really need and how they really feel by looking into their hearts. The current belief about the repetition compulsion is that adults who were abused as children love people who resemble their abusive parents because they are still seeking the parents' love.

I don't disagree with this analysis. Only it is like a prospector looking at a pile of brush and not clearing it away and digging to see what lies beneath. Beneath is where we find the gold. What gives force to this compulsion, this shallow or nonexistent digging that can lead only to failure? Why do we not learn from receiving no reward from our efforts? Or is there a secret reward, one that does not serve our adult purposes? Calling the repetition compulsion a habit in which we seek a different outcome from behavior that has always failed avoids the part we don't want to deal with. It doesn't deal with fear.

We seek love from those who can't give it, to cover our fear. We are more afraid of losing this defense than we are of experiencing our repeated failure to be loved. We try to disguise this fear from ourselves. The reason we seek love from similarly abusive people is to reassure us that what we fear the most will not happen. The original fear is of being hurt, even destroyed, by our parents, and now by lover X. People do what they fear the most to suppress their fear of it. What of Evel Knievel, who jumps vast spaces in his motorcycle? He has broken almost every bone in his body. Do you think he keeps doing it for the money?

Sometimes we dispense love in destructive ways to reassure ourselves that we cannot be harmed by the one we love, because we are hate's purveyor. At the base of all of this is fear. Finding abusive lovers is akin to using a drug that suppresses symptoms but does not remove the disease. That is why we need to take it ever more. Denial moves us toward the very thing we fear in a trance of pleasure and excitement. We grow to love the thrill of danger.

The adult mind, when attempting to know itself, feels the depth of childhood terror in a dissociated way. They say, "I don't know why I feel this way," or they may have terrible memories that lack associated feelings. Feeling while remembering a hurtful situation can be overwhelming to a child and later to the "child" within the adult mind. Defensive disassociation is like watching a scary movie from the point of view of humor, or saying, "That is supposed to be scary, but it doesn't touch me."

The adult minds of those who pursue abusive lovers often cannot comprehend that to them, love and fear are a unit. They sometimes feel madly in love and sometimes are rigid with fear. But secretly and often, they feel the two together. Feeling without memory—memory without feeling—is of little use. The mind is easily led by the internal "child's" need to pretend it isn't so. It is the union of the two that reveals the mind's ungodly pact and asks you why.

The "child's" fear of being snuffed out by an aggressive parent is carried as a lethal nugget tucked inside the brain. The internal "child" sheds fearful tears and issues self-instructions to the current adult mind. It tells you to surrender to your abuser. It is this nugget of fear, like that in the mind of a prisoner headed to the gallows, that generates inexplicable feelings of love for the executioner. Love is a secret bribe that the condemned man hopes will stay the executioner's hand. It is the "child" within on bended knee that loves.

People are capable of finding something slightly fearful to distract them from what they deeply fear. We need to see how we stop ourselves from knowing what we feel so that we can get a purchase on what takes us away from love and moves us toward abuse.

People don't believe that they have a need for fear connected to love, although love without fear doesn't call them. They do not notice it because they do not want to notice. The adult mind is out of touch with feeling their "parent's" abuse while seeking "parental" love and their "child's" attempts to deny the abuse in order to feel loved.

There are many ways we keep ourselves from knowing why we love those who cannot love us, or why we reject those who do. These ways include burying fear in fear. People are capable of finding something slightly fearful to distract them from what they deeply fear. We need to discover the ways we stop ourselves from getting in touch with what happened to us, how we felt before we turned off our ability to wholesomely love and be loved. Wholesome love does not wound. Wholesome love heals wounds. We need to get purchase on what has driven us in order to end a lifetime of painful denial.

Let us look at the kinds of parents who generate a desperate need in their children to take care of and adore these unloving folk. They were parents only in name. They came to the role of parent as babies in disguise. They never received the love and nurturing they needed from their own parents, so these feelings were in short supply. They do not know the experiential meaning of love, and even if they recognize their inadequacy, they still cannot give it. Love is an emotional state, not one of empty words and gestures. You cannot give to another what you lack.

Fear of Being Rejected

Fear of rejection is overemphasized by those who were rejected from the start. It is a kind of emotional reflex learned in childhood that later shows up in all your relationships.

The man who snowplows your driveway went way over the gravel portion of the lane, into your perennial garden. He plowed a part that took years to get started, due to the proximity of a black walnut tree whose roots exude a fluid that is toxic to many plants. From the extent of gravel sprinkled over half the garden, you can see he used some kind of blower. Between shoveling and blowing, the man's work was destructive.

You have to call and ask him to visit so you can show him what needs to be done next year. What if he walks off in a snit? Then you will have to find someone else to do the job or to do it yourself. Which is better, more plant destruction with all the work and money involved, or someone feeling hurt and quitting? And what if he gets angry? What about it? If you are female, his fit of pique will not remove your nail polish. If you are male, his getting angry doesn't prove you are a wimp. You do not need to fight him to prove otherwise. Who are you trying to impress? There is no need for you to shake in your boots in fear of his reaction. That is your ancient baby habit.

Here is another example. You have to tell a friend who is always making insulting comments, as well as giving orders, that her behavior is aggressive, hurts your feelings, and is unacceptable. She has been told this many times by many people. She returns the blame by calling all of them crybabies, pushing them away with some kind of diagnostic label, or by calling herself "impulsive." How long can the word *impulsive* operate as an excuse that gets her off the hook? It is too easy. Do you want to be in the company of someone who approaches you with fangs and knives, to feel continuously apprehensive when you are together? When will you next be gored?

What delays you from making a decision? Your internal "freezing parent" waves threatening fingers in front of your face and yells, "Save yourself by surrendering!" *Save from what?* you should ask yourself. Your internal "frozen child" quivers in fear and defensively grows smaller. But you are a grown-up and do not need to heed these ancient signposts to direct your adult self.

Are you afraid of letting go of friends and lovers who aren't friendly? Do you fear that no one else will like you? You got this idea from parents who did not sufficiently love you in the first place. Why do you believe what they said? Are you still trying to win their love? That no one else will love you is a childhood myth that has long dominated your thinking and serves no purpose except to glue you to your parents. The maze they created and in which you still wander has no way out.

Spit in the face of this myth. Let unfriendly friends and lovers go. If you want to give them a final try, put a date on the calendar for their becoming more civil and let them know it. If the required behavior does not happen by the specified time, turn the page. Go on to the new. If you think that everyone must love you to prove your rejecting parents wrong, and if the first one you meet doesn't do it, you are not to think that no one will. If you believe such a thing with scanty evidence, you are once more bowing to your parents' prediction.

You repeat what they said about you to the point that it becomes belief. Belief is not based on fact. It is based on wishful thinking. It is based on fear. Your parents didn't love you as you needed, yet they said only they could do it. What an amazing contradiction. Lack of love is not love. It is like out of George Orwell's *1984*: "Hate is love." The fact is, they never much loved you and never will (alive or dead). Their lack of love is not your fault. Take yourself out of the guilty box. Don't keep yourself on trial.

Fear of being abandoned by the one you love starts in early childhood with rejecting parents. You clung to them so as to not be left behind. The fear of being abandoned remains with you as an adult. It keeps you from fully loving others and unable to believe that they can love and remain with you. Fully loving makes you feel too vulnerable. Believing yourself to be unworthy of committed love goes back to your parents' rejection. It keeps you standing on the doorjamb, ever ready to depart.

Adults need to recognize what moves their internal "child" and "parent" in order to understand the early experiences that currently paralyze and distort their adult selves' quest for love. Adults need to become strong and autonomous enough to not be controlled by these fearful messages. Then they can find and love loving partners.

CHAPTER 4

Forced to Serve

Parents Who Must Be Served

Let us look at the kind of parents who generate their children's desperate need to take care of them. It is not a normal expectation for grown children of parents who are middle aged and able to care for themselves. It is natural for elderly people who once did the same for their children. The grown children of such adults will wholeheartedly care for them.

Parents requiring ongoing care to the point of self-sacrifice are not of a certain age. Their age is irrelevant. They have always been this way. They were this way before their children were born. They come to the role of parent as babies in disguise. As children, they never received sufficient love and nurturing to grow into independent beings. Their childhood left them empty. As parents, they cannot give to their children what they lack.

As parents, they often are belligerent due to their reservoir of need even in their silence. They cry like frightened babies. They accuse with fists and loud voices. They know what they need and are out to get it. They scream for emotional feeding. Partly they seek revenge for what never happened. They treat their children as their inadequate parents and behave accordingly. It's all about demand. They are ordering their offspring as only an upset baby can to "take care of me now," which turns out to be for life.

They fantasize without recognizing that the child will be their parent. Once the baby is born, the parent is frequently angry that the baby needs to be fed, held, and changed. When the child grows a bit and needs greater stimulation, creativity, planning, and interaction with the parent, the parent as baby resents it. It isn't stated and perhaps not consciously recognized, but the parent thinks, *What is going on? I am the baby here.*

The parent has baby modes of saying no. He or she turns into a bully or is largely unavailable. The child has to live on the parent's schedule—don't dribble on my good blouse—and on the parent's need to control: Do it when I say so. I want to hold you now. You are to smile, not frown and pull away. I want you to sleep now, eat now, stand and walk now; I want you to not make my apartment unsafe by pulling out plugs and putting everything in your mouth. The parent bears down on the "misbehaving" child like a polar bear about to eat a seal.

The child becomes a bull's-eye for the parent's dissatisfaction. As time goes by, the child weeps silent tears and becomes wishfully invisible. Eventually, he or she becomes a helper who knows what the parent needs even before the parent asks for it and does everything possible to provide. The child accepts the parent's rule of "No talking back." The child comes last in the parent's planning, including broken appointments. The implication to the child is that he or she is not that important. The child is related to by the parent as a servant or as a slave. When the child doesn't do things when they are demanded, he or she is treated as a delinquent.

Such parents, as babies masquerading as adults, are never satisfied. They rationalize abusing their children as justified by the children's "misbehavior." They paint themselves in beautiful colors, which is a form of rationalization. They project their own dissatisfaction onto the children, who "ask too much" of them. They blubber and yell their discontent as would any uncomfortable baby. With such overreactive and dissatisfied parents, these children never learn what is "right." Everywhere and whatever they do, there are sharp edges to nick them and quicksand to bring them down and swallow them up.

Fear and the need to placate the parent in order to avoid being slaughtered are carried into adulthood as motives that shape the adult's love life. The terrified internal "frozen child" lives within the brain of the servile adult. The "child" defers to the internal "freezing parent" in the form of choosing abusive lovers. The adult seeks love from those who do not give it. The "parent" requires the adult submit to their mistreatment.

Those who stand primly aside and criticize you for loving abusive people may be covering up their fear of doing the same. When one condemns another, often there is an aspect of that person inside the critic's self.

Avoiding awareness of terror blinds us to self-knowledge. To stop choosing unloving lovers or mistreating those who love us, we have to become aware of our internal "child" and "parent." It is the "child" who clings to life through submissive worship and the "parent" who demands it and punishes noncompliance.

The "parent" part is played in our adult life by our lover as parent stand-in, an adult who acts emotionally cold and damaging. If we are the ones who play the damaging parent, we damage our vulnerable lovers, one after the other. Critics focus on the lack of love in these pairings. We need to look at our history to explain it. There always is a payoff. Loss of life is more frightening than missing love. As bully or victim, you are trying to stay alive.

Copying the parent who mistreated you is an attempt to cajole the internal abusive "parent." You will not hurt/kill me if I am just like you. In effect, I am you. The Stockholm syndrome involves falling in love with your kidnappers. All abused children feel kidnapped by mistreating parents whose hatred stimulates them to fear, adore, and cling. Oh, powerful one on whom my life depends, I love you so. Please love me.

Loving parents create a secure and loving atmosphere for children who have no need to learn violence or submission. Such children grown to adulthood continue to love people who love them back. They are loving equals. Grown-ups whose parents offered tentative love at best and more often offered hatred, court harmful people to stay the killer's hands. It is an endless reenactment to still their panic. The internal "child" is too frightened of the consequences to tell the adult to leave the abuser's clutches. The "child" bends before the whip, and the adult concordantly surrenders.

Arms Outstretched to Hold You Back

To many who know you, your stuck and familiar behavior is their place of security. These are teachers and intellectual adversaries, people who take you as their model or as a dunce whose behavior they declare inadequate in order to declare themselves superior. These are the lovers who need to run the show and have you come out second or last. It is these who need to worship you as a star which remains in a fixed position, not a person growing and changing through his or her try-it-out life. A growing life is a changing life based on experience and your response to it. Those who fear acknowledging their own underlying conflicts do not want their hero or antihero (a person designated a failure), to change.

Whether emitting negative or positive words toward your thinking and behavior, their need for a place of comfort—which is associated with a fear of change—causes them to cling to your pregrowth position. It keeps you as a known constellation in their mental universe. Your image is their anchor and your chain. Even having something they can always hate is a stable, albeit lifeless, position. Stability creates security. Hooray for the constancy of your arrested development.

Nevertheless you are growing. They see you making changes, some of them subtle and some of them obvious. The intellectuals in your crowd become alarmed. They ask if you have read a certain book, if you have studied some important thinker, and what his or her position is on a stated matter. Many suggest that you should read the hallowed tome before you speak again and that there are dire consequences if you don't. They fill your mind with anxiety over being wrong. They make you worry about being rejected by your lover or your "pack."

Critical and controlling people don't want to be stirred by new ideas. Those who see themselves as having power over you don't want to be trounced by the force of your increasing autonomy. Those who think of themselves as erudite don't want to question philosophies they have been relying on for years. Your taking a position that differs from theirs turns them against you. It is fear that conquers their interest.

However, not every friend or lover runs for the hills. Some are at first fearful, then interested, and then stimulated by your ideas, and they want to try them on for size. Some want to debate you in a spirit of fun from which both of you expand your understanding. However, whether or not your lover agrees with you and whether your "almost" friends accept your emerging personality should not determine what you do. What you decide to think and do has to come from your reason as well as from the call of your heart. The past may educate, but it needn't corner you. Sometimes you simply have to move into the untried and new, to grow into it. You may need to find new friends.

Recognize that often behind a lover's or friend's reactive anger there is jealousy. Usually, what they attack you for comes from the threat of their internal "freezing parent" for your leading them to question its rules. The "parent" feels threatened by the danger of being removed from its "chief" position. Its jealousy moves them to ignore you.

Perhaps the way you speak your ideas might be improved. You may or may not have the time or interest in developing your communicative skills. In all decisions we make, there is always the issue of time. What do we want to do with the time we've got?

You need to deal with your fear of abandonment by your crowd, with the terror of your internal "child" in the face of their disapproval. You need to recognize that the magnitude of your fear dates back to a childhood with rejecting parents and assign it to the dustbin of history. It is possible that for a while, no new person whose ideas are in sync with yours will come along and become your friend. Associates are not friends. A friend offers a deeper and more meaningful interaction, one you deeply feel and will not soon forget. But given the number of people you contact, if you let yourself go out and meet them, it is unlikely you will not eventually meet such a person. The same thing goes for meeting a lover who cares.

As you grow into new understanding, acting the role your parents, relatives, friends, and lovers are accustomed to is being false to your self. If you keep your friends by playacting, you have no friends; the same thing is true with a lover. A lover is a friend who knows you and loves/likes you as you are today. Although good behavior certainly is required, being who you are is a rule.

Addicted to Pain and Suffering

What is the strange allure that pulls you back? Why are you always feeling anxious about the connection with your loved one and holding on lest he or she escape? Will your loved one be there as promised, call back, make plans that he or she will keep … or will the person suddenly be "too busy"? Will he or she remember my birthday? Can the person be counted on for anything? Will there be a conflicting appointment? "Sorry. I can't make it." You ask, "How about sex?" "Don't feel like doing it now." Is your loved one a borrower? "Lend me some money. I'll pay you back." All kinds of demands can be made which require that you sacrifice.

You experience hurtful words. You wait for the next accusation, something you did that hurt the person's feelings. You are asked to give up doing what you want to do, because he or she tearfully needs you to stay or to do something else together, regardless of the negative consequences … for you.

How can you say no to your lover (or friend) who expresses disappointment as if it is a major disaster, even though you told him or her in advance of your appointment? If you stay, you will miss your friend's video show and party, with all those films he has edited, including yours, before he leaves the country. Your lover says, "You can do it later." This is a one-and-only event, a celebration of your friend's life as a videographer.

If you don't attend because you choose to stay with your lover this night—as if there were no other—you end the friendship. How can you even consider doing it? But you do. You sink into a fog of confusion. Which action is best for you? What is love? Does love always involve sacrifice? What kind of sacrifice? Must pleasing the lover come first? You don't leave your lover as you intended to do after drinking or smoking some grass, so your thinking becomes hazy.

When your partner praises you for giving in, your elation is outrageous. Your sense of loss is laid to rest. You feel relief. No disaster is visible on the immediate horizon. That the friend who expects you will greatly disappointed has passed from your mind. It is the black-or-white thinking of a child. What you focus on is all there is. If it isn't bad, it's good. Your fear about displeasing your lover has been alleviated. Your hope that the relationship will last is based on crumbs of evidence … and at what cost? You have ignored the loss of a friend. Your adult mind has surrendered to the internal clinging and fearful child. Your grown-up self has been fooled.

Paradoxically, with so much anxiety and worry, with only occasional and unexpected moments of love—mostly after your giving in—your romantic attachment increases. You can't live without him or her. You feel pain in your stomach and shortness of breath. You are obsessed with that person. It's love. Isn't it?

Any habit becomes extremely strong when its reinforcement is aperiodic. Aperiodic means that there is no rhythm in positive reactions responding to your effort. Sometimes there is a reward and sometimes not. As a result, you expect that sooner or later you will get one. Feeling hated with unexpected moments of love sinks you deeper into the habit. You believe because of the aperiodic reinforcement of affection, that despite all of your suffering and possibly because of it, love will happen. The searing pain in your heart, the worthlessness of your needs and plans, the extremity of joy once you are embraced … that's love. Isn't it?

Your idea of union associates a lot of misery with minuscule hope. You react to miserable treatment as love's preamble. Most people would be repulsed and turned off by such experiences. Not you. Misery lights your fire. A state of fear, worry, mistreatment, and deprivation, interposed by kisses, is what you respond to and what you seek in all your love affairs. It is an addiction you need to shake.

To shake the addiction, you have to understand your love construct. Your idea of love needs to be studied in a bright light. You need to examine all the elements in how you come to choose whom you do. You have to experience your ongoing pain without covering it with the fig leaf of thereby "winning" love. This experience will help you stop responding with desire when your lover harms you. Enjoying pain as a prerequisite to love is destructive. Pain is not a reward. Pain is not the equivalent of love. Being on tenterhooks waiting for love to happen brings you back to your rejecting parents.

People equate or cover their suffering with love as a kind of disguise. Especially during childhood, when the love construct first evolves, a painful experience is made more tolerable if the child can make it wear the mask of love. A child says, My daddy hit me because he loves me. Hitting me when I have done something wrong proves that he cares. In this way, all abuse, be it physical, mental, or financial—even if it is done in an alcoholic rage—at some level can be labeled caring. Such parents may think this way about themselves; they look on the caring side rather than know themselves as abusers.

To say the parent loves you, no matter how he or she treats you, converts the terrifying home situation into something you can live with. But why would adults, once out of their parents' fearful home, continue to label abusive behavior loving and seek abuse in current partners?

Mentally, they have not left their parents' home. The early family situation lives on in their mind. Each new lover is chosen who fits into that ancient scene. Like a bird responding to the male of her species' courting tune, the adults respond to the love song of abuse. They are controlled by their need to see the abusive, uncaring parent as loving. It is an experience endlessly reenacted to keep their mind away from the stored and seething experience of fear.

One's addiction to abusive people must be consciously known if it is to be discontinued. All the characteristics of an addictive choice, the seductive ideas and denial of personal harm, must be clearly seen so that we are forced to recognize what is happening to us again. We are not to allow wishful thinking to keep us from becoming aware. We are not to forget and fall into a sea of rationalization. We need to know the danger and feel its pain in order to avoid it.

When the Sirens' song of destructive desire streams across the water, we need to recognize its danger and decide to sail away. The Sirens' song is that of your abusive parent. Odysseus had his sailors put wax in their ears after tying himself to the deck so that he could listen to the Sirens' song but not succumb to it. Children of unloving parents need to rehearse leaving when they hear their own version of the Sirens' song, regardless of their desire to draw near. They need a modern version of wax in the ears or of ropes tying them to the mast of the ship, whose wheel and rudder are set to sail away.

Their Feelings Are More Important Than Your Own

The issue was disturbing her. It was like being trapped in a spider's web with the spider constantly spinning threads to more heavily bind and hold her. Why was she willingly contained? She frequently is adversarial to her feelings. Her mind had long been programmed to accept those who stated that they had authority over her as well as superior knowledge.

She was seeing Carol, a counselor for support in taking her work project to its completion rather than giving in to childhood doubt. Carol stipulated that she had to come each week at a certain time for a certain fee or not come at all. Feeling cornered by this, she accepted the woman's rule. In choosing Carol to talk to, she thought, *At least I know this woman.* But did she?

She had trouble withdrawing from the relationship, which was changing its shape and turning into a trap. This is not the first time that this has happened. She is overly concerned with the other person's feelings: should she ask for a change in the style of their interaction? And if she does not receive it, should she leave, and how? Her parents were rejecting, her mother a "rage-aholic." She long ago learned to give in out of exaggerated fear. Giving in was her answer to any problem that seemed to lack a solution. Giving in represents her loss of self.

She tells Carol for the third time, "You are my 'coach,'" with its implicit limited range of interaction. The counselor was slightly miffed after hearing this. You could see it in her rigid, angry posture, which she tried to conceal under the guise of intellectual inquiry. She responded, "I am not like your original therapist," as if she had been put in second place.

She went home and thought about it, and then the following week she responded that the original therapist was her coach. A coach offers work on how you play the game. He or she does not go beyond this analysis and attempt to guide your life. If coaching is what you need, he or she gives it.

She had been raised by parents who always told her what to do. They disregarded, criticized, and attacked her plans. She has an inventive mind that did not need to be led into deepening insight. She needed someone to support her making a decision, creating a work of art, doing something entirely unconventional, and living her life.

She spoke to the woman about the value of a coach as giving what you come for, but was she understood? A spider is entangled in its own web of desire. Every filament is attached to the spider's need. The web creation is driven by hunger, the need to contain its prey. A spider makes its web strong enough to hold on to what it catches as well as to remain intact through windy storms.

The teapot of her brain, finding herself one more subject to another's will, was beginning to boil and whistle. She was paying money and using time to maintain a relationship whose value had dwindled to zero, if not fallen into the negative. She was remaining out of fear. By continuing this relationship, she added to her childhood-created doubt about her understanding, intention, and judgment. The counselor demanded an allegiance she did not feel, because she was not being understood. Intimacy is based on being mutually in touch. When another's understanding is superimposed and sold to you as if it is your own, intimacy dies.

She recognized that she was mentally ahead of the counselor. She had a better idea about what was going on. Many years past, she had had the same kind of uncanny "it can't be true" experience with her claimed-to-be-all-knowing parents. Eureka! They didn't understand.

The counselor was unable or unwilling to give what the client clearly asked for. Perhaps the woman was too full of self-doubt to be led by her client's request, so she improperly asserted herself. She had an "I can analyze this" mode of speaking that rendered the listener useless. She was operating from a brain that spun its wheels in space rather than from her heart, which knew better. But the client had enough of being submerged by others falsely claiming to know what she needed. She needs to speak to someone who listens to her and speaks the truth. Most of all, she needs to listen to herself.

It is true that sometimes we think we know something and it turns out to be wrong. But that is a matter of self-discovery, not of someone pushing you into accepting what they state you should know, so it never becomes your own. Everyone grows at his or her own rate. The respectful "helper" waits—be it lover, friend, or therapist.

The client's seeing the counselor has a superstitious air. She saw Carol to keep her mind away from her internal "freezing parent," which would put an end to her creative effort. But the counselor was turning into one herself. It was like childhood with parents who rarely came through. She courted them in hope that they would be around if ever an emergency arose. Needing them to understand her without their understanding was itself an ongoing emergency.

With Carol, it was a similar emergency of not being understood. She was paying a mighty dollar for this gap to a person claiming to be truth's vendor. A person raised by parents who did not understand her often does not recognize a similar gap in lovers, "authorities," and friends. She is used to being misunderstood and blames herself for its occurrence. Perhaps I didn't say the right thing in the right way at the right time. Self-awareness of this acquired guilty stance is needed for her to stop doing it.

She was at the point of saying good-bye to the woman but felt the same kind of incomprehensible fear she had with her parents, who would reject her if she did not go along with their program. She took an indirect approach by repeating yet again that she was only there for coaching. She was about to say that the coaching job was done.

Instead of helping her make a graceful exit with the relationship intact, the woman gave a bull-in-the-china-shop response and said, "How about doing psychotherapy?" The woman's statement was an inelegant power-ridden comment said to tie her down. The spider exudes silk to catch the fleeing bug. It was entirely the wrong thing to say, with threads of intellectual pride concealing greed.

The client felt an attack of rage upon hearing this and responded, "I am not interested in psychotherapy. The bread is already baked." The woman questioned her bread analogy. She explained, "I am not cutting myself into little pieces to be reassembled." Then she added, "The part of me that is currently developing, what I am learning to do right now, is to say no." She added, "I am saying no to you."

The woman looked at her with an expression that lay between shock and rage. The submissive child had turned onto a raging lion standing on its hind legs, paws extended with nails outstretched. The woman repeated, "You are saying no?"

She felt a surge of power when she humorously responded, "I am practicing saying no to you." Feeling power comes from self-affirmation, from setting your own limits.

Then she smiled and said good-bye without rejecting the woman's expectation that they meet the following week. Her courage failed her at this point. The woman undoubtedly would work on a rebuttal that would draw her in. During the week, she replayed the meeting and felt increasingly outraged that the woman suggested psychotherapy after she so clearly had rejected it. She thought of all kinds of responses she could make, including, "You should see *me* for psychotherapy."

Yet, in her mind, she equivocates. Her internal "child" is ringing the alarm bell. Under her "child's" influence, she tells herself, *I will go to the next session and say I am leaving you the session after this.* It was an act of procrastination. Why a session after the next? Why a next? Who was pleasing whom? She feels obliged to do a good deed, but what does this good deed do for her? The good deed done for the woman probably will do herself harm, since the woman is clearly set against her plan. Does she need to fight for the freedom she possesses?

She befuddles herself by toying with how she will announce her intention to leave at the *next session*. Should she state her departure at the beginning, or at the end to avoid an argument? She worries about being polite. Always, the other person's feelings come first. She cannot simply say, "I am done. Thanks for your help," and, "Good-bye." She can't give herself permission to leave a good-bye message on the woman's answering machine and drop the entire matter. What is the basis for her sense of obligation?

She needs to look at this experience as a model of self-sacrifice in order to learn from it. How many times has she done what a manipulative person presented as for her good? The woman is a hungry spider spinning silken threads to bind her. Using the word *psychotherapy* guarantees the longevity of their tie. The word *coach* is limited by its focus on developing a technique for doing something, in a game or in a season. The one who was spinning the thread of psychotherapy was creating a focus without parameters. Her view of Carol's offering is that she does it out of selfishness. Carol proposed *psychotherapy* out of the counselor's need to prolong their interaction rather than provide what the client needed.

How does the difficulty in stating her needs, of being autonomous, infuse and undermine her love affairs? How many times has she done what a lover or friend (or parent) required, setting her own needs aside? Does succumbing to another person's need make her feel more loved? Does it make the other person love her more, and what is it they love? You cannot feel loved unless you show yourself. Purchasing love through acquiescence is purchasing nothing. Getting the woman to love her by submitting to psychotherapy is an expression of her antiself position. It is as useless to do it here as it is everywhere else.

Guilt about Separating and Leaving

If you were raised to cater to your parents, often at your own expense, the habit is deeply felt, especially after people point the finger of blame at you for not doing what they expect. As a result of this need to be and do what other people desire, you have a poor sense of who you are and what should be expected of you. You do not know the right amount to give. There is not a developed you inside to judge.

This is all about setting boundaries. Boundaries concern what you will allow others to do to you and what you will allow yourself. They are about setting limits. While boundaries may be as facetted as the situations you encounter, they all encapsulate to give you a sense of self. Self is feeling yourself to be a unit, not a scrambled concatenation of unrelated parts. Self has integrity and is ongoing.

After careful self-examination, you need to conclude that you cannot develop a sense of self when following another person's plan. You need to strike out on your own, to make your own mistakes—which you can regard with mischievous joy since it is you who are making them, which is a sign of freedom. You will learn a lot from trying out different approaches until you find one that works and, equally important, one that you like doing.

But what about your parent's pain over your abandoning the dependent person's "court" and no longer being an extension for him or her? If the one who leans on you is your parent, he or she describes your intentions as foibles. The parent tries to fill you with fear by describing what you are planning to do as disastrous—like lemmings walking toward a cliff and then falling into the sea (although the idea of mass suicide by lemmings appears to be incorrect). Your parent's desire to reshape your plans is something that you not only do not need but also must regard as serious interference. You need to be free to make your own mistakes in order to grow your self.

Much of the energy that fuels the arguments they present to you comes from the pain you are causing them by going off on your own. Shouldn't you cancel your plan for that reason? You already have canceled many. It hurts to think of all your lost experiences. Your parents may ardently and sincerely believe what they are telling you, but their belief, whatever its foundation, is not your reality. Their need to protect/contain/possess you is not your own.

Do not argue with them about their advice. Say you will consider what they have said. Wait a moment or two, and change the topic. Terminate the discussion in a friendly way. If they try to overpower you with noisy speech and finger-pointing, do not be pulled in.

Theirs is the pain of a crippled person who is about to lose a crutch. But their paralysis is not physical. It is emotional, a very different kind of problem. By their assessment, if you love them must you remain their crutch. This is their assessment; is it yours?

When you go away, they will need to find another crutch, since without one they will fall. Do you have the right to leave them psychologically leaning against a psychological wall and wailing about their helplessness? Do you have the right to choose to consider your life instead of theirs? Are you responsible for their emotional well-being? Many parents fantasize their child as parent in the garb of a nurse. The parents' need-created fantasy should not be your own.

The weakness that makes your parents lean on you comes from their own inadequate parenting. Their parents did not give them what they needed to grow into strong and independent people. They were crippled this way before you arrived. Their need to lean on you represents their crippled state.

Your leaving gives them the problem of having to face and hopefully heal their injuries. Those who recognize that they are emotionally wounded will get into psychotherapy. Those who cannot bear to see the origin of their problem will look for another person to lean on, using the philosophy of concealment found in a "we are one" state they call love.

You need to look at your readiness to feel guilty in order to not fall prey to it in all of your relationships. You are not responsible for your parents' early deprivation. You are not to be blamed for their feeling empty and adrift when you leave. You were not put on earth to serve them. If you find a lover who enacts a similar "you must stay with me, or I will die" approach, you have found another version of your weak and needy parents. Childhood creates a debt of love, which is not what your parents seek, even if they call it that.

Your tendency to feel guilty and frightened when moving away from your parents (also from your dependent and/or tyrannical friend or lover) comes from the operation of your internal "frozen child," which is fearful of the internal "freezing parent." Developing an adult self, you separate from these aspects of your early experience with their rigid views. You need to develop a that-was-then attitude when guilt and being forced to cater comes to mind. You recognize the "child's" fearful dependency and the "parent's" critical opinion. Your adult self decides not to continue acting as a crutch for anyone, since it is an improper nonsolution for you both.

Tell your parent (friend or lover) the truth. Lying betrays and eliminates the real you. Say that you will do what you can to help him or her but will not remain an enslaved nurse. The "internal child" may worry about the "parent's" rage, but your adult self is not part of this historic internal duo. The adult self feels separate and knows better.

The Need to Heal Your Parent

The matter of autonomy—of separating from your parents, which is part of growing up—includes not taking on responsibility for curing them of the pain that comes from their unhappy childhoods. Not only is it not your responsibility, but you can't do it.

What makes recognizing this fact so difficult is your parents' fantasy that you can. Without knowing it, or with only dim awareness, they saw you as a parent who was supposed to love and nurture them, to know what they needed and provide it, and by doing all of this to heal them. The child of such parents, once grown into adulthood, continues to play this assigned role.

We learn more from what our parents do than from what they tell us. A parent's need, fear, and anger shape the child's truth and are his or her earliest culture. Children have to believe that their parents have good intentions. They cannot think they are living in a cave with beasts that may eat them when hungry, or attack and kill when angry. They have to deny this potential threat even if the parent is violent. To take the blame for the parent's aggressive behavior absolves the parent of having bad intentions and keeps hope alive in the child for receiving the parent's love. All the arrows of guilt are aimed at the child.

Such parents may not directly say, "You are supposed to care for me," but their behavior clearly states it. The parent is annoyed, withdrawn, ruffled, explosive, and demanding; the parent acts sick and helpless. The parent has tantrums and enacts vindictive behavior, for which he or she blames the child. The child quickly learns that it is wrong to make demands on a parent who basically is a child. The child gets the message, I am the cause of my parent's misery and have to fix it.

Eventually the children are grown, and their parents, whether alive or dead, remain central in their thinking. The grown-ups honor their rage, which resonates within their mind, and they find raging types to love. They seek ways to placate and gratify the lover, who has the same destructive and dependent features. If the parents were violent, the grown-ups find lovers who will beat them. If the parents yelled and blamed the child, a duplicate lover will be found. Each of the parents' out-of-control "save me from this pain you are causing" actions leads to the choice of lovers who will do the same. Submitting to the lover's abuse is an attempt to heal the parent. The grown child is living in the past but does not know it.

You allow yourself to be mistreated in order to placate and heal your internal "parent." You try and try again. How are you to know that it is the "parent's" demand that drives you? How do you get in touch with the "frozen child" that submits? You cannot imagine this to be true, because part of you is so angry at your actual parents that you want to hurt them. Your anger is a response to feeling helpless and used. The conscious mind feels angry. The internal "child" feels guilty, and fearful, and cringes before the abusive internal "parent." Whichever has greater force in controlling your self establishes what you do.

Having been shaped by your parents' view of you, you lack of sympathy for your cornered self. Your adult mind, which is flooded by your "child's" guilt, does not know that you cannot heal your "parent." You cannot heal backward to previous generations. You cannot heal sideways to a mate or friend. No one can heal another person. We can only heal ourselves.

You need to surrender the illusion of responsibility that the parent imposed on you. By shedding the absurd requirement that you be your parents' parent in order to heal them, you can step away from this burden. If you do not see it as unfair as well as impossible, if you cannot give up the imposed responsibility, you always will be trying to heal someone who needs to play the baby role.

You may have to mourn the loss of seeing yourself as healer. You mourn to release false commitments. To release is to be free. Then you can choose to love a person who is an emotional adult and loves you back.

Change Is Frightening

A defense is an operation our mind creates to protect us. This protection has the possibility of our seeing more, but more often it results in our seeing less, because an overreactive defense system closes us down and shuts out information. If our parents were too frightening, we tend to be overreactive.

An overreactive defense system has a childish origin. Such a defense is primitive and concrete, like a little girl holding her hands in front of her eyes so as not to see what frightens her. I don't see it, so it doesn't exist. Many of our defenses go back that far. Defenses that seriously narrow our vision to that extent make us blind. People insist that what they see is reality, but the extent of their perception tells the lie. Beyond our perception are realities that contradict our defensive understanding.

Two emotions that especially lead people into defensive blindness are fear and greed. Momentary anxiety that causes us to leap back from a swerving car is different from fear that is a constant part of life. Fear may be a continuous part of our childhood experience if it comes from frequent parental criticism, rejection, and beatings. We always are worried about what is coming next. The abusive parent becomes a threatening figure that looms in the back of our mind watching all we do and feel. Despite declaring itself to be helpful, it causes emotional, psychological, and often physical disaster.

Our thinking went along the lines of, Am I doing something wrong? What will set my parents off? What they thought of us and the attendant punishment became our world. As children, mistreatment was what we expected. Uncannily, it becomes what we seek or enact in our adult life. We are mentally submerged in our inner "parent's" judgment.

We learned what our parents feared and made it our own. Believing what the elders believe is part of belonging to the family. We do the same with our larger reference group, be it religious, political, national, etc. The need to belong to a certain group can blind us to its destructive premises.

When it comes to choosing friends and lovers, our acquired fears and values run the show. We lock our attention onto the characteristics our group thinks are important without seeing the entire person. If people have traits we learned to label "good," our heart is allowed to open. If we see traits that were labeled "bad," the people are disregarded. If they argue to support their innocence and to win our love, we grow alarmed and may retreat or attack. Once they are labeled "outsider," they turn into the enemy. Nothing they can do changes our opinion—or rather the opinion of our group, which foisted it on us. We call those we meet good or bad, enemy or friend, based on characteristics we have learned to see that way, which have little to do with our basic needs and with who they are.

Our love life goes through similar changes. Suddenly (or always), people we love are seen as our enemy or our victim. We do not discuss why we feel abused by them and ask them to stop doing what disturbs us. We do not question our urge to mistreat. A grudge is set in motion when our learned behavioral buttons are pushed. Many people in such relationships, if they are not peremptorily dropped, remain permanently at war.

We have plunged into our childhood experience when communication with our out-of-control parents did not happen. We experience ourselves as child/victim or as parent/bully with its attendant weakness or power. There is no talking back.

When greed enters a relationship, it is associated with the desire to have more or with the fear of having less. It is all about ownership. I feel that you are holding out on me. You have what I desire but won't give it. I fear that another person will take you from me. Greed rules when I plan or hope to steal someone's love partner. Fear rules when I play victim and resort to clinging, weeping, threatening, or defensive giving up. Better I should say good-bye to you before you reject me. Instant surrender is a childish defense.

Actions fueled by greed are destructive to love feelings. We no longer respond to our lover as a person whom we love and hope will love us. Greed causes us to "commodify" our partner. We see the person as an object with high or low "market value," depending on certain traits. The high-value person is some thing to possess. The "thinging" of greed dictates what we love and hate.

Greed keeps us from embracing those we love as people with their own needs, which we will happily try to fulfill. Although we want to make them happy, greed causes us to demand what they do not offer or to take it despite their saying no. This includes having sex. Greed causes us to think it's either yours or mine. You have to give it to me. There is no questioning of your feelings.

For one whose parent was abusive, the child learns to hate and, strangely, to love the abusive parent, a variant of the Stockholm syndrome. The grown children of abusive parents fall for people who rob, lie, cheat, physically attack, two-time, etc. Such people are ruled by the inverse of fear. The more they fear a certain type, the more they are drawn to love it. They curse the person they are courting. They run after the one who will do them harm. They know the person will eventually damage them in a variety of ways, but still they "fall in love."

Changing our self is terrifying because it moves us into the unknown. We are comfortable with the devil we know. We put into our expectations of change, an exaggeration of our worst experiences. Fear of what will happen to us brings loving to a halt. We cannot experience an empathetic union with the "other" unless we drop the scale of, How much am I getting or losing, or of, How will I be destroyed if my lover turns into an enemy? Even the idea of a lover's becoming an enemy is related to your parent's rejection and destruction of your love. All this valuing, possessing, and fear of losing interferes with feeling love.

Merging into a love union is full of terror. What if our aggressive internal "parent" should appear when we are unguarded and destroy us? We are not in a fighting position when we merge. Fighting is the opposite of love. Especially for those with aggressive parents, war is far easier than peace.

We fear that we will permanently lose ourselves in a state of love and be unable to return. There is a fear of madness as well as a fear of enlightenment. Madness happens when the sense of self dissolves. According to psychologist R. D. Laing, a new and healthier self can be built when our defenses fall apart. It is healthier because self's dissolution uncovers the original parental injuries that keep us from developing a self. As far as dissolving into enlightenment, meditators spend a lifetime trying to achieve it.

Falling in love has an element of surprise. We are caught off guard and plunged into pleasure. The security of love is an oxymoron. One both rejects and implies the other. We cannot have security and love. We cannot have security without love. We have to wing our way into the security of knowing that the person we love is flying beside us into the unknown. We have to accept our lack of control over the other's flight so that he or she feels free to love. Love is not a net or a ball and chain. Love is an experience to which we surrender.

It Feels Easier to Give Up

The internal "frozen child" is frightened of attracting attention by exhibiting any kind of behavior which that the "child" believes unacceptable to the internal "freezing parent." These two operate together as once happened in actual childhood when the child deferred to its aggressive parent. The sense of what is accepted by the internal "parent" and the emotions that attend defying the "parent's" rule spread like an energy field through adult consciousness and thence into the adult's behavior.

That is why, in the midst of a particular struggle to change some aspect of yourself, like giving up following the orders of a tyrannical person toward whom you have wavering feelings of love, or wanting to give up a hurtful relationship, you are cautious and unsure if this is your true desire as well as fearful of the consequences of doing it. To your adult mind the consequences are miniscule and insignificant, but they certainly are not to your "child." You are flooded by the "child's" what-if, its feelings of terror, and take them seriously. How can you, the adult, disregard its anticipation of disaster? You are not yet sufficiently separated from your "child's" mind to make an independent decision.

At the same time, you have difficulty phoning your accountant to make an appointment. You want to write your will, which raises the fear of death combined with the decisions about what to give to whom and questioning who will outlive you. The anxiety over doing the wrong thing spreads. It shows up in your procrastination and indecision. There is difficulty deciding what to do with old unused summer clothing. There is hesitation about making phone calls to those who await your call. Procrastination is like dust falling onto your eyeglasses. It creates a fine mist under which the constituents of every decision become vague.

Some say you should put your mind on your primary problem, how to deal with an abusive lover. They say that once this decision has been arrived at and carried out, other pieces will fall into place.

There is a lot of truth to this conclusion. At the same time, disorder in the lesser aspects of life has a tendency to spread into the major arenas, so that these little indecisive and disorderly events cannot be ignored. Unmet chores create the confusion over what to do next, which is like confetti blown in the wind. It is good to get the little things done while moving toward the big one. Getting small things done gives you a sense of power.

It creates a habit of making decisions. The consequences of doing them wrong have little importance and are easy to correct.

Take care of the small things. On the other hand, do not allow yourself to be swallowed up doing small things so that you do not get around to the big ones. Item number one concerns what to do about the partner who poorly loves you and whose presence causes you distress. Do not be distracted by myriad small necessities, since aside from doing what provides for your survival, love is of the greatest importance. A life lived without love is a shallow distraction, one that is haunted by what you miss.

Chapter 5

Leave the Trap

You Cannot Force Someone to Change

You desire someone to love you, but he doesn't. You are obsessed with that person and pressure him to drop the wall that stands between you. He says that his mind is on the wrong side of the wall behind which lie his feelings. As a consequence, he cannot relate. If he manages to get over the wall, he finds that his "freezing parent" is angry and has turned its back on the world, which includes on you. He says he has no control over this situation.

You argue and beg and cry but to no avail. You cannot force other people to change, and doubly so when they are emotionally out of touch—or at least claim to be. Love is like a plant that needs soil made rich by composted organic material, not by chemicals that force the plant into phony empty growth; it needs sun, air, wind, and vitality that comes from the soil. After providing all the necessary ingredients, it will grow the way its spirit moves it.

The same thing is true with people who were traumatized as children. When all the necessary (originally missing) ingredients are provided in adulthood, such people will grow into loving at their pace. Pressuring them to give love prematurely interferes with growth.

Children need a loving environment in order to become loving adults. Without this, they remain entrenched in a babyhood of deprivation and sometimes develop a defensive façade of cruelty, indifference, or submission. Sometimes they swivel back and forth from one defensive operation to another, depending on the situation, but behind it all is the undeveloped self.

People who have been closed off by an unloving childhood act unloving/unlovable as adults in order to not feel their emptiness and pain. Forced to pretend that you feel love puts you out of touch with self. Parents who require their children to act more loving than they feel push the children to assume an antiself position. It engenders phoniness that continues as a way to pass scrutiny throughout life. The children are afraid not to act the way their parents desire. Since they are acting but not feeling love, they do not know how love feels.

Later when partners plead with them to act more loving, they are back with their love-demanding parents. They do not respond to their partner's pleading to become more real, because they are afraid of knowing and feeling the emptiness that lies beneath. Their empty feelings are regarded as dangerous to approach, since feeling empty, which has some reality, also is a defense against feeling something worse. Beneath this emptiness there is an enormous mental cavern filled with need and rage. The defense against feeling the latter is, "I can't go there." Emptiness is a no-man's-land they will not cross.

There is no avoiding the fact that it if one wants to love more fully, all the bad stuff has to come along with it, since love comes from the place of all-feeling. You have to feel your grief, anger, fear, unmet needs, and love. Anger-dominated bullies, who push around masochists who readily submit, do not want to open their personal Pandora's box. Their internal "freezing parent" forbids it. To know/feel/remember childhood torture at their parents' hands moves the grown-ups into the childhood helplessness that lies behind it all. Feeling this is necessary to get them to renounce the bully role and to develop real, not punitive, strength.

To pretend to feel love, offered and received, is a cover for nonfeeling. To experience love is the only thing that will get a childhood-injured person to open up. Love, whose meaning is endlessly debated, has acceptance at its core. There is a contradiction in this for those who seek love from those who can't give it.

The internal "parent" and beaten "child" are at the helm. You are not to take as your goal curing a bully of aggression. This endeavor likely will not succeed and will continue at great cost to you. You are not to stay with someone who abuses you in order to win his or her love, nor to stay with a masochist who cowers in the corner and who responds only to mistreatment. You cannot cure people of their early damage by sacrificing yourself to their antilove defenses.

Bullies and masochists need to know that they are emotionally injured and should seek psychological help. A therapist appreciates the suffering of their internal "frozen child" but does not fall for a defensive cover-up. Therapists are paid for their services. They do not need patients to love them. They do not put a calendar over the patient's head. They insist that clients drop their defensive posture at a rate they can tolerate and begin existing as full and feeling people.

Patience is another thing the parents did not offer their child. The child either had to get it, do it, or be it now or never. He or she either was or wasn't what they needed, which means the child was totally rejected when he or she failed. The therapist has patience and can support the person's taking baby steps or giant steps, or anything in between.

Submitting to Them Makes Them Weaker

Every time you submit to bullies' demands, it makes them weaker. They feel elated at having power over you, but by giving in to that negative aspect of their personality, the part that mistreats others to feel strong, they are increasingly separated from their sense of self. To win by mistreating another person sends a message to the self of worthlessness. Self-worth comes from feeling loved and loving.

Bullying is like any addiction. It makes you feel good while doing it, but you need to do it more, because the more you enact the opposite of how you feel, the more you believe its contradiction. People tend to call addictions "chemical," which means craving a physical substance. Those who use this definition do not deal with and perhaps do not want to face the emotional emptiness that underlies turning to a drug. The quest for false power reflects and comes from a sense of weakness. To act like the one everybody loves ensures only that you are unworthy of love and that nobody loves you. Marilyn Monroe, raised in orphanages and foster homes, would go crazy if someone in the audience looked distracted, possibly due only to something physical like feeling a cramp or to some problem totally unrelated to her. All the fans screaming her name meant nothing; only the perceived rejection counted.

Children of self-centered parents who are demanding bullies later choose similar types to love. They feel guilty about not giving what the bully demands using fists or tears and whining. Or they reenact the bully role, and whatever method works to push you around will be employed. They may complain about your withholding; they may call you unloving and all kinds of names. Their enactment is that of an addict begging for a fix. The addictive substance of whatever nature is a cover for the emptiness beneath.

If you are locked into the role of victim who loves to get the bully off your back, you do not want to be a codependent drug "pusher" who creates further addiction. You are not withholding your love only to see the bully suffer for mistreating you, although that is not entirely absent in your thinking. His or her bullying has to fail. No love is given. Having mixed ideas and feelings should not erase the good behind your decision. Whether or not you relish the embarrassing downfall of bullies, giving addicts the drug they ask for is bad for them.

You want to emerge from this relationship with your head held high, not to scurry out of sight in shame over the damage you have caused. Do not give in to pleading. Do not give in to fear. Do what you know is right for both of you. Being coupled with a bully is intrinsically destructive. It is ill-advised to stay until he or she changes. It's better to say good-bye. Separation is necessary for your growth.

Hatred Is a Form of Attachment

You hate many people, including your mate and friends. You think that others hate you as well. You find evidence in their petty, misguided behaviors, in a word here and a gesture there. Sometimes you totally imagine it. You are immersed in hatred and are used to feeling it, since that is how you were raised.

You have never been happy for long with anyone who chose you. You hate the one who loves you for all his or her real and imagined faults. You expect, as has happened before with other lovers, that this lover will eventually say he or she hates you and will leave. Or you will hate and leave the person first. Or you two will remain together, hating, as happened with your parents. You expect hatred fore and aft because you hate yourself. You expect hatred, and you hate because that was your childhood form of attachment. It was better to think of yourself as connected to your parents by their hatred than to be totally unimportant and ignored.

Your family's roaring rage or quiet condescension was present from the start; no matter what you said or did, it wasn't good enough. You learned not to argue with them, because if you did their words or fists would beat you down. You learned to inflict the same kind of verbal punishment on others. You also mentally inflicted it on yourself whenever you made a mistake. You slapped your face and called yourself obscene names after discovering the least mistake.

You believed what your parents said about you, slunk away, and made yourself scarce. It seemed that power went to the one who first or consistently rejected the other. Power seemed to figure more than love as binding glue. Hatred was the bond in commitment.

Now as a grown-up, you play underdog with your friends or you treat your lovers as underdogs. Your lover dreads hearing your mean words. That smiling, happy face that once thrilled you, now is rarely seen. He or she is retreating into an emotional hiding place. You are doing to this person what your parents did to you. The poisonous words your parents once said fly out of your mouth. The internal "parent" makes you feel ashamed of your partner's traits, behavior, this, and that and of yourself. If the adult mind that receives these messages from "parent" and "child," takes them to be true, love is set to fail.

Not all of you agree with your internal "parent's" hostile mumbling and its orders to abuse. Part of you thinks that you are with a sweet and loving person. It tells you to wake up and know that you and your partner are comfortable and happy together, so different from being with your threatening mom and dad; different from all the critical parent substitutes you have chosen to "love" before.

The internal "parent" that rejects this person is echoing your actual parents' hatred for almost anyone outside themselves you ever chose to be with. Parental attachment also underlies the way you hate yourself. You hate yourself to be in sync with their chronic dislike. You have to stop hating yourself the way they hated you, before you can stop hating those you love.

You need to start speaking a language that lacks vituperative words. Your parents hated your autonomy, but their opinion is not your problem unless you make it so. Say past is past, and remove attention from the malevolent voice of your internal "freezing parent." This means to stop listening to words and feelings that tear you apart when it claims it wants to help you.

Pay attention to the feelings of your adult self. Love your partner as you love your self. Love.

Your Anger Has a History

You were raised by an angry mother, by angry parents. Now grown to adulthood, you are angered by many things. You are especially angry at your mate for not living up to your dreams. He or she is seriously flawed in many ways. Also, your mate is wonderful. Still you become angry at the drop of a hat. What are you supposed to do about your feelings? Should you turn the anger against yourself? Anger is a force to be reckoned with.

The path to follow is one of questioning. Why are you so angry? You blame it on events outside yourself. You react to their occurrence with anger as if you are a hate machine. Such thinking is shortsighted. Anger is a natural experience that happens to all humans. It showed up in the caveman and got him to act with courage in the face of formidable odds.

However, what makes post–cave-dwelling humans angry and how we express our feelings has to do with our personal history. You need to look at the shape of anger in terms of what happened to you in childhood. Were you allowed to feel anger and to show it? Were you allowed only to receive it? You remember that your angry mother treated you as a thing to be berated for wanting to express its own natural ways. A lot of her anger focused on your wild aura of kinky hair that naturally framed your face. She was set against it. She forcibly washed and braided your hair, even though you wanted to do it yourself and set it free.

The general parental assumption was that you were unable to do most things. You said no to your mother, who chased you around the apartment until she caught, dragged, and hoisted you onto the covered sink. She forced you to lie upright on it with your head in the basin and your feet on the stove. There were lots of struggle, tears, and shampoo in your eyes.

You wanted to be free like your hair. She wanted you and your hair tied down. Your father agreed with her but mostly stayed away.

She needed your helpless obedience. She needed to control you under the guise of serving. She needed to turn you into the slave she had been with your father—and probably far earlier with a family that could not fend for itself. So she had to run the family and thus had no life. While she learned to enjoy the power, her loveless life made her angry beyond expression. What was she to be? Whose cause was she to serve? She alternated between slave and master.

She served you, her child, and reacted to any evidence of your disobedience in the most picayune way as an outlet for her fury. Not daring to confront her, you grew up as a rage-filled balloon about ready to burst, and you did to others what she did to you. This is an aspect of the repetition compulsion, repeating the forms of antiloving you received. You pass on this anger to those who seek your love, partly to reunite with your attacking parents. You mistreat those you love to prove that your abusive parents loved you.

Since doubt of the initial loving does not go away, you will continue mistreating those you love without end. It is the terrified internal "child" which cannot face that its parent did not love it, or did not love it much. In wanting to emerge from this unloving and constricted maze of hostility, be assured that your adult self can take it.

If you behave lovingly toward the one you love, belief in your parents' love for you may be shaken. Your opinion of them may change, and not for the better. You will have some understanding of why they did to you what was done to them by their own parents to ward off comprehension of their own childhood's unloved state. Anger does not equal love. Giving up your fantasy of having loving parents who incomprehensibly abused you will allow you to experience genuine and reciprocated love.

Give up expressing anger to your loved one. Do it on an experimental basis, and see what happens. No matter how angry you feel, do not use cruel words. How does it make you feel if you talk about the issues without resorting to personal attack, and your partner responds by considering your words, agreeing with some and offering alternatives to others? There is a solidity of connection you have never felt before. You continue talking about your reactions as part of growing closer. Closeness is not about denial. It is about knowing and feeling.

It may be more difficult to experience love coming your way than you can imagine. Everyone longs for love, but many cannot handle it. After a childhood of abuse and rejection, closeness makes you feel vulnerable. Some react to their partners' reaching for them by becoming cold and distant. If you avoid using harsh words to push your partner away, your fear of intimacy will lessen and you will begin to react positively. After all, nothing bad has happened yet. People who were victimized in childhood may wait a long time before they remain open, ready to receive and knowing they are loved. They live their lives in the "yet."

Eventually, you will have greater objectivity about your partner's love. It may be disappointing when measured against your fantasy, but it will be real. Letting love in bit by increasing bit, you surrender your need to cover up. Holding your breath and expecting love to disappear is related to your "yet."

If anger from the past remains and feels too much to bear, take up an aggressive sport like Ping-Pong or tennis. After you try to "kill" your opponent on the court, win or lose, shake hands, leave the court smiling, and go home to your loving mate.

The Grief of Losing Unreal Love

There are two kinds of lost love. One of them is real. The other is imagined. Real love ends because our lover has died or has been unwillingly taken away. Imagined love is a horse of a different color. It is a wished-for experience, slaved for, paid for, but never had. The love experience has only been imagined.

Oh, yes, there may be moments when you think that love has happened, but true love it is not. What you have experienced soon disappears. Imagined love is only an impulse, a toss in the hay, an illusion shared by one or two, a passing fancy. Imagined love is intrinsically unreal. Real love is the love you still are waiting for.

The internal "freezing parent" supports your painful clinging to hope for receiving love from your latest ungiving lover. Clinging to this hope is an aspect of submission. It does not refer to what you have experienced.

True love is different. It is solid, real, and shared. You will grieve forever for true love lost. It does not end the same way as illusory love, since the one you love has become part of you as you are part of that person. You lose the body but not the spirit of your lover. Even after losing the physical presence, you are richer. With imagined love only the person's absence remains.

Endlessly grieving over what you are deprived of and what will never happen is the grief of an unloved child. There a sense of satisfaction in trying to please your "freezing parent" with your endless quest for its love. The repetition compulsion of falling for people who cannot love or of your not offering love to those who do love you, is a work of fiction created by your bullying "parent," which forces the "child" to comply.

Sometimes you get angry at the withholding person and then turn the anger against yourself and suffer more. For your unrequited love you suffer guilt and shame. But you do not change the object of your search. You direct your need for love to the same person or to a different unloving person, which leads to frustration, pain, anger, and guilt, and then back again to longing.

The "frozen child" sweeps you into an endless quest for what isn't offered. The "freezing parent" forbids you from seeking love from one who offers it. Under the guidance of these internal forces, you will never experience the fountain of love. To be caught in grieving for love never received as if it once existed traps you in a fantasy that is connected to denying your parent's abuse. Your actual parent could not love. There was nothing you could do to change this fact.

The conscious adult needs to stop being guided by the "frozen child," which tells the adult to be guided by endlessly wished-for love from one who cannot give it. You need to recognize the glue of denial that keeps you stuck. If you hold on to an unloving person by blaming yourself for love's lack, it is an act of penance. The repetition compulsion is self-punishing. Unearned guilt ever rehearsed by your "child" binds you to further suffering.

The person to fix is not you. There is nothing you can do about another's closed heart, just as it was with your parents. Give up a life of doing penance and seeking forgiveness for errors you did not commit, or are not as serious as you make them. Give it up so that you can choose a loving partner.

The Courage to Say No

Does fear stop you from attempting to create a pleasurable life with another person? Do you not put into words the love you feel, which the other longs to hear? Perhaps you do not know that behind your fearful inhibition is the issue of being seen. Your fear comes out of childhood. The way you were treated by self-centered parents showed that you were supposed to be invisible. You were to be noticed only when it was requested for some reason unrelated to your need. If you did otherwise, you were in trouble.

Creating happiness for yourself affirms your identity. Happiness does not come from selling out. As a grown person, you are dealing with a lover whose inflated self-image shadows your relationship. His or her opinions are supposed to take precedence over your viewpoint, intentions, and feelings. You are to be pleased by all the person says and does. You are not to dispute anything; you are not to recognize that the person's rejection of your ambitions, desires, spontaneous utterances, inner poetry, and song is abusive.

The way out of self-surrender is to learn to say perhaps the mightiest word in the language. No. You have to say no to an invitation for greater contact with someone who abuses you. You have to point out that mistreating behavior has been upsetting you and has to change. You do this even if the person seems unable to understand. Then you can give yourself credit for trying to correct things and eliminate an excuse for returning to the relationship. Passivity is a poor excuse to hide behind.

Most bullies are emotionally confused. They are too involved with affirming their shaky power to know what is going on. You say no at the very least, to define their cruelty to yourself. You say no to set your boundaries, which is intrinsic to having a self. You say no to recognize that you exist. It is a variant on *cogito ergo sum*. I state that what you do is hurting me and tell you to stop. I tell you what I need. There is an *I* in the sentence. Ergo I exist.

You have to remove yourself from cruel behavior, not to hold your breath, make pleasant noises, give gifts, and pray for change. You have to say no every time you are drawn into accepting/doing something that isn't good for you. The person may attempt to seduce you by telling you what you are missing. He or she is not attempting to persuade you for your own sake. The person is doing it to prove his or her flawless state and to gain power over you.

You have to hold on to your understanding so as not to be tossed about. You will know that something is bad for you if afterward you feel a lessened sense of self. "Self" means body, mind, and feelings experienced together. A sense of self is a solid position here on earth. It makes your existence real.

Once you give in to behavior that robs you of your sense of self, you tend to do it again. You would think that if something hurts, you would do it less. Giving in to it is like falling down a hill and gaining momentum due to gravity. It is like hurting yourself by accident or due to confusion and then doing it again to punish your self for having done it in the first place. It is done to please the internal "parent" which gains power by your acquiescence. Self-punishment is an act of giving in. I punish myself for having acted independent. I now see myself as less. The "parent's" power over you is reestablished.

When you ignore the realistic advice of your adult mind, your internal "frozen child" and "freezing parent" call the shots. How are you to get out of this experience once it has been set in motion? You need to reestablish your self's control. No matter how frightened you feel about attempting to reverse your abdication, that fear means you are wearing childhood's robe. Put on the brakes and reject your "child's" impulse to surrender to the "parent's" judgment. Say no to your "child's" urge to repeat and fail. Regard your error as an event to be learned from and only that. Do not take a submissive role. Life is a serendipitous adventure. You never know what it will bring.

If you are with a verbal bully, tell the person to stop issuing attacking words or you will depart. If the bully keeps it up, state that the relationship is over. Do not convince yourself to try again because one day it will be fine. Do wait for future love. A neurotic life is all about ineffectual waiting.

If you are with a physically abusive person, get out of the abuser's reach. If that person lives in your place, bid the person a polite but definitive farewell. Do not get into an argument, which invariably would be abusive. If you are in the abuser's place, return to your home. If the two of you cohabit, immediately find a place of shelter. If it is too difficult to immediately do this, move in with a friend or contact an agency that will provide a safe haven until you find a place.

Silence and noncommunication may be the best path to follow with a physical abuser. The absence of your clothing, furniture, and self tells the tale. Withhold your subsequent address to restrict visitation. Put a period on the sentence. This really is the end.

Tell your story to a friend who will support you and help you make the needed changes. If you have no such friend and/or feel too weak to do it alone, seek psychotherapy to strengthen yourself. You may think leaving is an impossible act, that it will take a miracle to become strong enough to separate, but strengthening is a step-by-step progression. Like developing any muscle, the more you use it, the stronger it gets.

Feeling Like a Failure Links Us with Our Abusive Parent

Loyalty can be a very strange thing when it has to do with our parents. It can be good or bad for you, depending on its definition. If loyalty to the other means being disloyal to yourself, it is bad. Starting in childhood, where we first come to understand the term *loyalty* as attending to the needs of destructive others, it will negatively change your life.

Self-centered parents assume that a loyal child will perform self-sacrifice when the parent needs something that deprives or is adverse to their child. The parents may be so self-indulgent that they don't see the child's behavior as sacrificial. Wearing their emotional blinders, they think it is the "right thing to do." A child who pleases such a parent is considered "good."

Insecure parents who need to inflate their image pull their children into their cheering squad. The parents need to be seen as better than everyone at something, or at almost everything, including those that are done by the child. Either that or the child is seen as identical to the parent, and then both of them are called "the greatest." Designated as inferior and below, or as equal and sharing the throne, the child loses a sense of self.

One woman, whose father endlessly put her down, failed a typing test for a clerical job, although she types like a whiz when alone. Her gifts are way above those required by a clerk's job. She takes no credit for her abilities. She quakes in her shoes if she is ever asked to meet the boss or to receive an award for excellence! Only her father is worthy of receiving it. She thinks that no man can ever be interested in her and runs from those who show signs of interest. She is terribly lonely and bereft. She believes this is her fate and that she deserves it.

If you don't understand what is holding you back, you can't correct it. What is unknown about your inhibition is found in your unconscious mind, which orders you to fail and labels you a failure, regardless of the result. Failing to get a job, you feel worried, hopeless, and incomprehensibly satisfied. Satisfaction comes from having pleased your tyrannical internal "freezing" parent.

Say your mother had to be the only sexually attractive female in the family and treated you as ugly. You, with your corona of glorious red hair, were regarded with hostility by your mother on the verge of high school graduation. She insisted you get it chopped off, which made you look mangled for graduation pictures. Even the hairdresser pleaded with her to leave it, but she would not be stopped. She called your choppy hairdo "practical." Your hair for once attracted no positive attention. You heard your schoolmates shriek in horror when they saw it, but your mother seemed oblivious. Secretly, she probably was pleased. Mom was a beauty who would not share the stage.

You absorbed her message to be unattractive, and now you don't notice if anyone draws near. You think of yourself as a kind of leper. If someone who is attracted touches you, you feel a kind of fury, as if the person had climbed over your guarding wall and invaded your sacred space. That sacred space belongs to your reigning internal "mother," who owns you—body, heart, and mind.

The one who threatens a child's existence owns the child. Terror causes the child to surrender. "If you own me, you won't kill me," is the underlying philosophy of giving in. Your sense of being a person with independent needs and wishes is buried beneath your parents' view of you as one of their possessions or as a cursed heap of junk. You are a girl whose father rarely touched. You are compelled to see this as justified by your ugliness. It was assumed or even stated that he saw you as unappealing, so that became your law. You are not to be touched by anyone.

Do you want sexual and affectionate touching? It is your deepest desire. Will you let yourself have it? No. In your mind, you are so ugly that no one will want you … and besides, touching is forbidden. Your parent's restriction set the law.

Deprivation offers you a peculiar satisfaction. Years ago, you learned to take a barely noticeable moment of calm when your mother or father wasn't attacking you and transmute it into the relief of love. Are you sexually and emotionally starved? You are empty to the bone but do nothing to correct it. First of all, you must receive your parents' love. Who established this priority? You did, thinking it was a solution, although it was only a wish.

You thought it was the way with parents like these. You lead a princess-locked-in-an-ivory-tower kind of life.

Since your mother had to be the only one admired as the family's sexual star, you must live without a lover. Accepting emotional deprivation is regarded by you as an act of loyalty to the parents who mostly loathed you. Dad called himself loving for never striking you with his hands. Feeling so unloved, you reasoned conversely that parents who strike their children truly love them. But striking with words and with hands are both abusive. It your parent had been a hitter, you would have felt no better.

Anything done by unloving parents can be read as showing you to be unworthy. Mom called herself loving for doing all your laundry. She never had any interest in how well you played the piano or what you wrote for the school magazine. Your parents' relationship to you was all about proving how much they gave and how little you merited it. The spotlight was on them.

All roads have the same destination for children who are loyal to such parents. These roads lead to pain, which is seen as love or as a justification for its lack. How do you know if you are still choosing the pain-oriented way? Are you uncomfortable, even frightened, if someone admires you? Do you think that an expression of love that you experience as unadulterated and direct is false? Do you mistrust love that is simple and openhanded? Must you seek love in a concatenation of confusion and mistreatment, like a prize in a box of poisoned Cracker Jacks, and just as small?

Are you attracted to people who lack proper feelings? Do you spend a great amount of energy trying to get them to show you love? If the person whose love you seek doesn't offer it, do you take the blame? Are you glad that your lover hogs all the listening space so that you can't manifest your stupidity? Do you fall only for people others call abusive? Do you have lovers and friends who put you down and have cruel ways of describing your mistakes? Do you magnify the importance of your errors? Are you usually waiting for the next attack?

Note that you feel strangely reassured by negative comments that tell you what you need to change. It is like being back in your childhood's torturing home. The pain you feel with such friends and lovers reinforces the tie you have with your attacking parents. Loving them despite the abuse they give is what you call loyalty. The crust of this pie is love; the filling is hate. It is not a proper meal.

Chapter 6

Awaken

Sometimes It Takes a Dream to Wake You Up

This book is all about dreaming. We know it to be a dream when it comes to us during sleeping. It is a different kind of dream that controls our waking life. Our blindness to the influence and presence of our past creates this dream, but we do not step back and analyze its message.

We are channels for what our parents verbally droned about us. These abusive or unrealistically idealizing parental statements were absorbed by us without a blink (even if we protested). What they poured into our thinking has persisted through adulthood. It is our waking dream.

You can free yourself of your parents' dream by studying your own. Your self uses dreaming to send a message. It desires freedom from illusion. All dreams send a message. Sometimes the message is obvious. More often it is symbolic, a concrete image or an enactment that needs interpretation. A dream is like a poem that was written by you which only you can interpret. Dwell upon its imagery, and see what comes to mind.

Dreams bring your attention to what is important, to what needs to be done or heeded. They tell you about an incipient flat tire or how you feel about a lover or a friend. It tells you when your parents' needs are overreaching or that their thinking about you is fantastic and unreal. A dream is like a splash of cold water in your face. It takes you out of your speculative view of life and moves you into action. Or it does the reverse and takes you from action into deep thought. Einstein dreamed his theory of relativity. Imagine that! Dreams ask questions about behaviors, decisions, and feelings. Dreams open the lid to Pandora's box. Once the box is opened, you cannot close it. And why would you?

People are afraid to relate to their dreams, because considering their meaning takes them from their comfort zone. The proper attitude to have toward a dream is one of fearful pleasure. You fear the unknown and pleasurably revel in it. A dream leads you into life's great adventures. A dream is your best friend.

A neurosis is a kind of partial dream state; it leads its sufferers by their rationalized blindness like you'd lead a bull by a ring through the nose. It causes the people to do things that have terrible consequences, to engage in behaviors that humiliate and impoverish them, and drive away lovers and friends. It leads them to do what their logical minds reject. Sometimes they recognize that their intentions are destructive and then do things anyway. Their reasons and excuses are all cover-ups. They do not understand what moves them.

Aren't we supposed to learn from our mistakes? Are we making inadvertent mistakes like the slip of a finger on a piano key, or is our behavior deliberately devised by some incomprehensible part of our mind? Is hurting and pushing away our lover the way we choose to love? Who is it that chooses? Our conscious and unconscious intentions are butting heads.

Does being hurt and pushed away represent what we call love? Why do we choose people to love who can't love us back? We are living in a dream state without knowing it.

Developing a neurosis is like inhabiting a bomb shelter during a childhood filled with violence and then remaining there for life. Neurosis is ignoring that the war which once raged around us is now over. Neurosis stops us from tuning in to reality in order to free ourselves from our childhood's constricted and self-protective life.

Neurotics never leave the confines of their mental bomb shelter. We see the world as at war and find evidence to support our belief—or we totally make it up. We choose people to play meaningful parts in our bomb-shelter life. They are shelter people too.

Hence we find the prevalence of certain kinds of people there—abusive, apathetic, unreliable, fearful people who share an omnipresent fear of attack. Choosing harmful partners serves a valued purpose. It supports our defensive stance. The negative behavior of lovers offers a peculiar kind of reassurance. Their attacking us while we are "loving" them proves that the world is an unsafe place. Our reenactment of the neurosis of leading a bomb-shelter life surrounded by serious enemies is experienced as saving us from destruction. But the bomb-shelter life actually injures us. It is a state of unnecessary deprivation.

Often, it takes a sleeping dream as distinguished from a waking neurotic fantasy to alert us to our fantasy enactment. Not knowing that our life is colored by distorted feelings, needs, expectations, and perceptions, we can use a sleeping dream to help us see what is going on. Sleeping dreams are full of cues created by the less externally controlled mind. The dreaming mind is trying to get our attention. It bears a message of who we really are. Pay attention.

The Self

How shall we characterize the self? Is it a unitary body inside the mind, or is it multiple? Is the heart involved, and how? If we observe the messages our mind sends us, we find more than one identity. Some of our selves are well known to us, but many are vague or are in hiding. All of them have strength and purpose. Let us call them "islands of the self."

One of these islands represents the child. Its characteristics remain infantile forever. The internal "child" is a copy of the original child and represents its relation to a slew of early experiences. The "child's" self can remain an active force in our adult life. If the original child's life was with parents who threatened and frightened it, whose interactions told him to hide or surrender, the internal child became a "frozen child" who is stuck in a pose of fearful supplication like a statue carved of ice.

If early experiences were full of the adventure of trying to know, taste, and do new things, if the child's escapades were met with acclaim and support by the parent(s), then the internal "child" is a "warm child," full of life and vigor. As an adult, the "warm child" sends messages that tell the adult to love the person who attracts and loves him or her, to build a new invention, to travel where no one has gone before. The "warm child" is a joy to have around, although sometimes the adult mind has to recall its common sense. The "warm child" helps the adult to develop the self rather than hold it back.

The internal "frozen child" has feelings of need, and is shaky and clinging, fearful of the world and ready to reject it. It draws the adult away from engaging in interpersonal relationships and into endless catering to the internal "freezing parent." The more the adult caters to the "frozen child" and "freezing parent," the more powerless he or she feels. The adult surrenders his or her thinking to the two of them and loses the sense of having an adult self. The individual is living in the past.

The mental island of the "internal parent" is formed in the same era as that of the "internal child" and is shaped by the responses of the actual parent. If the parent was unreliable, irresponsible, mistreating, scolding, hitting, starving, critical, unavailable, etc., these become the attitudes of the internal "freezing parent," which suppresses self-development.

Every child needs to develop the image of an "internal parent" so as to not feel alone. An "internal parent" modeled after a loving parent is available to support the child's self-esteem and adventures, exploring whatever interests him or her, or of doing things just for the heck of it. It supports the right to love. The internal "parent" may fade into pleasant obscurity over time but always is available and can return. This is what we call a "good parent."

The internal "freezing parent," framed by the parent who rejected the child and did not help him or her develop self-respect, remains center stage throughout the adult's life. This "parent" attempts to direct the adult and persecutes him or her for diverging from its advice. Grown-ups with such a "freezing parent" spend their lives trying to win the "parent's" approval, which rarely comes and never lasts. The internal "parent's" need for power shows the original parent's deficiency. It is an important for adults to free themselves from the "freezing parent's" control so that they can lead happy lives. The lives they then lead will be theirs to choose.

Other islands of self, which are obscured by the fog of denial, are extremely important to the evolving destination of an adult. Carl Gustav Jung sees the "shadow" self as part of one's identity. What is denied occupies a bigger space than what is accepted by those around you. In the shadow are the loves, needs, interests, and talents that were/are not accepted by the family or by society as a whole. Your family, and later society, unconsciously conscribe to have these inner forces suppressed and as much as possible, entirely out of mind.

Let us say that you have chosen to love the kind of person your family and society approve of, and the same thing with your job, hobbies, pets, travels, and clubs. You are fitting in so neatly that you do not know anything is wrong. But in fact, over time if not from the start, a great deal of this is wrong. You are wearing an emotional "zoot suit" not of your choosing.

Some people get in touch with their shadow during the midlife transition when they ask, Is this the life I want to lead? Others do not, because they are bound by the fear of losing membership in their referral group. Belonging to a social group as the predominant feature in self-awareness is not a healthy state. However, the internal "child" under the threat of the internal "parent" did not learn there is any way but fitting in.

It is you, the adult, who has to ask, given the pressures of making a living in a failing economy and all other negative features, Who am I? What is my shadow, and where does it want to go? What does my shadow desire? Whom does it love? Your shadow, now and always, has been part of your true self. It is time to listen and pursue.

Their Pain Is Not Your Pain

The tendency to meld into other people's projections goes back to childhood, in which the parents expected us to be what they claimed we were, even if their perceptions were false. The falsity came from their self-denial or self-aggrandizement, which means seeing in the other what you want not to see in the self or seeing in them the greatness which you claim. Glorified or denigrated, due to parental projection, the child is not seen as he or she is.

They got rid of what they hated in self by finding and hating it in us. The development of and hatred for these features were acquired from their own parents, who hated it in themselves … and then back and back with permutations through previous generations.

Children have to accept their parents' perceptions by taking blame for what they claimed to see in hope of receiving their love. All of this is unconscious. Children do not see it as an out-there percept. To accept blame for it is an act of love. If the parents seem to hate it, it has the corollary: if I get rid of that hated behavior, I can be loved. It is love, its absence or presence, that runs everything. Even more twisted, the child's mind converts the parent's hatred for that trait into an act of love and keeps doing/being it to gain further love.

If no matter what the child does, the parent keeps on hating, the child is stuck with being the unloved one who attempts to cure the breech between parent and child by choosing similarly rejecting people to love and then trying to win their love by changing the self. Accepting blame lies at the heart of the repetition compulsion. Children will dance to any tune to please the parent. They deny who they really are and make themselves blind to their forced acquisition of that hated part by parents who could not stand it. They accept the challenge to win their parents' love, as their parents did before them.

Children grown into adulthood continue to accept projections of those whose love they seek. They take their partners' side against themselves. Their philosophy continues to be, "That must be me, and it must be true," which makes their experience of punishment seem benign, although it isn't.

To find your real self, you need to give up hoping to receive love by playing "culprit," which doesn't mean you are flawless. None of us is. You may hear your partner complain about the pain you are causing. You need to examine the charge to see if it is justified. If it isn't, this should make you wonder if you have united with a person who plays the role of a vindictive parent or victimized child whose pain is not yours to fix.

The internal "parent" that moves others to attack you was created by identifying with their own abusive parent. You are not there to alleviate their "frozen child's" suffering if what they complain about is largely fictitious or exaggerated. It takes practice to learn how to assess charges brought against you, whether they are true or false, magnified or reasonable. To claim perfection is no way out.

Will you feel guilty about stepping away from false or exaggerated charges? Likely, you will if your parents always blamed you. You need to take a new position vis-à-vis false attack. This change may be difficult and require a degree of playacting until you get the habit. If your partner unfairly accuses you and then retaliates with hostility, tell the person to stop. Say, "Your words are hurting me. If what I have done has caused you pain, I am sorry. I will try to correct it. If you keep attacking me after hearing my explanation and/or my apology, I will have to leave." If your partner's verbal abuse continues, you need to live by your stated limits and depart. You need to put an end to your being an emotional (or physical) punching bag.

How to Deal with Fear

Fear is part of the body/mind's alert and alarm system. It calls attention to what threatens you. A baby needs to be in arms. It loves to be jounced up and down when its mother moves around. It feels exhilarated when Dad throws it in the air (not too far) and catches it. Closeness and movement, a ready breast, and a dry bottom are the baby's idea of heaven.

Fear is felt by a baby who is deposited in a distant corner or a separate room, feeling cold, hungry, and wet. Where is its warm connection? A baby has limited means of expression. When it feels uncomfortable, it uses tears, smiles, and clinging. If these don't work, it screams. If screaming doesn't work or if the should-be-helpful figure threatens, it falls into quiet stasis like a deer caught in the headlights. It enters a preverbal state of helplessness.

It is the adult mind that develops the responses of flight or fight when confronted by something harmful. The adult mind is able to assess a situation and call on its defenses or see their lack. The adult mind is both imaginative and realistic.

The child part of the mind is as it was back then in a world with fewer options. Everything came from the parent, who was their world. The internal "child" formed at that time, and it continues to have access to the adult mind and to send it signals. Not only does the adult pay attention to these signals, but it often is led around by them thinking them to be his or her "real self" and deepest truth.

It is the adult who is puzzled by his or her need for helpless clinging or relentless attack. Adults are puzzled by the severity of their reactions, although they act accordingly. The impulse is to punish people (and also sometimes themselves). It gives the adults a peculiar kind of satisfaction to see lovers and friends submit to their abuse. Attacking themselves for making "errors" also gives them a sense of doing "the right thing."

You cannot change the thinking and feelings of your internal "child" and "parent." They are locked in to their attitudes and feelings. Feelings sent by the "frozen child" or "freezing parent" are not to guide your behavior. If the "child" is fearful of your meeting a potential lover, it is you, the adult, who decides to make the approach. If the person you speak to doesn't please you or become enamored of you, it is the "parent" that calls your quest a failure. You need to ignore your "parent's" abusive thinking, to say to yourself, "Win a few; lose a few," and move on.

The adult needs to separate from the signals from the attacking "child" and "parent," since they do not represent the grown-up self. If you want to stop being at their command, which leads to misery, you need to take a giant step. You have to see the historic nature of who they are that leads them to what they see and say. Historicity means seeing it as of another era, not applicable to the now.

If adults investigate their history, they'll be less puzzled by their compulsions and constraints. Then it will be easier to stop being controlled by the "child" and "parent." Testing whether there is danger ahead, and seeing the consequences of your actions, need to be repeated until separation from these historic people is relatively stable. You need to see that they lead you into the kind of behavior which doesn't suit you. You need to develop faith that you can make up your own mind. Experience will support this idea.

How Are Your Gifts Received?

Someone has offered you his love. For the first time, you have deeply and clearly felt it. You are like a sleeping princess awakened by a kiss. This person gives from his heart and receives what you have given, treating it as something to treasure. He saved your birthday cards, saved all of them. He wore the green velour sweater you gave him to smithereens. You saw yourself in his acceptance. Love had no boundaries.

History denied this experience for you in childhood. You remember a time. You were about seven and saved some of your allowance. No. You didn't save your allowance, because your parents didn't give one. They needed you to ask, even beg, for money and to justify your request, which made them feel bigger, more important, and in control, while you felt equally smaller. It was a seesaw of self-respect. Theirs went up to the extent that yours went down. You secreted unspent money in an unsuspected place that was hard to find. Your mother never had a conversation with you except to give orders and ask embarrassing questions, and she spied on you and investigated your every move. It was a prison of antilove that masqueraded as loving care.

But even so, you managed to buy your mother what you thought was a beautiful gift, a scarf of silk, all bright blue and red and yellow. You think she thanked you for it, but not effusively. She said some words, but her acceptance was not given with much joy. You think she appreciated it. Didn't she? You had little experience with appreciation and were not a good judge. Afterward, you were watching and waiting to see her in the scarf. But it didn't happen. After a couple of weeks went by, you asked when she was going to wear it. You thought she had tucked it away in a drawer and forgotten all about it, which would have been bad enough.

But no, it was not bad enough. It was far worse. She said that she returned it. "I didn't need a scarf." She didn't see your love, your sense of self, your need to give it to her. She casually rejected your love. She casually mentioned that she kept the money. It was as if you were totally erased from the act of giving. It was just any scarf, worth a few dollars. That was all. You felt tossed into nonexistence. Erased.

Your mother continually treated your love as worthless. One might consider it an act of spite, which superficially it was. But more than that, she erased you as an independent giver to establish herself in isolation. Her internal "freezing parent" saw receiving your gift as an act of weakness. I, the great one, am complete unto myself. Relating to another person's offering as if it was of value and, even worse, as if it was needed was taboo. She erased your gift and the love it carried to deny her own feelings of need.

This mother cannot allow herself to see the emotional side of her child's gift. Her internal "freezing parent" related aggressively to the needs of her "frozen child." This reaction was expressed by the behavior of the parent, who wasn't allowed to be a joyous receiver. Historically, the act of not acknowledging love received is passed from parent to child. This cold mother who returned her child's present was similarly negated as a child. This mother's child learned that she is to receive only when her parent feels like giving. She learned that giving to her parent cannot happen.

The child saw herself as an empty shell, a person who feels the absence of self. A lot of self is learned by seeing your loved one's reflection of it … from you to that person, reflected in tears and smiles.

With this mother, there was no mirror. By not accepting her child's gift as worthy of keeping and wearing, Mom denied the pain of her own childhood trauma, of her own love offered, rejected, demeaned, and ignored. She pushed away her pain of love denied by doing it to her child.

Her daughter learned from her mother's behavior that love has to be forced onto the other as an act of violence. And who has the courage? She learned that love has to be extracted from you, not received in response to your giving. What is the worth of extracted love?

Remaining in a freezing state was her mother's defensive posture, with occasional attacks of rage. She went from total control to its lack and back. The daughter learned that there was no peaceful way to reach her mother. Mom was either a storm or the calm before a storm. How can you love when you need to tie yourself down against the wind?

This working mother paid for her daughter's college education, which was only partly on scholarship, but the daughter never knew it. She did not know where the money came from and had long ago learned not to ask. The mother, whose internal "freezing parent" forbade her from being visibly warm to her child, told her to hide herself as the giver. The child did not know that her mother loved and cared for her. She did not learn it until long after. But that is another story in which each one met the other's self and loved.

The child learned from a repeated "scarf" experience with her mother not to openly offer. She learned to work like hell for a cause, as would her mother, but to be equally invisible and impersonal in her giving, and after giving, to fade away.

After many years living on the borderline of barely giving or receiving love, her eyes opened and she saw a man who was love. She saw him as immensely beautiful. She had to be with him, to feel and see him. And he did the same with her. It was an awakening. This experience began her struggle to remain loving in the present. They received love from each other and declared it to the world. Their love existed. They existed.

What If You Don't Know Love?

You feel that something important is missing from your life but really can't define it. Since our early parenting experience had too little love in it or was a distorted kind of loving, our definition of love is twisted and confused.

Two people come together who light a spark between them. Is it love? It sure feels good. Is it good enough?

People raised in abusive or disinterested families have a poor and limited understanding of love. But that does not mean they cannot react to love when it is offered. Of course, sometimes their reaction is to run away in fear. They can't let anybody get too close.

When people are raised to expect the worst and to be on the defensive, it is upsetting to encounter someone whose approach is friendly. It sets off your alarm. You think that the goodness is a phony act to get your guard down. You lead a Trojan horse existence—the friendlier the approach, the more severe your expectation. Your parents also sometimes approached with a smile, the belt with which to whip you held behind their back. Your parents took pleasure in surprising you. The shock of their transition made you feel more pain. They measured their power by your surprise and horror. You always are on the alert now and are not going to be fooled again.

A person raised without love has to take it as an article of faith that there are people who are capable of loving. You have to be willing to drop your guard a little bit and, later, more than a little. How else can you learn? If you don't drop your guard, nothing can get through.

You need to remind yourself that you no longer are a helpless child, especially if you are attracted to marauding bullies. Moving toward those who will hurt you as your parents once did relates to your acting the role of a helpless child. It this is occurring, you need to seek therapy to help you end your need to court the bad. Learn the difference between acts of chance and choice. One bad love experience after another is no coincidence.

In order to find a person who loves you, you need to meet various people. There is nothing wrong with meeting as many as you wish, spending time together, having fun (or its lack), although if there is no pleasure here, inquire whether you are too uptight to feel it or if the person you are dating is not appealing. If chemistry is absent, you are not meant to be together and should end it from the start. Do not keep yourself from moving on because that will hurt his or her feelings. It is the wrong basis for a relationship.

You are not to keep meeting in order to fix that person in hope of someday receiving love. You are not to stay out of fear that the person will harm you if you leave. If you are not having fun because you are abused, do not fall into your habitual stance of taking the blame. You are not to be saddled with directing the person's hatred away from you, or even with letting him or her explode in your direction. Potential for abuse is not a minor issue. You are with a grown person who can do you harm.

If the abuse is minor, you are to call attention to it and see if the person stops. If the abuse is severe, politely end the relationship. Polite speech avoids stimulating further attack. You can say what everyone does to harmlessly end things: "The chemistry is wrong between us." Ending a relationship means not returning to it—even if there are promises made of change … then more experiences of abuse … then more promises of change … then abuse … in an endless cycle.

You do not know who will offer you love, but after you date for a while your defenses will increasingly seem uncalled for. You find that there is nothing to fear. All you have to do is be yourself. These people are not with you to prove something, not there to make you unhappy. If there are aspects of life over which they grieve, you can share these too. Do they have problems? Who doesn't? If something they do upsets you, like not helping to clean up after eating together in your apartment, you can mention it and they will comply. If they delay doing it, one wonders if their own "freezing parent" requires them to fail.

If you express hatred for a person's faults, you very likely feel such hatred for yourself for the same or different faults. Hatred is like a terrified beast that runs around biting everyone. Some avoid self-attack by directing self-hatred at their partner. You have to be on the lookout for projecting your self-hate.

People are not identical twins. Each has habits and approaches utterly foreign to the other, which is part of the excitement and sometimes the frustration of cohabitation. Do not allow negative moments to take your mind away from the fun. You are together to share joy and also sometimes pain. The ability to be together when confronting the hazards of life can lead to pleasure and increasing love.

You will know love when you encounter it because the feeling will fill you up. Mere words can only approximate the feeling. After you meet someone who radiates love, you will absorb it without measure and will send it back. When you find an appropriate lover and mate, you have a lasting feeling of warmth. Do not settle for less.

Each Time You Go into Confusion

You take a break from seeing someone who claims to love you but causes you great pain. Once the two of you are apart, you are plunged into a state of confusion, which comes from the contradiction between the other's words of caring, even of apology, and your experience of pain.

You are having a cognitive breakdown that ultimately benefits you. You are separating from the fear and need that come from your "frozen child," and from the orders of your "freezing parent" that direct you into loveless love affairs.

The prevalent defense that pulls you toward bullies who hurt you is denial of your "parent's" cruelty by calling it love. By recognizing the punishment that hides behind your (and their) dissimilation, you disengage your current adult self from the internal "child" and "parent." Denying your parent's mistreatment cannot be said only once and then forgotten. The defense against awareness must endlessly continue. You can deny hate received from them only by looking for lovers who offer more of it. If you should end up with a caring person who would not inflict pain, your parent's excuses fall apart. You no longer can accept the defensive equation that "hate equals love." Feeling real love undoes the love illusion.

Mistreating your lover is linked to your identification with the punishing parent. You mistreat the one you love as your parents mistreated you until your lover physically leaves or leaves you in his or her heart. Or you find another grown and once-mistreated child who will accept mistreatment from you and, if you also need to be psychologically beaten, will play "parent" and mistreat you as well.

Observing the childish aspects of your offensive or submissive behavior breaks your unconscious connection to the internal "parent" and "child." You feel lost and helpless having lost their guidance. What are you to do now?

Each time you undergo a painful cleansing, you initially will feel lost. Enduring your anxious disconnection creates the space of freedom. You may need to cut these destructive connections many times. If you avoid dealing with the emotional pain of change, you will remain stuck in it exactly as you are today.

Recovering Your Pain

We develop defensive amnesia as children to keep from being overwhelmed by the pain caused by our critical, rejecting parents. This amnesia applies to pain directly caused by them, which is not the same kind of pain as that of skinning your knee when you are having too good a time playing sports or exploring caves to notice.

Amnesia of a different kind comes if your parents overreact to the skinned knee and attack you for being "careless" at play. The attack comes from their need to be godlike and in control of everything you do so that nothing can go wrong. Instead of sticking with their exaggerated guilt for your exaggerated "injury," they pass the blame on to you. They turn a minor event into a guilt-laden tragedy. It goes from them to you. How did you do this to yourself? with the implicit or stated, How could you do this to me?

They take the joy out of playing wild games, like in Maurice Sendak's *Where the Wild Things Are*. Sendak really loved the special imaginative life of children who involved themselves with things most adults don't want to know and see. Sendak was totally unlike parents who are intent on proving how infallible they are. The kids took risks. The kids faced danger. There was magical all about. It was a total turn-on.

When we suppress awareness and memory of the pain that came from our parents' attack, we think we are doing something right and also something wrong. The feeling of doing something right comes from accepting our parents' description to be true. We were what our parents needed. As they said, we were careless or fearless; we had an extremely high pain threshold or an extremely low one. We were doing something wrong, because they said we were doing something wrong. Wrongness was part of our identity.

We were doing something right in that part of us—a very secret and hidden part of us—resented their intrusion in our play and their branding us with any name at all. That small and hiding part knew them to be the antithesis of freedom, the thing that only children have, value like they value their lives, and always look for more. That small part thinks the parents to be intrusive bullies who carve time and experience into controllable segments—good versus bad, right versus wrong, enough time for this but not that—rather than let children fall into time like into a magical space where anything they imagine can happen.

Children's self-image and reactions are like putty to the mold of their parents' directives. By deferring to our parents' accusations, we were acknowledging their power. By doing this we denied their weakness. Children are pulled into supporting their weak parents by applauding their illusory understanding.

Only weak people need their children to say that they are always right. The injury we received for doing this comes from learning self-denial. They frowned on our mentioning the pain we received from their fists or words, or by denying our reality in order to agree with them about what happened. We agreed to surrender the meaning we had for everything.

We stopped paying attention to our discomfort when they rejected our feelings of autonomy, and later we stopped remembering it. We forgot who we are all at once or in progressive stages as we were carried along by their rationalized attack. Losing painful or conflicting memories is a pejorative form of self-defense. We lose our self because it is embroiled in feeling the pain.

We were trained by our parents to be short in memory and out of touch with self. Forgetting what hurt us gives a kind of rest. It was a closing down of the mind. Without memory and awareness, the world seems to be a less dangerous place. However, emotional forgetting is a serious loss. Without the memory of our pain, we don't understand why we are attracted to or are creating negative relations. We feel the need to love certain abusive people. Where is this coming from? If we cannot find our history of pain, we cannot understand our present. One flows out of the other. The past creates the present road we follow.

Our feelings are unreachable and unaccountable, and are regarded as insignificant. Where did we learn to treat ourselves like that? Unable to pay attention to the pain we feel, we lose motivation to make important changes. Blank feelings and internal emptiness create stasis.

Without knowing our pain, we cannot feel another's. It takes sensitivity in both directions to know what people feel. If our behavior hurts people but we can't admit how it felt when something like that was done to us, our ability to react to them is nil or false. If we are set against feeling our pain to stay on our "parent's" good side, feeling historic pain again creates anxiety about displeasing it. But this is a step we need to take. Feeling early pain is associated with recovering our memory of the events that caused it. Having memory without feeling or vice versa deprives us of the experience of meaning.

Despite our fearful repression, how are we to return to our felt memory? One way is by observing what we negatively react to, especially to what we hate. We need to see what in our partner and friends we hate the most. Often this resembles a part of ourselves that we despise because our parents despised it.

Note which memories and associations come to mind when you have feeling without content. Let your mind soar free, and see where it goes. Feeling triggers memory and vice versa. Memory recovery goes on and on, painful and liberating.

We often turn to dreams. What are we dreaming about? What do we associate with our dreams' imagery? Dreams give us tendrils of association leading us to what we need to know. Dreams tell us what we fear. They show us things that scare us. They show us our unacknowledged strengths and talents. Dreams are great advisors. People have recognized this fact for millennia.

We need to know our "frozen child," to feel our "child's" suffering, in order to stop rejecting suffering in others. We need to know in order to stop identifying with our "freezing parent" so that we can accept our lovers after they drop their guard and let us know them. Our lovers show their strengths and weaknesses. We want them to feel comfortable being open. We want the same thing for ourselves.

How are we to know the right way to treat our lovers? If they are hiding their feelings, there is little said to alert us. If they take the risk of speaking openly, we need to dwell on what they say and see how it makes us feel. If we feel nothing, we may be out of contact with ourselves. It is an area of protective blindness we need to open up and see regardless of our pain. If they express joy, we can resonate with it unless we are beset by jealous feelings. We note that they have had something we lack. Jealousy implies we can never go there. Thinking this means we are listening to our "freezing parent." The "parent" would use our jealousy to break up the relationship.

If you overreact, it means that you have been trained to hate some aspect of yourself. If your lovers reveal deep sadness or shame, they feel the way you once felt and probably still do. To feel their pain, you must feel your own. If they are weeping over what you have said or done, say you're sorry. Say you were wrong. Say you can accept weakness, theirs and yours, and hopefully they'll do the same for you. You may cry.

You'd rather be a weeping, smiling human being, hand in hand with one you love, than a blameless robot. Find the place of love.

Whether to Stay or Leave

The issue is once you know the person you are dating, whether you stay or leave. In a healthy relationship, staying is a natural progression into an ever-expanding world of closeness and pleasure. There also is some "pain in the ass" behavior, since you two are not identical and have ways that do not match and to which you need to adjust. There also are neurotic habits and contaminants from childhood. The latter are best overcome, but this adjustment cannot always be done quickly, since the unconscious mind holds hold on to these behaviors without the owner's understanding.

One of the first principles in staying is whether commitment is possible. There are people who at first seem to be loving, but when the going gets serious, run for the hills. We live in a time when there is little commitment. People remain together like two turtles sunning on a rock. You're here, and I'm here. That's all. Commitment is a two-way thing not dependent on one's passing mood or petty grievances. It does not happen by chance. Commitment is like the foundation of a building. If there is no commitment, the whole thing will come crashing down when there is stress at the base. But commitment is not artificial. It has no value if it is pretended. It has to be something you deeply desire.

Commitment is not there with someone who constantly threatens to leave or who leaves you but then comes back, still threatening. You lack the experience of "I am always with you. We'll work out our problems." The potential for the other person to drop you is felt to be an act of torture as long as you are in love. You are walking on glass. What next will send him or her away? What must I do to keep the person? You are on your best behavior, like a child at an adult party.

Or you go to the other extreme and speak in such a nasty way that it shocks your ears. Nastiness can be defensive. You'd rather drive the person away than have him or her leave you after you've been your nicest self, which strikes too close to home. Some think that the absence of commitment makes the lover more precious, but it often makes him or her less so. You feel all kinds of misery while knowing it is only a passing fling. Why bother to invest yourself at all? There's the romantic heart, all anxious and aflutter, as compared with committed love, in which the lover is felt to be a part of you.

Another issue in deciding whether to go or stay has to do with how you fight. All couples sometimes disagree. Some may even enjoy a fight, a display of differing opinions. But it is a different kind of fight when people try to hurt each other by word or fist. Attempting to hurt is a sign of immaturity, a lack of control that can escalate to the point of causing damage. Why does someone attack? Is it done to make other people listen? You mean, they won't listen to you unless you abuse them or vice versa?

Is attack done to express the power of your internal "freezing parent" over the "child?" Neither "frozen child" nor "freezing parent" should be in control of the adult's method of disagreement. Adults have to take care of the infantile parts of their minds, which means to understand and keep them in their place. Only after setting them aside can adults commit themselves to loving other people fully, those who need to do the same.

Growing the Self

Islands of self that are obscured by the fog of denial are extremely important to the destination of the adult. Carl Gustav Jung sees the shadow as part of one's identity. What is denied occupies a bigger space than what has been accepted and is known. In the shadow are the loves, needs, interests, and talents that have not been accepted by your family or society as a whole. Your family and, later, society unconsciously conscribe to have these inner forces suppressed and as much as possible entirely out of your mind. They do it to help you fit in. But when is fitting in no longer good for you?

Let us say that you have chosen to love the kind of person your family and society would approve of ... the same thing with your job, hobbies, pets, travels, or clubs. You are so neatly fitting in that you do not know that anything is wrong for you in doing it. But in fact, a great deal of it is wrong. You are wearing an emotional suit not of your choosing. It is not your shape, color, and design. It is not you.

Some people get in touch with their shadow during the midlife transition when they ask, Is this the life I want to lead? Others do not, because they are bound by the fear of losing membership in their referral group. Belonging as the predominant feature in your self-awareness is not a healthy state. However, the "frozen child," under the threat of the "freezing parent," did not learn there is any other way. And so it is you, the adult, who has to ask, Who am I? given the pressures of making a living in a failing economy and all other negative features. What is my shadow, and where does it want to go? Whom does my shadow love? What must I do for my shadow to be myself? Your shadow now and always has been part of your true self. It is time to listen to it.

CHAPTER 7

Choose Love

Are there different kinds of love? Some divide types of love into those of the mind, the genitals, and the heart. Many see love in terms of sharing or possessing. We are happy together because we are one in the sense that I own you and you own me.

Is there greater stability for one kind of love compared to another? Those who subdivide love and choose a certain subset speak from limited experience. Their view of love is that of a scientist regarding an animal in a cage. They reduce love behavior to a mathematical equation or translate what they see into what supports their fantasy. Their grasp of reality is undermined by what they cannot see and feel.

In mind-love, there is attraction to another's analytic ability, to brilliance, which creates awe. Your minds play games together. Sometimes it is a game of hide-and-seek. Sometimes there is an explosive disagreement over matters big or small. You fight to the place of a shaky resolution until the next fight. This mental play or conflict stimulates interest and compels you to be together. The combative play of mind may be a distraction that takes you away from loving yet calls itself love.

We know there is something missing, which is why we try so hard to win a mental fight. But to win what? Is it all about cheap thrills? We do not know how to change our relationship into something deeper. We struggle to feel something that intellectual sparks cannot provide.

This experience is a replay of ancient history. We were raised by parents whose mental power was what they offered. We felt their emotional lack but had no name for it since we, like all children, spoke our parents' language. We dwelt within the field of their mind as our terrain like a fish dwells in the sea and does not question water. If we mentally soared as high as our parents and felt their pleasure, it was poor consolation for what they didn't offer. If we couldn't soar as high or if they didn't want us to soar with them, we moldered in the place of insufficient intellect and trod an emotionally empty ground. If they treated us as intellectually inferior, we labeled what they did as love.

In our adult life, we choose to be with people who also travel the path of the mind. We posit that their love must lie beneath. But the mind that stimulates us today fails tomorrow because the basic stuff is missing. Still we cling to the idea that finding someone "smarter" will do the trick, the same way our mind clings to the idea that our mind-besotted parents deeply loved us. So our next lover has to have more brainpower than the last. Brainpower flashes its signal and then dies out. It has to.

One kind of love is physical. We fall for people on the basis of sexual attraction, a beautiful body, a sexual tie in which passion is shared. Sometimes sexual attraction lasts a long time. Often it does not. At first the people are magnificently arousing. Then their bodies (and ours) age and get a little slack. Their/our sexual style and techniques become so well known that we feel jaded. We come, or we don't come. It doesn't matter much. Orgasm can be the peak of intimacy or something entirely private and unimportant. Orgasm can lead to greater emotional union or take us away from it.

With sex as the primary focus, we need to be with a new and different body to get our juices flowing. We have satisfaction, or pretend to have sexual satisfaction, while love fades away. Or we endlessly complain about its insufficiency until sex is given up. We may stay together so as to not be alone. We create a habitual, emotionally empty life together or leave and resume our hunt for the perfect sexual partner.

Then there is love of the heart. Lovers react to each other's feelings. There is a feeling of, "I need to share everything with you"—ups and downs, sadness and joy. I want to dance and have sex and sleep with you like two puppies in a basket. I look into your eyes to see your heart. What hurts you hurts me, and vice versa. When you are pleased, I smile and shout and hug. There is no competition, no winner and no loser. Heart-to-heart love is increasingly part of our thinking and feeling. It is like breathing.

Love has heart and sex and mind in it. My body craves your touch. I/you want to sink into the bliss of orgasm. I want to share your thinking, your doubts and fears, your excited discoveries. My mind and your mind go together. We flow from mind to body to heart and back, sometimes all three of them at once. There are no walls between us. We flow together in the energy of love. Love is what we do together here and now. Our future grows out of it. There is strength in a natural loving partnership. You cannot know this until you do it.

Do Not Accept Bullying

You have to confront bullies who secretly love you and you love back when you are strong enough to do it. If you are not strong enough, keep your distance and bide your time while developing your ability to speak. If you are strong enough but afraid that you might not be able to carry it off, do it anyway. Learning you are not yet strong enough is a fact to be respected and corrected. You are always aiming to take an autonomous position, even with one you love.

Take the example of this girl.

Her mother was a bully. Publicly, she was a defender of people's rights, head of her teachers' union unchallenged for thirty years. The idea was, "Don't take Tillie on." She had the courage and oomph to do what most people lacked; she had power, force, ambition, and courage. She also was willing to do it. At home, her image of control prevailed. Secretly afraid that she would be abandoned by the person she loved most, which was her daughter, she put a prison atmosphere into place. She would do things her daughter needed and wanted to do herself. She ignored but secretly enjoyed her daughter's school accomplishments. She could not openly state it, because every step her adored child took in becoming able to use her gifts took her away from Mom.

And so it went through the years, with the daughter avoiding and dreading her mother's critical input. The daughter became awkward at doing things—partly due to lack of practice, partly due to fear of Mom's attack. This awkwardness due to Mom's rages became the internal "freezing parent," who demanded that she please her mother by submitting to Mom's doing for her what she intended to do for herself. The "parent" demanded that she feel inept and unable to do what she wished. The "freezing parent's" critical orders and the "frozen child's" compliance are received as directives by the adult mind.

Offering love was seen as an act of pleading and defeat. Incompetence was repeated as an approach. Through many years of psychotherapy and beginning to do things that showed her abilities, the girl, now grown, invited her mother to spend a weekend with her. She rented a cabin on Daniel's Pond in Vermont and drove up in her own car, and Mom drove up in hers. The weekend was going nicely—with nothing serious and nothing deep happening between them—when she told her mother that her father's recent girlfriend's daughter and boyfriend would be dropping in.

That news set her mother's anxious brain on fire, which the daughter had not expected. She had forgotten that Mom had to have exclusive possession of her. As the couple showed up to share tea and some snacks, Mom bolted out the back door and ran to the beach. She got into a boat and rowed around the lake until she saw the couple depart.

Then she came back, walked into the house, berated her daughter for doing this "to her," and announced that she was leaving—so like the tantrum-ridden mother of her childhood. But the daughter no longer cowered in the corner. She stood up and said, "You are not leaving. We have to talk this over." Mom was shocked. Her daughter was defying her. And then she gave in.

One might think that she gave in because secretly, as had always been the case, she needed to be close to this child she so much adored. Mom so feared losing her daughter that she enclosed her in a fence of fear. So she listened. They talked and talked and talked.

Who can say what they didn't talk about? It was a mighty sharing. The daughter learned for the first time that Mom had paid for all her school expenses except for those covered by a grant. Dad, with his trips to Mexico and Europe with girlfriends, lacked the dough. Mom learned that her daughter took great pleasure when her mother seemed to enjoy anything she did, instead of knocking it down and saying, I'll do it for you.

The weekend was filled with tears and laughter. They embraced more than once. It was a weekend of transformation. Each one learned that she loved the other and had always done so. These were the times they cried. Mom learned that her daughter would not tolerate bullying. The daughter learned that Mom had loved her from the start. Each one became the other's forever-after friend.

At War with Your Partner as if with Your Parent

Love for our partner can reveal ancient wounds in order for them to be healed. The experience of self-awareness can be unpleasant and full of pain. But also it is an opportunity to heal through interaction with the most important person in our life, with a mate who relates to us as friend, brother/sister, self, and parent, often sequentially or all at the same time.

For many grown children of unloving and often attacking parents, childhood injuries cause them to be hypersensitive to similar wounding behavior enacted by their partner. Such reminders may cause a fight. Sometimes, the person fights an imagined opponent, thinking that something assaultive has happened when it has not. Often they fight because they have exaggerated the hostility of their partner's behavior.

Is such a reaction to real or imagined slights a good thing for the partnership? It forces the ones called "abusive" to look at the way they are behaving. Are they are talking down to their partner and thereby mistreating him or her, or is their partner overly sensitive to neutral actions that they call abusive? Or is the partner even making the whole thing up?

Self-designated "abused" people have to look at the larger picture in order to see what happened. They need to learn how to evaluate their "wounds." Does the same feeling happen with other people? If nothing supports their experience of having been abused, they need to recognize that sometimes childhood agony flows into one's current perceptions, which renders them bleak and hurtful.

The experience of ancient wounding invading your present love life gives you a time to understand and move into a new reality. One cannot easily live in the present while denying the hurtful past. The past lives on inside our mind regardless of our intentions. We have very little energy left if much of it is spent keeping the hurtful past out of our consciousness. On the other hand, one leads a very unhappy partnered life if there is little happening but conjured-up injury and rebuke.

Take Vinnie and Marie. Vinnie was totally bullied by his father and older brother. He was endlessly put down. His father was a vain, drinking egomaniac, a lecturer who went from job to job because he so often offended his public and his boss. His mother was a spineless pushover, the kind who would marry such a bully. She ran her son's life by whining, complaining, and asking him for favors.

Vinnie's wife, Marie, had been raised in a large, spread-out family with twelve unplanned children. All the children were called "accidents" by their mother and were treated as such. Dad was off drinking, eventually in his own bar, and Mother was inclined to hang out with her friends, away from the kids. There was a good deal of criticism from their mother should any need be directed her way. No kid was treated as special. Marie could not get her favorite brand of cereal. The kid who did the shopping made the choice. The children were mostly ignored by their parents as well as by each other. Each developed an "I take care of myself" philosophy. Marie learned to do what she needed to do, and she claimed to need very little. This defense was used to keep her from feeling any craving for care. An ocean of pain lurked beneath.

However, when she married, she wanted to express her need and took it to a childish extreme. It was an all-or-nothing experience. Finally, she was with a person who would do exactly what she needed. A deluge of desire flooded her mind, and now she felt entitled. As a result, when her husband didn't want to go her way or do her thing, she became extremely insulted. When he reacted with loud, defensive speech, she fell into a first-class snit. She was furious even when his no was soft and troubled. Any form of no was taken as a personal rejection.

He, on the other hand, had trouble saying no to anything. Perhaps that is one of the reasons she fell for him. She assumed that he would always do what she wanted. Saying no was an action he needed to learn to do with ease. He felt that he always had to do whatever was asked of him to avoid giving insult, since disputing with his father had led to physical attack. He seriously resented the inexorable need shown by his wife because of the way his mother played on him with her teary requests.

The task for Marie is to express her needs but not to go off the deep end should her husband be unable or unwilling to comply. The task for her husband is to say no without having to be in a state of rage to do it. He needs to accept that his partner also has flaws and shortcomings. This doesn't mean allowing her to attack him like his father did for his failing to comply. It also doesn't mean that he is to attack her for being needy and overdemanding like his mother. Not attacking does not mean giving in. It means to peacefully stand your ground. It means for each to take a good look at how the experience of past mistreatment intrudes on the present.

They can be happy with their differences. They can enjoy learning to say no as well as yes without attendant disaster. They can be happy about what each brings to the marriage and not endlessly dwell on the inevitable disappointments. We all need to give up our infant's view of paradise to find happiness on earth.

The Power to Disconnect

People who get into disturbing and harmful relationships often remain stuck there because they do not know how to disconnect. Sometimes, they think that they are not allowed to end a relationship or they do not know how to end it. Ending relationships is a skill that seems like light-years ahead of them, since their parents never allowed them to say no to anything. Not knowing how to end relationships that harm them keeps them from trying out new ones. They do not know that ending what doesn't suit them is their natural right.

Ideally, people are able to tolerate anothers' displeasure in reaction to what they say or do so they can take an independent stand. A woman home with children and dependent on her husband is in a weakened state. Let us say that the woman is self-supporting, and the one she has "fallen in love with" turns out to be a vindictive, aggressive type. She needs to get away from him but is afraid to hurt his feelings by leaving. It is a strange conflict when the abusers' feelings are more important than your own. Compulsive caretakers lack freedom to do what is best for themselves.

Some are afraid of being hurt should they ask for separation. If they are with a hurtful bully, the words they are most afraid of using, and not without reason, are, "I am leaving you."

If they have fallen into the vulnerability of early childhood, their fear of abuse may not be a realistic assessment of their partner's potential to do harm. Of course, some lovers will injure their partner as they would harm a weaker child. The couple found each other to play aggressive and submissive roles. The one who plays the child needs to emotionally grow up in order to escape before there is serious damage. She may need psychotherapy to do this.

You have to assert your right to assess a situation, to find out what kind of person you are with. If your partner is very stubborn when you present your point of view, he or she may refuse to consider what you say. Since you are not there to cure the person, nor can any partner do this, you are not to remain until he or she understands. If you think that the relationship still has potential, you need to insist that he or she see a psychotherapist for couples and/or seek individual treatment, or you will immediately leave. Note the word *immediately*. Talking about leaving without doing it loses its potency over time.

You need to set early limits pertaining to what you find intolerable so that the person has a chance to change. Stating what is important to you helps you decide whether to stay or go. It eradicates the timelessness of childhood. If what you say is disregarded, if all the blame is placed on you, your partner is irresponsible and the time has come to pack your bags. If children are involved, the issue becomes more difficult. You may need to see a divorce mediator to work out a financial and visiting settlement. If your partner is set against divorce, you both need to see a marriage counselor. It is like a ball game. Trying to fix a marriage requires both of you to move toward a mutually agreeable position. Otherwise it is "strike three—you're out."

You develop courage by moving forward step-by-step. You speak about what bothers you and discuss what needs to change. Your partner also airs his or her concerns. The consequences of speaking out are rarely as bad as your "child" imagines. If your partner's reactions are, "It's all your fault" or "Forget it," the potential for becoming a happier couple seems to be lacking. Waiting for it to happen bears the dust of magical thinking. If violence is involved, you are with an abuser and may need the action of police to remove you and restrain the person. Do not remain in a relationship due to fear. Seek psychotherapy to strengthen and support your ability to depart. The consequences of remaining together may be life-threatening.

Look at your fear of disconnecting as a remnant of childhood spent with parents who threatened to abandon you and frequently did by making themselves excessively scarce. Children have to feel connected to their parents so that they can venture forth. Initial courage comes from this connection. After a while, a connection to your parents remains inside the mind. A supportive and loving "parent" is always there. If the parent did not establish this connection, no internal "warm parent" develops and there remains a sense of being alone.

An adult who never developed a "warm parent" has to create his or her own island of safety, a rock to cling to when venturing forth. This can be a friend who understands, or, better still, a therapist who knows about spousal abuse. You can call when you are in a panic or when needing advice. Therapists or friends do not need to deal with their own panic. They have already gone through the pangs of separation and are happily on the other side. They can share your panic without falling into it. You are not alone.

Unhealthy Connections

Healthy parents in their imagination see through their offspring's eyes. They feel elated when they hear that their child has done some kind of daring deed. "Hey!" they yell. "I never could have dreamed of doing such a thing. My kid is such a trip!" To healthy parents, if their children don't surge forth into a courageous and exploratory life, the parents feel they have done something wrong. They encourage their children to take adventurous steps by recounting some of the crazy things they did when they were young.

It is an altogether different kind of life with parents who have trouble seeing the child as a separate being and have troubling views of self that enter their view of and treatment of their child. Such parents can deal with their self-hatred only by giving it away to their child. A terrible bond exists between them in which the child must disappear as a separate person in order to feel connected with his or her parent. The child is sacrificial from the start.

Such children bear a heavy mantle of obligation. They are not free to explore; to make mistakes and to laugh about them; to fall and fall again in rough play with their pals; to have skinned knees ("who cares"); to try out different ways to achieve their goals; to change their objectives depending on what calls them just today; or to have old, new, and different friends.

Change is one of the wonders of childhood. You can do it as you please each day.

Restrictive parents may not allow their child such freedom. They are trying too hard to be "right" parents, in control over everything. They put their children under such supervision that the children see it as the only place to be, a kind of permanent jail. It is a sad loss imposed on the children that is rarely, if ever, needed.

Here are few example of the distortion imposed by a parent:

Undeveloped parents who live through their children permit only behaviors they need or approve of, which creates a universe of pressure and misunderstanding. These parents project unacceptable parts of themselves onto their children, for which they scold, direct, and hate them. Or they see themselves as failures and need their children to mistreat them. Or they bully their children and create children who bully back. It is a back-and-forth assignment of error, guilt, and punishment, of inflated or vastly poor self-esteem.

Our life as a lover starts with how our parents see us. With dependent parents, we need to separate from them in a way they do not like. Our "freezing parent" issues prohibitions from inside our mind. The actual parent may state that our straying from their control will kill them. They are attempting to reinstitute a submissive relationship by stimulating guilt.

The adult self needs to develop a wryly stated "really?" in response to negative statements that try to put on the chains of obligation. Saying "really" indicates that you are not going to fight about it. The parents' opinion is not your problem. It may be difficult to learn to act this way, but it is up to you what you choose to discuss with them, no matter how they question it.

We may feel guilty about leaving the parents, since the relationship was founded on our giving. Now that we are separating, how will they fare alone? Should we be forced by their fear of the consequences to accede to their pleading that we stay?

Does the mother of a baby bird now grown release it to fly across continents and oceans, or does the mother climb on its back and say, "I can no longer fly across oceans; you must carry me"? No. The parent who has separated from the child, which means to fully love him or her, would not ask for that. The parent's mind accompanies the child, gliding and soaring with joy. To bring it down by burdening the child with a need for symbiotic union would be a loss to the parent.

It is a natural, necessary, and beautiful action for every child of every species, including humans, to take off as soon as it can. But it is hard for the child raised by a grasping parent to say adieu and depart. The parent long ago reversed the assignment of who takes care of whom. The child has to separate from a parent who cries, "I need you to stay near because I am helpless."

The assertion of freedom by such children does not come easily. They have to explore their history in order to understand the parent/child reversal, which never should have happened. They have to know that it is not their responsibility to cure their parents of their inability to stand alone. They have to know this even if the parents calls them traitors whose actions betray the parents' love.

Grasping love, no matter how deeply felt, is not true love. Love is a giving and a sharing. Love adores the loved one even if the person's abilities take him or her far away. Love is not stopped by space.

Parents who were inadequately loved by their parents deny the insufficiency by pretending it was more. If in touch with their deprivation, they blame their own unworthiness for the lack. They later pass a permutation of love to their children. They express love that isn't so with its charade of self-denial. The children remain unhealthily connected to their love-distorting parents to help the parents deny their paucity of love. The children care for their parents by sharing this lie so that the parents will not feel the pain of being unloved. Children in each generation help their parents lie about the missing parental love. That the children lie because their parents are too scared to face it, keeps them all from healing.

Sometimes, parents who lack an adequate sense of self can't recognize that anyone exists outside themselves, so they relate by incorporating their children. The children are treated as if dissolved into their parent's image. Constantly treated this way, children feel themselves to be dissolving in a kind of fog. The parents use the word *we* when they speak of them, but they mean "I." The children, who are older now, feel that their parents' "we" represents a kind of bonding with their nonself. The children are like a canvas for the parents to paint upon. Accepting this designation as the only way to relate to their parents smashes the children's feeling of existing. To perceive their self as real, they have to remove themselves from the parents' mental universe, no longer to do and be what is expected. It is an either-or decision.

Refusing to allow your parent to deny your identity is a fearful step to take. The parent's you-are-part-of-me relationship with you is all you've got connecting you. You fear that your parent may retract his or her love. But what kind of love will you lose? It is an emperor-is-naked kind of love. You are told you are loved, but you don't feel it and are forever waiting for love to arrive. Grown children need to keep an eye on the clock to unmistakably discover that hope for receiving love is unrealistic. How long have you been sitting on the platform? It's too much time spent waiting. Once grown children admit this to be the case, they have to martial their resources to separate from the parent in order to restore a sense of self.

All parents who give their children too little love are needy in a way that breaks the flow of life. Parents who need their children to parent them move the energy backward. Parents who hate their children for moving away or as a carrier of the parents' self-dislike, retard the children's natural velocity and confuse their direction.

The parent takes from the child the love he or she needs to give. When the time to seek outside love arrives, will the grown child seek love from a similarly empty, needy, and blaming lover? To move in that direction justifies the parent's mistreatment, which deadens awareness of the parent's pain. The child's life is sacrificial.

Parents who were insufficiently loved as children have an incomplete sense of self so can't handle the coexistence of together and separate with their children. They need to superimpose their image onto their children to feel that they are whole. They take a rejecting stance toward the children's movement away from them, which presents the children with an unsolvable problem: how can I meld with my parent so as to be loved and still be me? It is an unworkable situation. To be identical with the parent in all you think, feel, and do interferes with the development of your self.

If children heed their parents' demand that they not be independent, they obey out of love, fear, and guilt. If they say no to their parents' request that they remain in this antiself-connection, they take fear and guilt with them and subsequently are afraid to love. They feel like a culprit rather than a fleeing victim of their developmentally arrested parents. The escaped grown children need to accept that they have a right to become separate people.

Time to Warm Up

What are the things that make us warm? Most of all it is being with people who appreciate and love us, who make us feel okay about who we are. We are warm with people who don't make us feel wary about what they will say and do. We share a common vibe. Getting together is a happy occasion. They appreciate our accomplishments and support us during down times. They are there for us, and we are there for them. We are friends.

Who are the ones that cool us down? They are sometimes appreciative but more often not. They attack us for doing something "wrong," according to their standards. They hang attack on the final loop of praise, such as, "You are good at this, but …" Then out comes the knife. They send us cards with mean descriptions that are to be taken as a "joke." They say, "I saw this card and thought it was meant for you." The card features the same kind of nasty characterization they sometimes state in open speech. You laugh on cue at this indictment and feel the pain. Why do you laugh? Why do you accept their aggression as an act of affection?

People who attack you speak your parent's cold language. Like the internal "freezing parent," they are there to freeze you. They claim to love you and need to see you. They call to say, "Let's get together." You do not call them back. Then they call again. You feel trapped in the web of their reportedly loving embrace, give some paltry excuse for not having returned their call, and make an appointment. Why do you not turn them down?

Here comes the grasp of history. Our parents verbally assaulted us. Loving the hurtful parents and taking blame for what they said left us confused. Our "freezing parent" says that we are being too sensitive. It says, "Who else would be our friend?" We are expected to see ourselves as the ones in need rather than our demeaning lover/friends.

We join them drinking booze or smoking grass or eating chocolate cake, breaking all our rules pertaining to health, mental clarity, and weight control. We are fitting in. Do we enjoy doing it? No. This behavior is associated with a feeling of loss. We have betrayed ourselves—again. These "cold makers" may call themselves lover or friend and may claim to love us, but we feel neither loved nor liked. We feel like victims.

We need to examine how we feel during and after time spent with them. Are we happy to be ourselves, or are we invaded by self-doubt? If we feel depleted and need to recover, meeting with the lover or friend has not provided what we need. Something is bad for you if it cools you down and exhausts you. You need to be warm during and after you get together with them. Warmth is a sign of healing and of life.

March through the heat of your rage after once more submitting to abuse so that your heat replaces the cold of panic. Be an adventurer who sails into the unknown. What will be the consequence of your speaking up and, if necessary, taking action? Will your parents step out of the dark to slaughter you? Does your lover/friend have power over you? Do you invent this power—or more likely, give it away? Do not be surprised that as your own power grows, you will feel yourself warming up.

Don't Think of Yourself as a Commodity

Treating all or part of you as a commodity leads to a loveless life. Treating your lover/mate/friend that way has the same result. Thinking of your self as an object to which we assign a monetary value or some other kind of assessment associated with prestige or its lack, is abandoning the essence of your self and the principle of love.

Parents who think of themselves in terms of commodity do it to their offspring. They plaster "market value" onto their entire world. Instead of seeing their existence as part of a greater sense of spirit shared by all living things, they own objects. Treating a person as an object you own, as a "mine," means you can't relate to that person.

"Thinging" is destroying the world around us. People can take it, eat it, splice it, sell it, kill it, and make it extinct without feeling any kind of connection or personal loss. They use it up, poison it, and spoil it because they do not love this earth and the creatures with which they share it. They spread the emptiness of "market value" onto the ones they "love." They spread pain and death around them because they lack a broad sense of family.

The "commodification" of people and living things, including of your self, comes from an unfulfilled childhood. Your parents were not in tune with you because they were not in tune with self. They did not welcome you into a loving community, because they did not belong to one. They taught you to accept your emptiness by focusing on acquiring things. Possessions, including lovers or friends, were thought of as "goods." If we empty the world of beauty and spirit, we lose it in ourselves.

The child was looked at as a kind of "product" of the parents' genes and training. The parents made remarks about the child's appearance, faults, and talents. The parents boasted about what the child inherited from themselves. The bad stuff came from the other. They divided the child into good and bad. Later, society does the same. Society can be seen as a group neurosis, a collective experience of what we learned as children.

Your parents pointed you toward what they thought you should pursue, which was a projection of their view of life. You should acquire better objects. You should become a better object. They pushed you away in a joking fashion if not an angry one. Sometimes with pleasure, they tossed you into the air and caught you with loud laughter. More often, they pushed you away from the divine experience of walking hand in hand. You learned to scream your unhappiness, which they decided was a demand for a new toy, a complete misunderstanding until they implanted this in your mind as a cover-up. Emotional isolation became a way of life.

They plopped you in front of the TV so that they could take care of chores, from which their solitary life gave no respite. You watched your own TV in your own room. You learned to zone out. You learned to live in your own space, unrelated, distracted, intent on not noticing that you were alone. Family life was all about emotional isolation.

Extended family was a bunch of unhappy people who got together but really did not meet. Love was lacking since it was blocked by the barrier of possession. Everyone in the group was counting and comparing and competing instead of feeling the pleasure of companionship. Family life taught the child to get something and hold on to it, and then to work to get more of that or of something else.

Sometimes your parents took you to play with other children. Moments of being with children who acted impulsively, who expressed like and dislike without looking at a scoreboard of value, offered you relief from emptiness but did not cure it. It is only in the embrace of older loving people in an ongoing loving community that the sense of self is created. A child needs the emotional feeding and holding of an adult community.

If your parents were cruel and rejecting or simply disinterested—which is common—you developed an internal "freezing parent" that related similarly. The parent directed you to take lovers and friends who were to be used and ignored, and who mistreated you and taught you to mistreat others or yourself. The parent triumphed when you focused on developing your muscles or having a job that you hoped would impress people. You were emotionally for sale.

Now that you are grown, you look outside for something to fill your emptiness—which doesn't work, because "outside" is no solution. You do not know, because it was not done with you at an early age. You move through life without relating to plants and animals and people as fellows in spirit to celebrate life. You do not know there is another way, nor do your lovers. People choose to be with those whose defenses interlock with theirs. They "understand" each other in a way that defies understanding.

You fall into angry, distracted, needy activities—buying, demanding, hating, drinking … using and being used. These behaviors have nothing to do with having a loving connection and in fact stand in its way. You bring your lover emptiness. You bring it to each other. Neither of you operates in the world of caring. You do not know your inner life, that your self needs fewer things. Self revels in meeting with friends, talking, dancing, creating and sharing pleasure. Self shares its pain with those who care. Self shares work. Self is full because it is related.

It is in our current society, so rapidly moving toward mass extinction, that most of us dwell. We lead the life of an addict whose need is never sated. If anything, need grows stronger after each indulgence because the relief it offers is a sham that creates the need for more.

Don't Let Age Stand in Your Way

Let us start with age and the need for romance by women. You think you are too old to meet a man. That is what other people tell you. Do you need Botoxed lips and all kinds of artificial adjustments to help you "pass"? Women are more conscripted than men into the myth that it's all over after a certain age, especially by corporations that sell them youth-creating products. Men are not so easily bound, or at least not so directly bound, although many want a much younger woman to support their image of having the virility of youth. Women get wrinkles. Men get "character."

The problem with the myth of aging and the fact that women outnumber men in the population is that people fall prey to a statistic, make it personal, and then live as if it inexorably applies to them. Statistics are only averages. They are not jail sentences. You can think and feel and move in a different space. There are two obvious ways that people let common bias against age dominate them. First and most important, they stop looking for a partner. They socialize with buddies of the same sex and age who hang the topic of sexual companionship out to dry. The second activity, which supports the first, is that they let their bodies go.

They act as if the muscle tone of youth; the idea of maintaining a certain weight and posture, shoulders back, stomach in; dressing in attractive colors; sending animal signs of sexual availability—all those things you did or should have done as a younger person—are no longer on your behavioral palette. Those who were raised to think of themselves as unattractive or unavailable do this from the start.

This is nothing short of a self-attacking crime. Who creates your rules, and why do you obey them? Why are you walking with the lonely crowd? Is there punishment for going your own way and meeting someone with whom to happily bond?

You let your body go. You walk in a slump. Your stomach pushes out, and your breasts hang down. Your penis is hidden beneath your overhanging stomach. Your haircut and clothing—nothing celebrates your sense of being a psycho-sexual animal on the prowl for a mate. Nothing is done to celebrate your sense of self. You look unattractive, and you know it. Only you do not take responsibility for your condition.

You point your finger at your age. You use the statistic of age as an excuse. In countries where fat is looked down upon for people at any age, even for women after menopause, after years of aging they are thinner than they were before. Perhaps you are afraid to break the mold of aging. It is strange how we fear to leave the statistics and expectations of our group.

Then there is your image established from your earliest days by your parents' treatment. The internal "freezing parent" is a copy of your rejecting parents, who put their self-dislike and ugliness into you. You were an extension of their unacceptable selves. Then there are parents who are afraid of losing their children. The parents have a hostile reaction to their children being socially successful, because the parents want to retain possession.

The parent insists you are faulty, ugly, and unlovable by anyone but him or her. This characterization continues in the mind so that the grown person hesitates to try his or her luck in love. If parents feature having an emotional collapse should their grown children leave, the children are controlled by the fantasy that they have to persuade the "parent" to release them before they can seek a mate. Making the internal "parent's" release a necessity means that you never will be free.

What must one do to reverse this trend? The first thing is to get in shape. This means achieving a proper weight, not one others would call fat if they dare to honestly speak of it, not listening to comments said to slow you down or stop you by negative ageists like, "But you know … at his or her age …"

You need to accept that your proper weight is most likely close to the weight you had when you were at your fittest. If you never had that weight, let the mirror be your guide. I suggest not buying new clothing after you have lost a little weight, because that weight tends to be where you stop. Buying clothing prematurely is a way of giving up halfway and not achieving what you seek. You can pin back your waistband on the old stuff and continue dieting.

You need to begin to exercise and keep increasing time and effort until your heart beats so fast that you sweat and breathe. Clean your body of toxic waste this way and live! Do weight-lifting exercises to improve muscle tone. Many people buy exercise tapes that they play and move to at least three or four times a week. Others join a gym because the group activity led by someone of good spirit with great music gets them going.

Another reason that some do not get in shape is that they are too afraid of failure. They do not try, or barely try, so that they can keep alive the fantasy of how great their success would be if they devoted themselves to it. These are the Walter Mitty "secret successes" who lead sexually empty lives except in fantasy.

Putting on weight before you start encountering the opposite sex is also a repetition of the way you were taught to handle parents who slammed you for transgressing their power by being good at something at which they had to be superior. You need to take your mind away from every meeting that did not go "right"; you need to accept that this man or that woman was not your type. Do not be taken in by appearances. They may look good and act winning, but their character is not right for you.

Do not think that your values have to be eliminated for you to find a partner. Rather, you need to note false matches, pairings with people who clearly would mistreat, abandon, attack, not love, take advantage of, ignore, or bore you. Note the kind of people you choose over and over again but barely enjoy. Swear off repeating these mismatches.

Those who do not give up do wonderful things. The greatest thing is to find a person to love who appeals to you and who loves you back.

Are You Not Good Enough?

The fear of never being good enough is so terrible that many people avoid the struggle to get good at doing anything. Many women do nothing but attend to their looks. Some of them don't do that. Many men are afraid of not being strong enough, so they do not lift weights, go to the gym, or play competitive sports. Instead they become slack. Many people think that they might like to be a potter, a musician, a dancer, a mathematician, a this, or a that, but they hold back because the parents of childhood called them failures and they believed their parents' words. What is a failure anyway if you like doing what you do?

You, the grown child coming from such a family, do not send signals of interest to the guy or gal you like. What if the one who attracts you turns away? It would confirm your self-hatred. You dare not even raise your eyes to such a person. Instead, you stay with people you do not like. You stay with abusers, people who use and fail to respect you.

You feel safe walled away from your true desires by staying with "inadequate" and inappropriate people. You do not fall into the failure mode, because if you do not win such a person, it doesn't count. This defense deprives you of love. You give up seeking what you want because you think your ego will be trampled for trying to do it and failing. You treat a one-time failure as an always. This is a faulty supposition. The ego always grows from effort spent and pushes on. Hiding away from the presumed "damaging world" supports the negative view you have of yourself. To not challenge one's self-rejecting beliefs is to endorse them.

Grown children who have absorbed their parents' criticism slink away from life, dreading to learn that the outcome of their effort—including their search for love—might confirm their parents' rejection. They don't see that each day's best is exactly good enough. They are saddled with a negative self-image, which they take with them everywhere. They see self and the world through it.

They are unable to appreciate each day's best because the internal "freezing parent" uses their minor mistakes to attack them. They do not seek a person they would love and who would love them back. Such behavior is considered dangerous. Life is dangerous with the internal "freezing parent" as your warden. Under the warden's rules, seeking love and expressing it are a major transgressions. The "parent" operates under the philosophy of, "You are mine."

To get out of this pitiful, depressed life, we need to welcome fantasies and wishes of doing different things, as well as of finding love. We have to take off the mental chains acquired from rejecting parents to take the first step, and then all the steps that follow.

The life that develops never turns out to be the one that we imagined. Rather than this being a disaster, it is an amazing experience that keeps growing out of itself in new and unexpected directions. It is full of excitement and thrills, like putting a kite into the air and feeling the wind take it away. Your kite surrenders to the wind's great energy. Your controlling self is blown away. It is like love.

Mourn the Loss of the Loving Parent You Never Really Had

You are locked in the repetition compulsion of falling for unloving people. Such a preoccupation may dominate your life. You choose parent-resembling lovers to find the love that originally wasn't there. This choice supports your parents' pseudo-giving posture. It underscores and validates their cry of perfection. Part of the glue that fastens you to this effort is your fear of exposing your parents' emptiness and having the internal "parent" turn against you.

The adult portion of the mind doesn't understand that its conscious needs are in conflict with those of its internal "child" and "parent." The adult mind doesn't feel strong and clear enough to unravel this web of constraint. The "child" is ruled by its fear of the "parent," which has always been in control. You need to reduce the power of these forces over your adult mind by pushing them into the past. You, the adult, need to experience what pleases you in whom and how you choose to love.

The childhood myth that fuels the internal "child's" deference to the "parent" is that the "parent" can destroy it. You have to dethrone the "parent" influence on your adult mind by recognizing and openly declaring that your actual parent's love was insufficient. It is not your duty to comply, support, agree, or cover up. You are not to be drawn into the child's ancient drama, which is all about what happened once but is not happening now.

Renouncing the myth that your parent deeply loved you is associated with an act of mourning. Mourning is a "giving up" of a connection. Good memories will arrive but also ones of failure. You will remember times the parent wasn't there for you. You will recall the lack of empathy and the tendency to dismiss you. You will remember being treated as inferior, and how you labeled yourself inferior to explain why he or she didn't love you. The more you look at memories, the more you will question whether your parent's lack of caring was your fault.

Memories tell a different story. How often did he or she come through for other people? You can learn about these instances by asking those who knew him or her. Are those who claim to have received your parents' love also children of egocentric parents? Do they create excuses for your parents' failures as they had to do for their own? Are many of their reasons self-rejecting? Remember if you can instances of being loved. Do not inflate such moments to make them seem more wonderful. Do not try to fill an emotional vacuum. Experience what is. Recognize how your parents' self-aggrandizing needs made them insensitive. If they sometimes did what you asked for, did they do it when you asked for it, even if the time was inconvenient for them? Were your parents' "loving" gestures attuned to your needs or merely done for show?

To be available when needed is a mark of loving. Love involves giving what the loved one needs. Love isn't a gift tossed out of a car window as your parents drive away, leaving you alone and stranded. Love isn't hastily drying your tears and then changing the topic to something that interests them. Love isn't buying you off with things. Unless what is purchased is very important to you, spending money rarely touches your heart.

Remember and review. Look at photographs. How is the family arranged? Where are you in respect to your parents? Who is touching whom? Movie stars preen for the camera. They are concerned with how they appear. Look at old letters. As you review the past, you will feel loneliness, grief, and rage. You will feel deep loss. Mourning is a process of resolving attachments. To mourn means to see your parents as they were, to recognize what they could and could not do. Mourning frees you from a further hopeless search for love from one who cannot give it. You will be free to seek love from people who show that they can love you from the start.

In your memories you can see a sprinkling of real love, but not enough to support the fantasy of a having had fully loving parents. You see that your parents tended to treat and mistreat everyone alike, unless the guest was someone "special." Remembering the multiplicity of experiences, you have to conclude that there was inadequate giving.

See if you feel guilty. You were taught to feel guilty by your parents' curses, tears, and reprimands. You felt guilty when they ignored you. All children take the blame for what their parents don't do. When you asked for what they did not want to give, they blamed you for asking. They blamed you for getting them in touch with their inadequacy and their failure, even with their selfishness. They couldn't admit that they failed at anything. Instead they denied the rightfulness of your needs. They took your request as an affront and counterattacked.

You were raised to be a sponge for their self-hatred. Know that you are not responsible for their rage. They projected the cause onto you. Their dispensation of love for your acquiescence caused you to think that you deserve to be hated. Accepting their hatred, being a target for their abuse, is not an act of love. You are not required to endlessly seek lovers who will similarly punish so that you remain connected to your attacking parents. You need to stop denying parental hostility by reliving it in your love life.

You may grieve that you cannot cure your parents of their inability to love, but accepting their hatred is no cure. You need to give up seeing yourself as some kind of doctor or, even worse, as a saint. You cannot cure them through self-abnegation. Nor will your sacrifice increase their love. They abused you to defend themselves. Your pain was overlooked or even needed, since you were a stand-in for their suffering. They traded being the victim for being the attacker. The victim was the role they had with their own attacking or ignoring parents. They felt relieved by giving it to you.

You probably tend to exaggerate your shortcomings. This stance helps justify receiving your parents' blows. You may need some kind of psychotherapy to help you stop taking this position and to see the entire story. Your parents' hate affair with you started long before you were born. Look at their parents. Were they self-centered and unloving? A damaged child becomes a damaging parent. This is the law for all. If you don't want to become a damaging parent, you need to free yourself from the negative image put into your damaged internal "child." You need to separate yourself from the curses and demands of your internal "parent."

Mourning is an act of healing. Mourning is a process of giving up, which makes room for something new. How much of your early childhood was spent in the fantasy of having a loving family? Did you imagine yourself to be part of a family of pigeons cooing in their nest behind the ceramic cornucopia by your window? How much time was spent in hiding and in pain? These memories are the building blocks for what you have become. Some of these blocks still help you. Others stand in the way and have to be removed.

How will you know when mourning is done? Your sense of inferiority and guilt will be greatly lessened. Feeling responsible for what befell you will be mostly gone. You continue to work on separating from your parents based on the reality of what happened. Mourning is over when you can choose a person who genuinely loves you. What a relief. What joy.

Early Places of Adaptation

In childhood, you developed ways to preserve your sense of self. An unloving and desperate life is countered by the creativity of the child who finds or creates a special place, a way of relating to the world that does not destroy him or her. These ways of feeling the world and expressing the self become islands of security that need to be sustained. These ways support the spiritual language that you speak.

We all have our own special places in which our self survives. Some of them may resemble the ways of the girl described below. Some of them are far different. Every person's way is important and not to be forgotten. It is an essential part of the self's knowledge and development.

Let us look at one example. A woman had parents who were unavailable, who left her to long hours of isolation. Her mother did not provide a house key, so she had to wait on the corner of her street until Mom came home from work. She felt like a refugee. Her mother did not encourage friendship by inviting other children to visit, and if she ever did, Mom gave them no privacy. She haunted her child's room, listening and later cross-examining. There was no way to bring friends home. The same thing went for phone calls. Mom stood by as she sat on the phone bench talking.

But more serious than being cross-examined, ignored, and disregarded was the constant verbal attack. She was not good enough for either parent in an endless variety of ways. Her mother focused on physical activities. She denounced her daughter's skills at doing small things like dish washing or hair washing or choosing what she would wear the following day. What she did was faulty, period. Mom redid or did it from the start. Her father focused on what she knew and how she said it. He labeled her some kind of ignoramus.

She did not join with girls on the block who spoke of things about which she knew little; her parents heartily disapproved of liking boys "that way" and equally of the current modes of fashion. She did not get a fuchsia satin jacket, a crinoline to bow out her skirt, or an early bra. Dad frowned on all of this as worthless acts of following the crowd (as most adolescents do), and Mom complied. The boys she rode her bike with began to pay attention to the girls and no longer were interested in her ability to ride her bike without hands or to leap over fire hydrants. She did not show her mother the wound she received the time she did not sufficiently clear the spigot, and to this day she is proud of the scar on her calf.

There was no place for her to relate with people, no place to be her self. What was her agency of coping? What did she do to deal with so much rejection and to find a wonderful place to be? It had to be a place that did not feature hollow, selfless talking. Her parents' speech was full of knives, endless ways intended to demean, attack, and wound her.

She went into nature. She related to the beautiful dragonflies, with their big translucent blue/black wings, flying, landing, and mating. She quickly followed to be part of the stream of beauty. She felt sexually aroused to see them connect tail into tail, flying, landing, and flying again. She walked after them, getting wet. She related to the turtles in the stream—so many turtles and frogs, all leaping off the bank when she approached them on her way to the water.

She joined the kingdom of living things, which recognized her in their leaping. She loved the minnows and hellgrammites scurrying beneath her feet as she walked in the stream. She loved the flowering of spring and the family dog that scampered with her. She vibrated to the sound of singing birds. She related to them all without having to speak. She lay on her back on a hillside with bees buzzing around her head. She heard the universal sound, the *Om* of life.

She related to them completely from her heart. The animals reacted to her in their quiet way, usually as friend. She felt connected to living things and the fecund earth that supported them. She had a real mother now: Mother Earth.

Later, much later, she had friends and lovers and teachers who emotionally touched her. They related to her without words. They felt who she was, and she felt them. They related without manipulation or evaluation. They spoke her "language." They offered her a place to be. When they said they loved her, she knew it and felt it and sent love back.

You need to recognize the places that supported your sense of self. You need to focus on places and actions that mean so much to you and develop them. It is through this that you keep developing your sense of self.

If you do not find a place in which your self can dwell, you continue to be an unreal person who "fits in" with other people's needs and views. Place can be physical, emotional, imagined, or all of the above. It is where you can be you. Fitting in keeps your self hiding in a state of fear. Overaccommodation to others' thinking establishes a negative expectation. It is a form of backward thinking. If you go along with this, you must have a reason to hide your self. If you are a grown-up, the reason cannot be a good one.

The part of you that is attempting to fit in has to play its role but not let the role take over. Your parents attempted to suppress, ignore, and deny your sense of self. Due to your need for their "love," much of you complied. The part of you that learned to accommodate became the decider of what is to be done. Accommodation cannot heal you. You need to return to your self … better still, not to leave it. Self and love go together. You can't have one without the other.

You Feel Compelled to Comply

Do not be surprised if fear does not go away. Do not be surprised if you continue to overreact to unloving words. It is better for you to avoid people who engender these feelings, but when such contacts and reactions occur, do not be surprised.

The vulnerable internal "frozen child" will always be afraid. It had terrible, felt-to-be-life-threatening experiences that impressed its memory. The internal "parent" warns, "Don't go there," in order to help the "child." While the adult mind knows better than to react this way, the internal "child' does not and cannot do it. The "child" lives in the danger of the past.

When you feel this kind of fear, recognize its origin. The "child," who expects to be put down and hurt, once more is crying out. And a lover perceived as destructive tends to arouse this. But is your potential lover actually destructive? The autonomous adult needs to become independent of messages sent by the "child." The "adult" needs to stand its ground, not only against a potential aggressive lover but also against its own internal alarmist "child" and "parent." The adult will assess the person as lover or friend and will act accordingly.

Some people use self-supportive sayings to keep their self on track. Some see a psychotherapist or attend therapy groups with people who state their mind, say what they see, and are supportive. The therapist, the friend, and the group all say, "Nothing comes easy. Do not give up." These people warn against falling into the arms of a destructive lover or friend. They keep each other on the path to love.

You need to forgive your parents for passing on to you the hatred that was passed on to them. Forgiveness requires understanding that their antilove was not relevant to you. Hating them for hating you binds you to the injured position which you will replay or reverse with your lovers. Forgiveness is an act of separation. Forgiveness cuts the negative connection and sets you free.

Choose Love

What is love? Do any two people agree about it? Some believe that love must last a lifetime, but for many this isn't so. Does this mean that they have never loved at all? Or is what they call love an emotional shudder that is quickly forgotten, like a yawn or a smile?

This question cannot be resolved merely through descriptive language. Love is an emotional experience. People who love are happy together. It is not the kind of happiness based on what they own. It is not fueled by alcohol and other drugs. If people say they love you and you do not feel it, either love isn't being sent, or you are not on the same wavelength and your ability to receive it is nil. It is the same from you to them.

Love comes from the deepest part of you when the barriers are down. Love and intimacy go together. Love has no sense of space. Love is an I/thou experience. Love creates a "we." If we were insufficiently loved as children, as adults we need to learn to love.

People who speak of loving may not know what love is. They may be lying to seduce you or be lying to themselves because they don't know how to create the mind-desired union. Those who did not know love in childhood often create a substitutive myth about love to still awareness of their painful needs. They did not receive love but want to say they did from parents who barely gave it, as did their parents' parents before them.

Poorly loved grown children now tell that myth to you. They tell it to themselves. The myth is used to cover a painful inner truth. The power of a myth comes from the extent to which people use it. The power is not its ability to fool you, the one who hears it. Its power comes from its ability to fool the tellers, who need to believe their words.

You need to stop living myths, your own and those of people you fall for. There are good consequences from being in touch with reality, even if they are sometimes painful. Truth can hurt. If you go through the painful experience of learning the truth of your past, it will help you grow beyond it. Truth heals.

How do you know when you have found love rather than the cheap version of a sexual thrill or the fantasy of being with an idealized person, soon to be dropped by one or both of you? You indulge in the myth of love to still awareness that nothing meaningful is happening. Is there a way to determine whom we choose to love, or is it something over which we have no control? What can we do to change what turns us on if it lacks love?

We know that love is absent if we feel depleted while we are with people or afterward. Something has been taken from us rather than put in. Love fills us up. The love experience is different from going through the motions. Pleasure may be there, but is pleasure the equivalent of love? We seek ever-newer objects and experiences to distract us from our emptiness. We go on buying trips; we have satisfactory but unemotional sex. We share sexual partners with others. We hippity-hop from one lover to another saying, "This time I know it's real." We skirt the issue of intimacy because intimacy means dropping one's shield, which leaves us feeling unprotected and terrified. We stay married for the security it provides but do not relish spending time together. The shared life is a chore.

You need to examine your feelings to move you to take a different path. The way people around you have loved, or have claimed to love, hasn't worked for you. It is only a journey of pain, boredom, and disappointment. You feel disgusted with what is desperately done to and by you so as not to be alone. You need a vision of love that involves all of you—body, mind, and spirit.

Raised without deep love, how do you begin to know it? Look for moments when you felt love at any time in your life. Love is a full body-and-mind experience. See what turned you on. What were the elements you felt then and need to seek again?

I remember meeting the "rabbit man." I was about eight years old on a vacation with my father, who did not converse with me—only lectured. He took me to a resort way up the Hudson River, where the river was less imposing. He told me that the people there were anti-Semites, so I shouldn't tell them my religion. If they asked, I should tell them I didn't know it. Why did he take me there? My father was a man in hiding. He hid his true identity, which he thought to be inferior. He took me along on one of his "don't let them know you" trips. He went to places where hiding his religion supported his need to be unknown.

Dad was busy reading something when I took myself off in a small rowboat, which I rowed along the river's edge. It was a quiet, peaceful, and beautiful day. I already was such a tomboy that rowing a boat on a river by myself did not scare me. I rowed easily until I saw a man on a rise above the riverbank. I grew curious. What was he doing?

I pulled my boat onto the shore and climbed the riverbank. He was an elderly man with white hair who was sitting on a chair inside a wire-mesh hutch. He looked at me and smiled. I saw that the hutch was full of huge white long-haired rabbits, almost half my size. He pointed to the chair opposite his and said, "Sit down." I came in and sat. Then he said that the rabbits were very friendly and liked to be held. The next thing I knew, an enormous long-haired rabbit was put into my lap with its head leaning against my throat, its whole body pressed against mine. It snuggled against me looking out and totally relaxed. I sank into the rabbit as well. We snuggled together. The old man smiled as we sat there enjoying the day. I do not know how long I sat there holding the rabbit. I was awash in pleasure. Minutes, hours, a lifetime later, I realized I had to get back to the hotel. It was a sad departure when I lifted the rabbit and handed it to the old man. He said, "Please come back. The rabbit is waiting for you." In my heart I never left.

It was the first time I remember being welcomed like that. I didn't have to speak. Speaking words was a family rule, even a fetish. They were a noisy bunch who competed for who was loudest. No one really listened. The rabbit man saw me and welcomed me into his world. He *really* saw me, knew who I was and what I needed. The rabbit also did. I had nothing to prove. I only had to be and allow the bunny to be with me. I felt together with the man, with the rabbit, and with myself. I call this love.

Heart-to-heart love is all about growing stronger and moving together. It is about finding courage to drop your defenses despite the fear of being rejected once you open up. Love is the essence of what is.

We Love and Heal Together

My "friend" said (as a compliment to make me feel good about myself), "You healed your husband. No one ever paid attention to him before, and he did not have the personal skills to make friends. You knocked on his door and said, 'Come out.' You saved his life."

I hated hearing these words. I felt that they were taking away an experience of great value. These words propelled me into a vague and dim place far from self. I felt like a denizen watching earth from another planet. My friend was summarizing a love match into that of giver and receiver. My friend's words dismissed the feelings between Malcolm and me so that the true event was lost.

I felt disturbed by my husband's being seen this way, so small and pathetic, the man I dearly loved. Yes, he was hesitant to speak his thoughts, but that was not all there was of him! I felt hurt for myself as well. Did my friend think that my relationship was only one of sacrifice? My husband was my friend. He was a friend to many; he did favors without asking for recognition. He was shy about revealing his rambling ideas and historic allusions, but his heart was fully involved. Above all, he didn't want to hurt anyone. He didn't want to damage people the way his selfish, insensitive family did. He wanted to hold my hand and laugh at the ridiculous predicaments we cause for ourselves. He wanted to listen to the music and to dance.

No, I did not save Malcolm. We knocked on each other's doors, and we opened and said, "Come in." I saw him, a man who radiated warmth. A spark flashed between us. We saw and loved from the start. We saved *each other* from the isolation of unexpressed love.

Why did my "friend" not see it as it was? Perhaps, despite stating otherwise, she had known only the relationship of unequals and wrongly called it love. We cling to defenses formed at a time when we were weak, young, and dependent. The fear of giving them up continues in the mind of our internal "child."

You do not expand your sense of self by denying how much you have received. To do that is to shrink. My husband always spoke his personal truth from a beautiful caring space. I had never known a man like this before, at least not known him in my heart. I loved his smile, his bony cheeks, and his Roman nose. I always kidded him by saying I married him for his looks. He would laugh at this and hug me.

When describing a plan I was afraid of doing, he responded, "You can do it. Go ahead. It's right for you." He never told me to stop. He never said, "You can't do it; you're too stupid and weak"; he never offered restrictions like my family always did. When I suggested we visit a certain country on our vacation, he always answered yes. He had not gotten it together to travel before but had always wanted to go. We went to ancient cities, where he studied the inlaid brick wall patterns of palaces, paying close attention to details I never noticed. We loved to walk the streets and look in windows. Neither of us had had an adequate family life, and we were looking at how other people lived. When I was nasty—and I was nasty sometimes, the way my parents had been to me—he always forgave me, saying, "I take the good with the bad." I found that love was an emotional miracle shared by people who are committed but do not possess.

The "friend" who said, "You saved him," did not understand that we saved each other. She did not understand this because of her childhood with a self-centered and malicious mother. My friend had to stop feeling the maternal connection, which is the first and most profound learning a child has about love. She had to close herself off so that her mother's aggressive speech couldn't reach her. She lived on an ancient island of emotional isolation, habitually guarding herself with self-centered thinking. This defense made her blind to the happy surrender of a woman to her man, a man to his woman, and all lovers to their love. To see what you have missed in the way of initial loving with your mother, you have to feel that pain again. The way to the truth of loving is walking through the pain of childhood when your need for loving went unmet. Then you can move on.

The defenses you develop in childhood to get through helpless suffering often are walls that shut out later understanding. The "friend" has to see her own internal "child's" helpless neediness. She has to see that she too is incomplete and imperfect in order to understand that this deficiency will not lead those who love her to reject her. A true lover is not your enemy, is not your rejecting parent. If you do not drop your walls of control, ownership, and pseudo-power, you will never know it.

She has to understand that all healing is a two-way event. I receive as I give. You and I are one. Healing is a shared event. You do not heal another. We heal together.

How I Learned to Love

Malcolm was not my first boyfriend—the first man I hung out with, slept with, even lived with. But he was the first one whose love I deeply felt.

Of the lovers who went before, the first was Dorian, an immigrant from Vienna. He truly loved me, but I was walled-off, numb, and mostly unable to feel much affection. He supported getting me what I needed. He helped me get my beloved dog, Effie, a German shepherd that became a major part of my life. At that time, I was best able to trust and love a dog. Its affections and loyalty were clear.

Dorian helped me laugh at my tears and terrors. We laughed together. He took a photograph of me splayed out and weeping on a stone jetty in Cape Cod where we vacationed. He called it, "Elan gives up." It was said in loving jest. He had been through too much himself to scorn another's pain. We played hide-and-seek in his huge apartment. We jumped out at each other from behind closet doors. We were reliving (or living) our first childhoods. We talked about everything. We made love, although he did not have a lot of fire in him. It was mostly the fire in his cigarette with which he extinguished the flame of grief over the family he left behind to the Nazi onslaught. I left him because of his smoking. I said he would die of cancer. The real reason I left him was that I didn't have a strong enough sense of self to tolerate that much closeness. For me, closeness meant inevitable rejection, although he did not do it. But childhood terrors run deep.

After Dorian I had a long string of men to whom I felt superior. François was a charming French artist. His grandfather was part of an artistic bohemian family that moved to Paris from San Francisco, where they took on a neo-Greek lifestyle. They wore sandals year-round with socks that accommodated their toes in winter. They told me that closed shoes were killing my feet, and they were right. They were vegetarians who had oatmeal for breakfast every morning and did not wash the bowls. They saw no need for that. They carded wool and made togas, which they wore every day. François was raised to be vegetarian. His mother was overshadowed by her parents, and her husband, a French filmmaker, was mostly absent. François knew the man more by reputation than by contact. François never developed a strong sense of identity.

Why did I break up with François? He loved me but could not get his act together to seek the career he desired. He spoke of architecture and rescued an antique desk whose top went up and down when you turned the handle set in front. We found it in the weekend dump in front of city hall, where cleaning men who knew nothing about antiques dumped it in the trash. He spent a long time sharpening his pencils and setting up his materials at the top of the desk, but very little time drawing. I felt exasperated, nagged him, got fed up, and left.

Then there was Mike, the poet whose way of eventually making money was not defined. He knew famous poets who liked his work, but how many poets in America can make a living from selling their poems? Sex with him was great, and he was very handsome, but still I had to criticize his money situation and push the man away. I was constantly rejecting him as my parents had me. I was hurt when he left me. I did not foresee his reacting to my hatred. I never dared react to my parents like that, so it was not part of my thinking framework. Shouldn't he have stayed with me and lived in rejected misery, like I did?

Then my program changed. I began to chase after men who did not want to be with me in any lasting way. They avoided commitment, probably to everyone. Now I was playing the role of my parent-rejected internal "frozen child." I was a dunce who sat in the corner as I had with Mommy and Daddy. My lovers were the smart ones. They had scholarships and were ambitious. One of them typically left without mentioning when we would meet again. Each meeting was an isolated event.

My trumpet-playing boyfriend left me waiting in the hallway outside his loft—in an empty building next to a deserted pier—till he came home from rehearsals in the wee hours. He never gave me a key, and I didn't ask for one. I didn't dare. What was I afraid of? You ask for something to symbolize acceptance, and you get less. It's better not to know. Fear was so much a part of my *almost* being in a relationship.

My psychologist boyfriend called another woman for a date as I lay there on the mattress (his bed was on the floor), recovering from the great sex we had just had. I thought that my pleasure drew him in. Not so. Perhaps it was the opposite. I listened to the phone call in a state of shock. I thought that he loved me but learned he lacked respect. Worse still, he was putting me into a "you mean nothing to me" place.

My Vietnam veteran boyfriend briefly left his girlfriend to be with me and then went back to her. I was getting too connected and wanted what he didn't offer. The center of his life was making recompense to the Vietnamese, even though they asked him not to return. They had had enough of Americans moving in on them in every guise.

It was true of all of them. I left them, or they left me. I frequently was used. I dated an Amazonian explorer who never took me on any of his kayaking trips, although I begged to join him. Sharing such events was why I contacted him after reading his personal ad in *The New Yorker*. He took other women along who adored him and gave him gifts. I discovered fancy underwear in his dresser drawer. He was famous. He was exploitative. I was going to break up with him—a tremendous step for me to take—when he got sick with prostate cancer that spread to his bones. I felt I had to care for him. Would he have done the same for me? Forget it.

Were there others after this one? Who can remember? Mostly, I felt hopelessly lonely. I was hungry for companionship and love; I was beginning to consider that criticism has no place in establishing a relationship. I no longer wanted to be above or below. Where should I go to find someone who shared my love of nature and my humanistic values, a person who cared for the little things like I did?

Sadly alone, I went to Allen Ginsberg's memorial service at St. John the Divine Church on the Upper West Side of Manhattan. There were people who had been involved with Ginsberg in so many ways—people from the sixties in tie-dyes, people in monks' robes with long hair. There were poets who read and dancers who danced to Ginsberg's verses and songs; there were Buddhists and Hindus, gays and straights, people who wanted to celebrate the unity of man. There was a bit of everyone. The atmosphere was celebratory.

I had been there for about an hour when I looked around this huge hall to see who was there—hoping, but not expecting, to see anyone I knew from the sixties—when I saw this gorgeous, tall, semiblond/gray-haired man sitting behind me. I was totally attracted to his gentle look. He had an aura of kindness. When I finally decided to get up and leave to go to work, he got up as well. I didn't know it, but he had been studying my ass with pleasure. We started talking in the lobby and continued out onto the street. It was one of those times when you instantly communicate with someone. It was more than that. He was a world I wanted to enter.

It was strange, but I knew right away that I wanted to go home and live with him. I had no idea of how to communicate this to an almost stranger. Does a woman do such a thing? I smiled and looked into his soft brown eyes. He took my phone number. I was ecstatic. I stayed near the phone for days, but he didn't call. Finally, I fell into the emptiness and despair I had felt before meeting him. And life went on.

Then a year later, I was walking down Broadway reading a newspaper, on the way to the supermarket, when this tall, gorgeous gray/blond man came over to me. He said something pleasant as I slowly began to know him. Aren't you the man I met at the Ginsberg celebration? Yes. We said a few more words, but my guard was up. I wasn't going to be abandoned a second time. We got to the supermarket, and I said a friendly good-bye, walked off, and entered the supermarket without looking back.

That night he called me. He had saved my phone number. He explained that when we met, his head said, "She doesn't want to meet you," although his heart said, "Yes." He was unable to listen to them both and chose his head. He wasn't used to receiving love, which undoubtedly I sent to him from the start. I laughed when I told him that he had ruined my life by not calling. Then he said, "Let's meet for dinner."

I said, "I know a great macrobiotic restaurant."

He said, "Sure"

We ate there. He loved the food. I invited him to visit my cabin. He said yes. I thought he would sleep in the guest room, but he naturally walked up the stairs to my bedroom and bounded onto the elevated bed—beneath a skylight through which we could see a great moon through the branches of a nearby tree. He said, "This is perfect. I feel safe."

I said, "Me too." I never sent him downstairs.

And so instantly, as it was when we first met, we bonded. We held hands in bed. When he turned onto his left side, the way he always slept, he drew my hand across his back. His hands were cold, and mine were hot. I would heat him up. We walked the country roads and city streets, hand in hand. We told each other funny stories until we cracked up. Sometimes we could get each other to laugh just by laughing … bent-over bellies that ached from going in and out. I loved his warm, open eyes, his cackle.

He was involved with me. No restraint.

How did this happen after a lifetime of coupling with fleeting or absent love?

I was fed up, despairing about leading a solitary life, alone even when dating. Alone. I'd kissed and held and then turned away from all those people, feeling detached, empty, and needy—like a child looking through a window at other people's Christmas celebrations. I'd chased after all those people for years, never counting in their eyes and hearts, feeling endless pain and blame. I would try to win them, always available, giving them all I had, but to no avail. What kind of life was this? It was all about emptiness and loss. It was a direct continuation of my childhood. It was the empty dance of the internal "frozen child" to the whip of the internal "freezing parent" that kept it hopping. I was tired of my "parent's" directions telling me to be a weakling and settle for less if not for nothing. What did the destructive internal "parent" know about life? I was tired of reliving my past. I hated the way things had always gone, and all of it caused by whom I chose to love or how I chose to love them.

I was interested in feeling love. What is love? I knew a tiny bit about love from Dorian, who was devoted to me; from François, who cooked for me and took me to meet his family; and from Mike the poet, whose lovemaking dazzled. Their love signals had been deflected and mostly ignored by a secretly terrified me. I knew a little bit about love from Effie, my dog. I did not feel threatened by her closeness; there was no need to act superior or inferior. My internal "freezing parent" did not consider the importance of my dog as it moved into my heart. Nothing stood in the way.

I was fed up with hatred in every form, giving and receiving it. My conscious adult mind knew that hate didn't get me anything I needed. I was tired of living the life dictated by my internal "freezing parent" who stated I wasn't good enough and had to chase after men who agreed. I refused to remain the self-deprecating child who always must fail and be rejected. I can't say I knew another way to live, but I was throwing myself onto the winds of change to let them carry me.

Malcolm came along and his love poured in. I will never be the same.

Index

A

abandonment
- expectation of, 46–50
- fear of, 103–4, 162
- guilt about leaving, 116–19
- loss of transitional object and, 2
- by parent, 31, 78
- threatening to leave, 94, 166

abuse, *see* mistreatment; physical abuse; verbal abuse

acceptance
- of blame, 144–45
- of gifts, 147–49
- love and, 127
- of mistreatment, 86
- by others, 20

accommodation, 183

accusations, 15, 27, 56, 67, 110, 145, 154

achievement, lack of, 31, 54

action, need for, 19

adaptation, 25, 181–83

addiction
- to bullying, 128–29
- to suffering, 109–12

adulation, need for, 14

affection
- aperiodic reinforcement, 111
- competing for, 40
- withholding, 67, 129

African Americans, in history, 51, 75

age bias, 174–77

aggression, 31, 66; *see also* rage

aggressors, identification with, 15, 65

alcoholics, 31, 56

amnesia, 153, 154

anger, 17, 120, 131–33; *see also* rage

animals, *see* pets

anxiety, 8, 17, 20, 44, 73, 124

apologies, 33, 85

appreciation, 33–34, 79

arguments, 13, 25, 157, 159, 163

arrogance, 34

assertiveness, 61, 84, 114, 166

attachment
- bad, iceberg of, 84–85
- to caregiver other than parents, 75
- development in childhood, 1
- between false selves, 25
- hatred as form of, 129–31
- ongoing, 2
- secureness of, 5

attraction
- to intellectual ability, 159–60
- to potential partners, 84–85, 91, 99
- sexual, 160

autonomy, 14, 18, 25, 55, 119

avoidance
- in adulthood, 2
- of conflict, 9

of parent's wrath, 5
sex, 16
of truth, 13
of unpleasant topics, 22

B

behavior
approach/avoidance, 16
compulsive eating, 86
habitual, 28, 49, 82, 91, 110
neutral, 11
obsessive, 36, 42
putting on an act, 37
beliefs, 82, 103
belonging, 21, 121, 144, 158
beloved objects, 1
loss, 4, 6
parental acceptance of, 2
replacement of, 4
sense of security, 3
surrendering, 6
blame
acceptance of, 144–45, 151, 171, 180
parent projection on child, 88, 119, 120, 153
partner projection of, 116, 166
self, 72, 114
swallowing, 85–88
"blindness," 78, 81, 91–93, 121, 140
bomb-shelter life, 141–42
bonding, *see* attachment
boundaries, 36, 62–63, 73, 117
bullying
confronting, 161–63
curing a bully, 127
in marriage, 26, 28
parents, 8, 26, 52, 106, 161–62, 163–64
submission to, 128

C

career choices, 16, 18, 78
career success, 31, 54, 56
caregivers
attachment to, 1
compulsive, 165
"mammy" as, 75
catering, to others, 20–25, 67, 116
cats, *see* pets
change, 74, 92, 94
fear of, 108, 120–23
forcing others to, 126–28
chaos, 4
child development, 1, 170
childish dependency, 5
childish thinking, 82
children
ability to self-entertain, 22
ability to understand parents, 70, 81
clinging to parent, 92
compliance, 47, 70
copying parents, 107
entrapment, feelings of, 8
exploration, 167
extensions of self, 1
fighting back, 69
hatred from parents, 69, 83, 85
invisibility, 3
as mimics, 77
self-image, 154
unhealthy connections to parents, 167–70
choice, 28, 91–93
church, *see* religious communities
closeness, 132, 133, 190
coach, role of, 113, 116
comfort, 71
commitment, 156–57, 191
compliance, 47, 70, 162, 183–84
compulsive eating, 86

conflict avoidance, 9
conformity, 20, 24
confusion, 8, 26, 152
control
 lack of, 157
 love and, 19
 over feelings, 19
 parental, 11, 14, 57, 65, 132
counselors, *see* therapists
courage
 lacking, 14
 to leave, 166
 saying no, 134–37
cover-ups, 22
criticism, 99, 107
 parental, 3, 72, 153, 161
 between partners, 94
 between spouses, 13

D

death, loss and, 53
deceit, 73
decision-making, 124–25
defeat, 7, 8
defenses, 81–84
 childhood, 12
 forgetting as, 154
 letting down guards, 150, 155
 narrowing of vision, 120–21
 nastiness, 156
 neutral behavior, 11
 pain and, 29
 protective shells, 11, 12
 slacking off, 55
defensive self-image, 19
defiance, 66
demands; *see also* submission
 for allegiance, 113
 of bullies, 128, 129
 of freezing parent, 28, 32, 107, 181
 of others, 9
 parental, 6, 15, 60
 of partner, 57–59, 60, 94
denial
 of attachment, 77
 as defense, 28
 emotional, 5
 of feelings, 10, 19, 75–76, 100
 of identity, 80, 142
 of love, 16
 of mistreatment, 25
 mutual, 67
 of pain, 25, 29, 152
 of reality, 25, 112
 self, 144, 154, 169
dependency, 5, 10, 23
depersonalization, 10, 18
deprivation, 13, 15, 98, 138
detachment, 16, 18, 46, 69
disagreement, 47
 with parents, 26
 between partners, 28, 157, 159
 rights to, 9
disapproval, 36, 109
disconnection, 23, 165–67
disguises, 42, 76, 111
dissatisfaction, 34, 106
dissociation, 100–101
distance
 from child, 15
 from internal child and parent, 18
 between parent and child, 4
 between spouses, 13, 16
divorce, 22, 166
dogs, *see* pets
doubt, 26, 46, 171
dreams, 48–49, 140–42, 155
drug use, 29
dysfunctional thinking, 81–82

E

eating disorders, 86

ego, 33, 37, 57
emotional denial, 5
emotional deprivation, 98
emotional isolation, 173, 189
emotional unavailability, 12, 126–27
empathy
lack of, 34
from partners, 59
emptiness, 10, 16, 18, 74, 127, 174
encouragement, 72
ending relationships, 136–37, 151, 165–67
enemies, 9, 63, 121–23, 142
escape, need for, 31
escapism, 3
estrangement, 31
existence
establishing, 11
independent, 14, 15
loving and, 11
exploitation, 30, 31, 60–63

F

failure, feeling like, 137–39, 168, 177
false identities, 22–23, 37, 42, 44, 50, 73–74
fears
abandonment, 47, 103–4, 109
attracting attention, 97, 124
change, 108, 120–23
confronting, 54, 166
and dependency, 5
disappointing others, 110
of frozen child, 28
group ejection, 20
harm of self, 37
hiding and, 50
holding on due to, 100–102
how to deal with, 146–47
hurting others' feelings, 165
incompetence, 23
intimacy, 53, 59, 133
nonsurvival, 28
parent, 8
rejection, 12, 102–4
staying in relationship due to, 165–66
superstition, 82
for survival, 92
feelings
control over, 19
denial of, 10, 19, 75–76
fear of hurting others', 165
memories and, 101
necessity of, 127
numbness, 8, 10, 11
others' as more important, 112–16, 165
pretending to have, 127
sensitivity to, 154
thinking and, 48
first love, 91–92
fitting in, 13, 20, 74, 144, 171, 183
forgetfulness, *see* memories
forgiveness
demanding, 33
lack of, 69
of parents, 184
free association, 48
freedom
children assertion of, 169
fight for, 86
from hate, 16, 41
parents not allowing, 168
freezing parent, 12, 15, 17, 18, 69–71
abusive, 18
calling for rejection, 25
catering to, 143
choice of friends and, 171
demands of, 28, 32
directing adult love life, 92
ignoring, 44, 49–50, 147
judgments by, 121, 136

model for, 5
needs that bind to, 20
negative attitudes induced by, 26
placating, 29, 120
separation from, 82–83, 147
friends
acceptance, 108–9
choice of, 171–72
fear of rejection by, 48, 102–3
harmful, 10
isolation from, 22
parental disapproval of, 26, 27
frozen child, 17, 18, 69–71
catering to, 143
changing thought of, 146
decisions by, 5
emergence of, 11
fears of, 28
ignoring, 44, 49–50
separation from, 82, 83, 147

G

gifts, reception of, 147–49
giving in, *see* submission
giving up, 124–25
grandiosity, 3, 57, 78, 85
grasping love, 2, 169
greed, 122
grief, 133–34
groups
belonging, 20, 21, 121
ejection from, 22
growth, 108, 126, 157
guilt
about separating, 116–19, 168
swallowing blame, 85–88, 153, 180

H

habits, 28, 49, 82, 91, 110
happiness, 135
hatred
acceptance, 70
covering with love, 88–90
directed at children, 69, 83, 85
as form of attachment, 129–31
freedom from, 16
loving behind walls of, 63–68
passed on through generations, 70, 144
self, 10, 30, 74, 151, 180
healing, 92, 181, 187–89, 199–20
helplessness, 10, 23, 57, 70, 85
hiding, 26
beauty, 97–98
false fronts, 22–23, 73
feelings, 10, 18, 19, 155
out of fear, 50–55
from parents, 8–9
raised to hide, 33–37
self-destructive acts and, 50–55
from spouse, 13
holding on
to being unloved, 96–99
due to fear, 100–102
to unloving partners, 133–34
homosexuality, 53
hopelessness, 18, 94
human interaction, 12, 20
hyperactivity, 29–33
hypersensitivity, 163

I

iceberg analogy, 84–85
identity; *see also* roles; self
adopting that of aggressor, 15, 95
affirmation, 135
denial of, 80, 142
false, 50, 74
hiding, 186
lacking, 12, 17, 190
multiple, 142–44

split, 77
wrongness, 153
image, 22, 27, 41, 174
imagination, 153
immaturity, 157
immigrant stories, 21, 37, 56
inadequacy, 177–78
indecision, 124–25
independence, 14, 15, 25, 48, 56
indifference, 69
indirect communication, 33
individuality, 20
indoctrinations, 15
indulgence, 79
inferiority, 38, 66, 96
inhibitions, 16, 137
insecurity, 37, 40, 96, 137
intangibles, 14
internal child, *see* frozen child
internal parent (good parent), 143; *see also* freezing parent
interpersonal relationships, 72, 143; *see also* partner relationships
intimacy
dropping defenses, 73, 186
fear of, 53, 59, 133
love and, 185
mutual understanding, 113
sex and, 17, 160
invisibility, *see* hiding
isolation, 22, 96, 173

J

Janus, acting like, 73–74
jealousy, 97–98, 109, 155
judgments
accepting negative as true, 7, 9, 86
of internal parent, 121, 136

L

leaving, *see* abandonment; ending relationships
lies, 22, 35, 70, 89–90, 169
loneliness, 5, 23
loss
of beloved object, 4
consequences of, 3
lessons learned from, 5
mourning, 4
pain of, 76
of partner to death, 53
of self-awareness, 14
as self-protection, 10
lost love, 133–34
love
acceptance, 127
as adults without grasping, 2
beginnings in childhood, 1
choosing, 184–87
constructs of, 111
control, 19
covering hate with, 88–90
denial of, 16
as essence of developed self, 26
existence and, 11
as exploitation, 60–63
giving to others, 11
grasping, 2, 169
of the heart, 160–61
identification and, 43
imagined *versus* real, 133
inability to give, 12, 102, 134
intimacy and, 185
kinds of, 159
lacking knowledge of, 149–51
learning to, 189–94
lost, 133–34
mother's reincarnated, 4
myths, 89, 103, 179, 185
need to destroy, 93–96

parameters, 8
of pets, 12, 14, 187
reception, 133, 147–49
security and, 123
sharing, 74
surrendering, 6
tendency to give up, 2
unrequited, 30, 31–32, 31–33, 134
loyalty, 137
parent, 26, 61, 96, 99
to partner, 62, 94
self, 17, 96

M

madness, 123
manipulation, 15, 67
marriage; *see also* partner relationships
accepting flaws in, 164
arranged, 34
bullying in, 26, 28
choice of mate, 17, 27, 90, 112, 119–20, 141, 178
extramarital sex, 22, 34–35, 45
hatred, 15–16
intimacy issues, 16, 17
saving each other, 188, 189
staying with abusive spouse, 25–29
marriage counseling, 166
martyr, 78
masochists, 127, 128
master, role of, 77–80
memories
dissociation from, 100
false, 89
recovery of, 155
remembering parents properly, 179–80
suppression, 2, 89, 90, 153–55
mental associations, 2
mind-love, 159–60
mistakes
accepting blame for, 85
freedom to make, 117, 167
learning from, 71, 72, 87, 141
mistreatment and, 139, 178
repeating, 49
self-punishment for, 130
mistreatment
acceptance, 86, 87
addiction to, 109–12
attraction to, 88
in marriage, 25–29
by parents, 52, 88, 137–39
physical, 52, 79, 136
rationalization of, 88, 106
recognition of, 86–87, 95
by step parent, 87–88
submission to, 26, 84
verbal abuse, 13, 98, 130, 136, 145
money, as life objective, 37, 38–39, 41
morality, 22, 78
mourning, 4, 20, 59, 120, 178–81
myths, 89, 103, 179, 185

N

nature, 182–83
neediness, 10, 32, 118, 165, 170
needs
to destroy love, 93–96
of freezing parent, 20
to heal your parent, 199–20
for mother's love, 20
of others, 6, 9, 14
of parent, 10
unmet, 13, 57, 58, 164
negative expectations, 46–50
negative self-image, 41, 42, 177
neuroses, 141–42
numbness, 8, 10, 11
nursery school, 4

O

obedience, 15, 59, 61, 85, 132
object constancy, 12
obligation, sense of, 114–15, 167
overreactions, 27, 106, 120–21, 153, 155, 163
overworking, 33, 39
ownership, 7, 98, 122, 138, 162

P

pain
- addiction to, 109–12
- avoidance with hyperactivity, 29–33
- denial, 25
- of disconnection, 23
- forgetfulness of, 2
- loss and, 76
- recovering, 153–56
- of rejection, 55
- surrendering to other's, 6
- taking on others', 144–46

parental projection, 86, 144–45, 173
parents
- absent, 1, 22, 33, 56, 61
- abusive, 52, 88, 137–39
- acceptance of beloved objects, 2
- acting like their parents, 5, 13
- angry, 131
- avoiding wrath of, 5
- as babies in disguise, 102, 105–6
- belligerent, 105
- bullying, 8, 26, 52, 106, 161–62, 163–64
- in competition with child, 38, 97–98
- connection with child, 13
- controlling, 11, 14, 57, 65, 132
- critical, 3, 72, 153, 161
- disapproval, 26, 27, 36
- disinterested in child, 7, 150, 173
- dissatisfaction, 106
- estrangement from child, 31
- expectations of, 8, 16, 20
- fear of own sexuality, 3
- fear of rejection by, 12
- fighting back against, 8
- giving in to, 6–7, 10
- healthy, 167
- ignoring children, 3, 13
- impulsive, 4
- insecure, 85, 96, 137
- invasive, 10–11, 26
- jealousy, 97–98
- objects that represent, 1
- rage, 4, 5, 130
- restrictive, 168
- self-centered, 26, 38, 96, 137
- self-image, 83
- service to, 105–7
- swinging from cold to hot, 70
- unhealthy connections to children, 167–70
- weakness in, 154

parent stand-ins, 107
partner relationships
- accepting flaws, 164
- age and, 174–77
- arguments, 13, 25, 157, 159, 163
- attractions, 84–85, 91, 99
- boss role, 14
- catering, 23, 24
- closeness, 132–33
- commitment, 156
- demanding, 57–59
- destructive, 184
- disinterest, 49
- embattled, 63
- ending, 136–37, 151, 165–67
- exploitation in, 30, 31, 60–63
- hypersensitivity to wounding, 163–65
- indirect communication, 17

intimacy, 16, 17, 53, 59, 73, 133
lover as parent stand-in, 107, 178
loyalty, 62, 94
promises to change, 94
resembling parent, 28, 74, 90, 100, 178
right to be separate, 25, 59
role swapping, 17
setting limits, 166
staying out of fear, 165–66
staying *versus* leaving, 156–57
superiority in, 30, 107, 190
unattractiveness, 175–76
understanding, 59
unfaithfulness, 55
passive role, 30–31, 54, 135
past
escaping from, 93
intrusion into present, 10
mental remnants of, 18
reliving, 17, 37, 58, 143
rewriting, 95
patience, 128
peers, *see* friends
penance, 18, 134
perceptions, 121, 144
perseverance, 72
pets
as companion, 6
competing for affection, 40
loving, 12, 14, 187
taken by parent, 6–10
physical abuse, 79, 136
pleasure, 185
popularity, quest for, 42, 45
pornography addiction, 53–55
positivity, 25
possession, 7, 14, 162, 172; *see also* ownership
poverty, 36, 37, 51
power, 52, 75, 78, 87, 172
powerlessness, 5
present, living in, 73
pretending, *see* false identities
pretenses, 37
prison atmosphere, 28, 161
procrastination, 17, 124
protective shell, 11, 12
protectors, 35
psychotherapists, 9
psychotherapy, 116
punishment, 14, 15, 18; *see also* mistreatment
put downs, 38, 66, 78, 96, 99, 163

R

rage, 24
parent's, 5, 26, 56, 69
against spouse, 17
rationalization, 76, 86, 88, 106, 112
reality
children's view, 61, 89
denial of, 25, 154
of feelings, 19, 48
versus myths, 89, 179–80, 185
perceptions of, 121
in touch with, 141, 185
rebellion, 3, 15, 16, 85
rejection, 7, 19
called for by internal parent, 25
expectation of, 43
fear of, 102–4
pain of, 55
of spouse, 13, 164
unmet demands as, 55–56, 59
religious communities, 21–22
religious fanaticism, 15
repetition compulsion, 58, 68, 91–93, 100, 132, 134, 145
resentment, 33, 41, 51, 164
retreat, 14
revenge, 105
role reversal, 19, 74, 95, 169

roles; *see also* bullying; submission
aggressor, 16, 65, 95
of boss, 14
parent stand-ins, 107
passive, 30–31, 54, 135
rejected/rejecting, 17, 19
servant, 24, 57, 58, 106
slave/master, 74–80, 132
switching between, 17, 19, 63, 77, 78
underdog, 130
victim, 46–50, 54, 95, 129, 180
weakling, 54
romantic relationships, *see* partner relationships
rules, 34, 48

S

sacrifice, 10, 62–63, 105
saying no
courage to, 134–37
to parents, 3
to partner demands, 59, 164
power of, 115
secrecy, 35
security, sense of, 3, 72, 89, 123
self
characterization as islands, 142, 143
commodification, 172–74
development, 170, 183
dissolution of, 123
finding, 24–25
growth, 108, 126, 157
learning about, 87, 161, 185
preservation, 181
sense of, 11, 12, 18, 19, 169
true, 11, 18, 19, 23, 24
view as limited, 12
self-attack, 50, 151, 175
self-awareness, 14, 23
self-centeredness, 13, 15, 26, 55, 57, 96
self-contempt, 73
self-denial, 154
self-destructive behavior, 28, 50
self-discovery, 114
self-esteem, 17, 31, 41, 42, 89
self-examination, 97, 111, 117, 171, 186
self-hatred, 10, 30, 74, 151, 180
selfhood, 23
self-image
children, 154
creation, 73
defensive, 19
inflated, 135
labels and, 52
negative, 41, 42, 45, 177
outer-directed, 42
parents, 83
selfishness, 34, 58
self-knowledge, 107
self-protection, *see* defenses
self-punishment, 136
self-respect, 6, 42
self-support, 184
separation, 5, 41, 76
confusion, 152
from freezing parent, 82–83, 147
from frozen child, 82, 83, 147
guilt about, 116–19, 169
from parents, 119, 167–70
from physical abuser, 136–37
servant mentality, 24, 57, 58, 106
sex
achieving orgasm, 30–31, 160
extramarital, 22, 34–35, 45
intimacy and, 17, 160
passive role, 30–31, 54
with strangers, 54
sexual attraction, 160
sexuality, 3, 16
shadow self, 143–44, 157–58
shyness, 13

siblings
rejection, 36
rivalry, 56
taking care of younger, 33, 78
Sirens' song, 112
slave mentality, 24, 28, 78–80, 106, 132
slavery, 74–77
sleeplessness, 29
social isolation, 96
solitude, 24
speech, lack of, 15
split identity, 77
spouses, *see* marriage; partner relationships
stability, 108
standing your ground, 66, 165, 184
status, 38
stepmothers, 87–88
Stockholm syndrome, 107, 122
strength, 161
submission, 3, 16, 96, 113
to abuse, 26, 28, 84, 135–36
to bullying, 128
circular path with rebellion, 85
making others weaker through, 128–29
obligation to, 10
to parents, 6–7, 10
to partner, 61
in sexual relationships, 30–31
suicide, by inches, 30
superiority, 30, 43, 107
support groups, 184
suppressed memories, 2, 89, 90, 153–55
surrender, 14, 17, 25, 103
survival, 28, 29, 97, 125
"swallowing the bad," 85–88

T

talking, 162
therapist-client relationship, 112–16, 128, 167, 184
transitional objects, 1, 2, 6
trapped, feeling, 8, 112–13, 171
true self, 11, 18, 19, 23, 73
trust, 14, 27, 65
truth, 13, 185; *see also* reality

U

unattractiveness, 175–76
unconscious acts, 35
unconscious mind, 48–49, 84, 89, 137
undeserving attitude, 29, 33
unhealthy connections, 167–70
un-lovability, 39, 45–46, 72

V

verbal abuse, 13, 130, 136, 145, 182
victim role, 46–50, 54, 129, 180
violence, 52, 141, 149, 166
vulnerability, 5, 12, 66, 165

W

warmed child, 71–72, 142
warming parent, 71–72, 167
warming up, 171–72
weakling, role of, 54
weakness, 52, 53, 57
making others weaker by submitting, 128–29
parading, 50
in parents, 154
weight issues, 175, 176
win/lose experiences, 42
winning, 30, 41, 63, 159
withdrawal, 15, 17, 35
worthlessness, 40–45, 50, 104, 128

Author Biography

Elan Golomb earned her doctorate in clinical psychology and her certificate in psychoanalysis and psychotherapy from New York University. She has been in private practice in New York since 1972. She is also the author of *Trapped in the Mirror: Adult Children of Narcissistic Parents in Their Struggle for Self.*

TRUE DIRECTIONS

An affiliate of Tarcher Books

OUR MISSION

Tarcher's mission has always been to publish books that contain great ideas. Why? Because:

GREAT LIVES BEGIN WITH GREAT IDEAS

At Tarcher, we recognize that many talented authors, speakers, educators, and thought-leaders share this mission and deserve to be published – many more than Tarcher can reasonably publish ourselves. True Directions is ideal for authors and books that increase awareness, raise consciousness, and inspire others to live their ideals and passions.

Like Tarcher, True Directions books are designed to do three things: inspire, inform, and motivate.

Thus, True Directions is an ideal way for these important voices to bring their messages of hope, healing, and help to the world.

Every book published by True Directions– whether it is non-fiction, memoir, novel, poetry or children's book – continues Tarcher's mission to publish works that bring positive change in the world. We invite you to join our mission.

For more information, see the True Directions website:
www.iUniverse.com/TrueDirections/SignUp

Be a part of Tarcher's community to bring positive change in this world! See exclusive author videos, discover new and exciting books, learn about upcoming events, connect with author blogs and websites, and more!
www.tarcherbooks.com

CPSIA information can be obtained
at www.ICGtesting.com
Printed in the USA
LVHW02*1741270818
588268LV00008B/35/P